TensorFlow Machine Projects

Build 13 real-world projects with advanced numerical computations using the Python ecosystem

Ankit Jain
Armando Fandango
Amita Kapoor

BIRMINGHAM - MUMBAI

TensorFlow Machine Learning Projects

Commissioning Editor: Sunith Shetty
Acquisition Editor: Nelson Morris
Content Development Editor: Rhea Henriques
Technical Editor: Dinesh Chaudhary
Copy Editor: Safis Editing
Project Coordinator: Manthan Patel
Proofreader: Safis Editing
Indexer: Pratik Shirodkar
Graphics: Jisha Chirayil
Production Coordinator: Nilesh Mohite

First published: November 2018

Production reference: 1301118

Published by Packt Publishing Ltd.
Livery Place
35 Livery Street
Birmingham
B3 2PB, UK.

ISBN 978-1-78913-221-2

www.packtpub.com

I would like to dedicate this book to my wife, Sneha, who has canceled outdoor trips, stayed at home for multiple weekends, read early drafts of chapters, and even patiently listened to me rant about how difficult it is to write a book. She did all of that and more with a smile on her face. This is only a testament to the fact that she is the most amazing person I know.
I would also like to dedicate this to my parents, Ranjan and Surendra Jain, who have given me nothing but unconditional love and unparalleled support. Their profound belief in my abilities has motivated and encouraged me to take up this massive project.
Lastly, I would like to thank my in-laws, Sudarshana and Pravin Runwal and my sister and brother in-law Ankita and Yash Gandhi for their constant support throughout this book.

– Ankit Jain

I would like to dedicate this book to Rhea Henriques from Packt for working remotely with me for many hours extending well beyond work hours, into late nights and early mornings, to provide quality content for the readers.

– Armando Fandango

I would like to dedicate this book to my PhD supervisors, Prof. Enakshi Khular Sharma and Prof. Wolfgang Freude, for teaching me the importance of doubt, taking joy in solving little problems, never giving up.

– Amita Kapoor

`mapt.io`

Mapt is an online digital library that gives you full access to over 5,000 books and videos, as well as industry leading tools to help you plan your personal development and advance your career. For more information, please visit our website.

Why subscribe?

- Spend less time learning and more time coding with practical eBooks and Videos from over 4,000 industry professionals

- Improve your learning with Skill Plans built especially for you

- Get a free eBook or video every month

- Mapt is fully searchable

- Copy and paste, print, and bookmark content

Packt.com

Did you know that Packt offers eBook versions of every book published, with PDF and ePub files available? You can upgrade to the eBook version at `www.packt.com` and as a print book customer, you are entitled to a discount on the eBook copy. Get in touch with us at `customercare@packtpub.com` for more details.

At `www.packt.com`, you can also read a collection of free technical articles, sign up for a range of free newsletters, and receive exclusive discounts and offers on Packt books and eBooks.

Contributors

About the authors

Ankit Jain currently works as a senior research scientist at Uber AI Labs, the machine learning research arm of Uber. His work primarily involves the application of deep learning methods to a variety of Uber's problems, ranging from forecasting and food delivery to self-driving cars. Previously, he has worked in a variety of data science roles at the Bank of America, Facebook, and other start-ups. He has been a featured speaker at many of the top AI conferences and universities, including UC Berkeley, O'Reilly AI conference, and others. He has a keen interest in teaching and has mentored over 500 students in AI through various start-ups and bootcamps. He completed his MS at UC Berkeley and his BS at IIT Bombay (India).

I am grateful to the Packt team for giving me the opportunity to share my knowledge. Special thanks to Rhea Henriques for her insights and superb editing skills. Lastly, I would also like to thank my co-authors, Armando and Amita, for their suggestions, and my acquisition editor, Varsha Shetty, for approaching me to write the book.

Armando Fandango creates AI empowered products by leveraging his expertise in deep learning, machine learning, distributed computing, and computational methods and has provided thought leadership roles as Chief Data Scientist and Director at startups and large enterprises. He has been advising high-tech AI-based startups. Armando has authored books titled *Python Data Analysis - Second Edition* and *Mastering TensorFlow*. He has also published research in international journals and conferences.

I would like to thank Rhea Henriques for her hard work in getting this book published with the highest quality and also for working closely with all the authors. I am grateful to Amita and Ankit for sharing their experience and knowledge.

Amita Kapoor is an Associate Professor at the Department of Electronics, SRCASW, University of Delhi. She has been teaching neural networks for twenty years. During her PhD, she was awarded the prestigious DAAD fellowship, which enabled her to pursue part of her research work at the Karlsruhe Institute of Technology, Germany. She was awarded the Best Presentation Award at the International Conference on Photonics 2008. Being a member of the ACM, IEEE, INNS, and ISBS, she has published more than 40 papers in international journals and conferences. Her research areas include machine learning, AI, neural networks, robotics, and Buddhism and ethics in AI. She has co-authored the book, *TensorFlow 1.x Deep Learning Cookbook*, by Packt Publishing.

Special thanks to Narotam Singh, without whose help in establishing the cluster it would not have been possible for me to complete this book. Sincere thanks to the principals, Dr. Payal, Ms. Richa, Dr. Punita, and Ms. Deepali, for sanctioning my leave. I would like to thank Armando and Ankit for their insights. I am also grateful to the team at Packt, with special thanks to Manthan Patel for getting me involved in the project, and Rhea Henriques for her support.

About the reviewers

Sujit Pal is a technology research director at Elsevier Labs, an advanced technology group within the Reed-Elsevier Group of companies. His areas of interests include semantic searching, natural language processing, machine learning, and deep learning. At Elsevier, he has worked on several initiatives involving search quality measurement and improvement, image classification and duplicate detection, and annotation and ontology development for medical and scientific corpora. He has co-authored a book on deep learning with Antonio Gulli and writes about technology on his blog, Salmon Run.

Meng-Chieh Ling has a PhD in theoretical physics from the Karlsruhe Institute of Technology. After his PhD, he joined *The Data Incubator Reply* in Munich, and later became an intern at AGT International in Darmstadt. Six months later, he was promoted to senior data scientist and is now working in the field of entertainment.

Packt is searching for authors like you

If you're interested in becoming an author for Packt, please visit `authors.packtpub.com` and apply today. We have worked with thousands of developers and tech professionals, just like you, to help them share their insight with the global tech community. You can make a general application, apply for a specific hot topic that we are recruiting an author for, or submit your own idea.

Table of Contents

Preface

TensorFlow has transformed the way machine learning is perceived. *TensorFlow Machine Learning Projects* teaches you how to exploit the benefits—simplicity, efficiency, and flexibility—of using TensorFlow in various real-world projects. With the help of this book, you'll not only learn how to build advanced projects using different datasets, but also be able to tackle common challenges using a range of libraries from the TensorFlow ecosystem.

To begin with, you'll get to grips with using TensorFlow for machine learning projects. You'll explore a wide range of projects using TensorForest and TensorBoard for detecting exoplanets, TensorFlow.js for sentiment analysis, and TensorFlow Lite for digit classification.

As you make your way through the book, you'll build projects in various real-world domains incorporating **natural language processing (NLP)**, the Gaussian process, autoencoders, recommender systems, and Bayesian neural networks, along with trending areas such as **generative adversarial networks (GANs)**, capsule networks, and reinforcement learning. You'll learn to use TensorFlow with the Spark API and explore GPU-accelerated computing with TensorFlow in order to detect objects, followed by understanding how to train and develop a **recurrent neural network (RNN)** model to generate book scripts.

By the end of this book, you'll have gained the required expertise to build full-fledged machine learning projects at work.

Who this book is for

TensorFlow Machine Learning Projects is for you if you are a data analyst, data scientist, machine learning professional, or deep learning enthusiast with a basic knowledge of TensorFlow. This book is also for you if you want to build end-to-end projects in the machine learning domain using supervised, unsupervised, and reinforcement learning techniques.

What this book covers

Chapter 1, *Overview of TensorFlow and Machine Learning*, explains the basics of TensorFlow and has you build a machine learning model using logistic regression to classify hand-written digits.

Chapter 2, *Using Machine Learning to Detect Exoplanets in Outer Space*, covers how to detect exoplanets in outer space using ensemble methods that are based on decision trees.

Chapter 3, *Sentiment Analysis in Your Browser Using TensorFlow.js*, explains how to train and build a model on your web browser using TensorFlow.js. We will build a sentiment analysis model using a movie reviews dataset and deploy it to your web browser for making predictions.

Chapter 4, *Digit Classification Using TensorFlow Lite*, focuses on building a deep learning model for classifying hand-written digits and converting them into a mobile-friendly format using TensorFlow Lite. We will also learn about the architecture of TensorFlow Lite and how to use TensorBoard for visualizing neural networks.

Chapter 5, *Speech to Text and Topic Extraction Using NLP*, focuses on learning about various options for speech-to-text and pre-built models by Google in TensorFlow using the Google Speech Command dataset.

Chapter 6, *Predicting Stock Prices using Gaussian Process Regression*, explains a popular forecasting model called a Gaussian process in Bayesian statistics. We use Gaussian processes from a `GpFlow` library built on top of TensorFlow to develop a stock price prediction model.

Chapter 7, *Credit Card Fraud Detection Using Autoencoders*, introduces a dimensionality reduction technique called autoencoders. We identify fraudulent transactions in a credit card dataset by building autoencoders using TensorFlow and Keras.

Chapter 8, *Generating Uncertainty in Traffic Signs Classifier using Bayesian Neural Networks*, explains Bayesian neural networks, which help us to quantify the uncertainty in predictions. We will build a Bayesian neural network using TensorFlow to classify German traffic signs.

Chapter 9, *Generating Matching Shoe Bags from Shoe Images Using DiscoGANs*, introduces a new type of GAN known as **Discovery GANs (DiscoGANs)**. We understand how its architecture differs from standard GANs and how it can be used in style transfer problems. Finally, we build a DiscoGAN model in TensorFlow to generate matching shoe bags from shoe images, and vice versa.

Chapter 10, *Classifying Clothing Images Using Capsule Networks*, implements a very recent image classification model—Capsule Networks. We get to understand its architecture and explain the nuances of its implementation in TensorFlow. We use the Fashion MNIST dataset to classify clothing images using this model.

Chapter 11, *Making Quality Product Recommendations Using TensorFlow*, covers techniques such as matrix factorization (SVD++), learning to rank, and convolutional neural network variations for recommendation tasks with TensorFlow.

Chapter 12, *Object Detection at a Large Scale with TensorFlow*, explores Yahoo's TensorFlowOnSpark framework for distributed deep learning on Spark clusters. Then, we will apply TensorFlowOnSpark to a large-scale dataset of images and train the network to detect objects.

Chapter 13, *Generating Book Scripts Using LSTMs*, explains how LSTMs are useful in generating new text. We use a book script from one of Packt's published books to bsuild an LSTM-based deep learning model that can generate book scripts on its own.

Chapter 14, *Playing Pacman Using Deep Reinforcement Learning*, explains the utilization of reinforcement learning for training a model to play Pacman, teaching you about reinforcement learning in the process.

Chapter 15, *What is Next?*, introduces the other components of the TensorFlow ecosystem that are useful for deploying the models in production. We will also learn about various applications of AI across industries, the limitations of deep learning, and ethics in AI.

To get the most out of this book

To get the most out of this book, download the book code from the GitHub repository and practice with the code in Jupyter Notebooks. Also, practice modifying the implementations already provided by the authors.

Download the example code files

You can download the example code files for this book from your account at www.packt.com. If you purchased this book elsewhere, you can visit www.packt.com/support and register to have the files emailed directly to you.

You can download the code files by following these steps:

1. Log in or register at www.packt.com.
2. Select the **SUPPORT** tab.
3. Click on **Code Downloads & Errata**.
4. Enter the name of the book in the **Search** box and follow the onscreen instructions.

Once the file is downloaded, please make sure that you unzip or extract the folder using the latest version of:

- WinRAR/7-Zip for Windows
- Zipeg/iZip/UnRarX for Mac
- 7-Zip/PeaZip for Linux

The code bundle for the book is also hosted on GitHub at https://github.com/PacktPublishing/TensorFlow-Machine-Learning-Projects. In case there's an update to the code, it will be updated on the existing GitHub repository.

We also have other code bundles from our rich catalog of books and videos available at https://github.com/PacktPublishing/. Check them out!

Download the color images

We also provide a PDF file that has color images of the screenshots/diagrams used in this book. You can download it here: https://www.packtpub.com/sites/default/files/downloads/9781789132212_ColorImages.pdf.

Conventions used

There are a number of text conventions used throughout this book.

CodeInText: Indicates code words in text, database table names, folder names, filenames, file extensions, pathnames, dummy URLs, user input, and Twitter handles. Here is an example: "By defining placeholders and passing the values to session.run()."

A block of code is set as follows:

```
tf.constant(
  value,
  dtype=None,
  shape=None,
  name='const_name',
  verify_shape=False
  )
```

Any command-line input or output is written as follows:

```
const1 (x):  Tensor("x:0", shape=(), dtype=int32)
const2 (y):  Tensor("y:0", shape=(), dtype=float32)
const3 (z):  Tensor("z:0", shape=(), dtype=float16)
```

Bold: Indicates a new term, an important word, or words that you see on screen. For example, words in menus or dialog boxes appear in the text like this. Here is an example: "Type a review into the box provided and click **Submit** to see the model's predicted score."

 Warnings or important notes appear like this.

 Tips and tricks appear like this.

Get in touch

Feedback from our readers is always welcome.

General feedback: If you have questions about any aspect of this book, mention the book title in the subject of your message and email us at customercare@packtpub.com.

Errata: Although we have taken every care to ensure the accuracy of our content, mistakes do happen. If you have found a mistake in this book, we would be grateful if you would report this to us. Please visit www.packt.com/submit-errata, selecting your book, clicking on the Errata Submission Form link, and entering the details.

Piracy: If you come across any illegal copies of our works in any form on the internet, we would be grateful if you would provide us with the location address or website name. Please contact us at `copyright@packt.com` with a link to the material.

If you are interested in becoming an author: If there is a topic that you have expertise in, and you are interested in either writing or contributing to a book, please visit `authors.packtpub.com`.

Reviews

Please leave a review. Once you have read and used this book, why not leave a review on the site that you purchased it from? Potential readers can then see and use your unbiased opinion to make purchase decisions, we at Packt can understand what you think about our products, and our authors can see your feedback on their book. Thank you!

For more information about Packt, please visit `packt.com`.

Overview of TensorFlow and Machine Learning

1

TensorFlow is a popular library for implementing machine learning-based solutions. It includes a low-level API known as TensorFlow core and many high-level APIs, including two of the most popular ones, known as TensorFlow Estimators and Keras. In this chapter, we will learn about the basics of TensorFlow and build a machine learning model using logistic regression to classify handwritten digits as an example.

We will cover the following topics in this chapter:

- TensorFlow core:
    - Tensors in TensorFlow core
    - Constants
    - Placeholders
    - Operations
    - Tensors from Python objects
    - Variables
    - Tensors from library functions

- Computation graphs:
    - Lazy loading and execution order
    - Graphs on multiple devices – CPU and GPGPU
    - Working with multiple graphs
- Machine learning, classification, and logistic regression
- Logistic regression examples in TensorFlow
- Logistic regression examples in Keras

You can follow the code examples in this chapter by using the Jupyter Notebook named `ch-01_Overview_of_TensorFlow_and_Machine_Learning.ipynb` that's included in the code bundle.

What is TensorFlow?

TensorFlow is a popular open source library that's used for implementing machine learning and deep learning. It was initially built at Google for internal consumption and was released publicly on November 9, 2015. Since then, TensorFlow has been extensively used to develop machine learning and deep learning models in several business domains.

To use TensorFlow in our projects, we need to learn how to program using the TensorFlow API. TensorFlow has multiple APIs that can be used to interact with the library. The TensorFlow APIs are divided into two levels:

- **Low-level API**: The API known as TensorFlow core provides fine-grained lower level functionality. Because of this, this low-level API offers complete control while being used on models. We will cover TensorFlow core in this chapter.
- **High-level API**: These APIs provide high-level functionalities that have been built on TensorFlow core and are comparatively easier to learn and implement. Some high-level APIs include Estimators, Keras, TFLearn, TFSlim, and Sonnet. We will also cover Keras in this chapter.

The TensorFlow core

The **TensorFlow core** is the lower-level API on which the higher-level TensorFlow modules are built. In this section, we will go over a quick overview of TensorFlow core and learn about the basic elements of TensorFlow.

Tensors

Tensors are the basic components in TensorFlow. A tensor is a multidimensional collection of data elements. It is generally identified by shape, type, and rank. **Rank** refers to the number of dimensions of a tensor, while **shape** refers to the size of each dimension. You may have seen several examples of tensors before, such as in a zero-dimensional collection (also known as a scalar), a one-dimensional collection (also known as a vector), and a two-dimensional collection (also known as a matrix).

A scalar value is a tensor of rank 0 and shape []. A vector, or a one-dimensional array, is a tensor of rank 1 and shape [number_of_columns] or [number_of_rows]. A matrix, or a two-dimensional array, is a tensor of rank 2 and shape [number_of_rows, number_of_columns]. A three-dimensional array is a tensor of rank 3. In the same way, an n-dimensional array is a tensor of rank n.

A tensor can store data of one type in all of its dimensions, and the data type of a tensor is the same as the data type of its elements.

 The data types that can be found in the TensorFlow library are described at the following link: https://www.tensorflow.org/api_docs/python/tf/DType.

The following are the most commonly used data types in TensorFlow:

TensorFlow Python API data type	Description
tf.float16	16-bit floating point (half-precision)
tf.float32	32-bit floating point (single-precision)
tf.float64	64-bit floating point (double-precision)
tf.int8	8-bit integer (signed)
tf.int16	16-bit integer (signed)
tf.int32	32-bit integer (signed)
tf.int64	64-bit integer (signed)

 Use TensorFlow data types for defining tensors instead of native data types from Python or data types from NumPy.

Tensors can be created in the following ways:

- By defining constants, operations, and variables, and passing the values to their constructor
- By defining placeholders and passing the values to session.run()
- By converting Python objects, such as scalar values, lists, NumPy arrays, and pandas DataFrames, with the tf.convert_to_tensor() function

Let's explore different ways of creating Tensors.

Constants

The constant valued tensors are created using the `tf.constant()` function, and has the following definition:

```
tf.constant(
    value,
    dtype=None,
    shape=None,
    name='const_name',
    verify_shape=False
    )
```

Let's create some constants with the following code:

```
const1=tf.constant(34,name='x1')
const2=tf.constant(59.0,name='y1')
const3=tf.constant(32.0,dtype=tf.float16,name='z1')
```

Let's take a look at the preceding code in detail:

- The first line of code defines a constant tensor, `const1`, stores a value of `34`, and names it x1.
- The second line of code defines a constant tensor, `const2`, stores a value of `59.0`, and names it y1.
- The third line of code defines the data type as `tf.float16` for `const3`. Use the `dtype` parameter or place the data type as the second argument to denote the data type.

Let's print the constants `const1`, `const2`, and `const3`:

```
print('const1 (x): ',const1)
print('const2 (y): ',const2)
print('const3 (z): ',const3)
```

When we print these constants, we get the following output:

```
const1 (x):  Tensor("x:0", shape=(), dtype=int32)
const2 (y):  Tensor("y:0", shape=(), dtype=float32)
const3 (z):  Tensor("z:0", shape=(), dtype=float16)
```

Upon printing the previously defined tensors, we can see that the data types of `const1` and `const2` are automatically deduced by TensorFlow.

To print the values of these constants, we can execute them in a TensorFlow session with the `tfs.run()` command:

```
print('run([const1,const2,c3]) : ',tfs.run([const1,const2,const3]))
```

We will see the following output:

```
run([const1,const2,const3]) : [34, 59.0, 32.0]
```

Operations

The TensorFlow library contains several built-in operations that can be applied on tensors. An operation node can be defined by passing input values and saving the output in another tensor. To understand this better, let's define two operations, op1 and op2:

```
op1 = tf.add(const2, const3)
op2 = tf.multiply(const2, const3)
```

Let's print op1 and op2:

```
print('op1 : ', op1)
print('op2 : ', op2)
```

The output is as follows, and shows that op1 and op2 are defined as tensors:

```
op1 :  Tensor("Add:0", shape=(), dtype=float32)
op2 :  Tensor("Mul:0", shape=(), dtype=float32)
```

To print the output from executing these operations, the op1 and op2 tensors have to be executed in a TensorFlow session:

```
print('run(op1) : ', tfs.run(op1))
print('run(op2) : ', tfs.run(op2))
```

The output is as follows:

```
run(op1) :  91.0
run(op2) :  1888.0
```

Some of the built-in operations of TensorFlow include arithmetic operations, math functions, and complex number operations.

Placeholders

While constants store the value at the time of defining the tensor, placeholders allow you to create empty tensors so that the values can be provided at runtime. The TensorFlow library provides the `tf.placeholder()` function with the following signature to create placeholders:

```
tf.placeholder(
    dtype,
    shape=None,
    name=None
    )
```

As an example, let's create two placeholders and print them:

```
p1 = tf.placeholder(tf.float32)
p2 = tf.placeholder(tf.float32)
print('p1 : ', p1)
print('p2 : ', p2)
```

The following output shows that each placeholder has been created as a tensor:

```
p1 :   Tensor("Placeholder:0", dtype=float32)
p2 :   Tensor("Placeholder_1:0", dtype=float32)
```

Let's define an operation using these placeholders:

```
mult_op = p1 * p2
```

In TensorFlow, shorthand symbols can be used for various operations. In the preceding code, `p1 * p2` is shorthand for `tf.multiply(p1,p2)`:

```
print('run(mult_op,{p1:13.4, p2:61.7}) : ',tfs.run(mult_op,{p1:13.4,
p2:61.7}))
```

The preceding command runs `mult_op` in the TensorFlow session and feeds the values dictionary (the second argument to the `run()` operation) with the values for `p1` and `p2`.

The output is as follows:

```
run(mult_op,{p1:13.4, p2:61.7}) :   826.77997
```

We can also specify the values dictionary by using the `feed_dict` parameter in the `run()` operation:

```
feed_dict={p1: 15.4, p2: 19.5}
print('run(mult_op,feed_dict = {p1:15.4, p2:19.5}) : ',
    tfs.run(mult_op, feed_dict=feed_dict))
```

The output is as follows:

```
run(mult_op,feed_dict = {p1:15.4, p2:19.5}) :   300.3
```

Let's look at one final example, which is of a vector being fed to the same operation:

```
feed_dict={p1: [2.0, 3.0, 4.0], p2: [3.0, 4.0, 5.0]}
print('run(mult_op,feed_dict={p1:[2.0,3.0,4.0], p2:[3.0,4.0,5.0]}):',
    tfs.run(mult_op, feed_dict=feed_dict))
```

The output is as follows:

```
run(mult_op,feed_dict={p1:[2.0,3.0,4.0],p2:[3.0,4.0,5.0]}):[  6.  12.  20.]
```

The elements of the two input vectors are multiplied in an element-wise fashion.

Tensors from Python objects

Tensors can be created from Python objects such as lists, NumPy arrays, and pandas DataFrames. To create tensors from Python objects, use the `tf.convert_to_tensor()` function with the following definition:

```
tf.convert_to_tensor(
    value,
    dtype=None,
    name=None,
    preferred_dtype=None
    )
```

Let's practice doing this by creating some tensors and printing their definitions and values:

1. Define a 0-D tensor:

```
tf_t=tf.convert_to_tensor(5.0,dtype=tf.float64)

print('tf_t : ',tf_t)
print('run(tf_t) : ',tfs.run(tf_t))
```

The output is as follows:

```
tf_t : Tensor("Const_1:0", shape=(), dtype=float64)
run(tf_t) : 5.0
```

2. Define a 1-D tensor:

```
a1dim = np.array([1,2,3,4,5.99])
print("a1dim Shape : ",a1dim.shape)

tf_t=tf.convert_to_tensor(a1dim,dtype=tf.float64)

print('tf_t : ',tf_t)
print('tf_t[0] : ',tf_t[0])
print('tf_t[0] : ',tf_t[2])
print('run(tf_t) : \n',tfs.run(tf_t))
```

The output is as follows:

```
a1dim Shape :  (5,)
tf_t :  Tensor("Const_2:0", shape=(5,), dtype=float64)
tf_t[0] :  Tensor("strided_slice:0", shape=(), dtype=float64)
tf_t[0] :  Tensor("strided_slice_1:0", shape=(), dtype=float64)
run(tf_t) :
 [ 1.    2.    3.    4.    5.99]
```

3. Define a 2-D tensor:

```
a2dim = np.array([(1,2,3,4,5.99),
                  (2,3,4,5,6.99),
                  (3,4,5,6,7.99)
                 ])
print("a2dim Shape : ",a2dim.shape)

tf_t=tf.convert_to_tensor(a2dim,dtype=tf.float64)

print('tf_t : ',tf_t)
print('tf_t[0][0] : ',tf_t[0][0])
print('tf_t[1][2] : ',tf_t[1][2])
print('run(tf_t) : \n',tfs.run(tf_t))
```

The output is as follows:

```
a2dim Shape :  (3, 5)
tf_t :  Tensor("Const_3:0", shape=(3, 5), dtype=float64)
tf_t[0][0] :  Tensor("strided_slice_3:0", shape=(), dtype=float64)
tf_t[1][2] :  Tensor("strided_slice_5:0", shape=(), dtype=float64)
run(tf_t) :
 [[ 1.    2.    3.    4.    5.99]
```

```
[ 2.    3.    4.    5.    6.99]
[ 3.    4.    5.    6.    7.99]]
```

4. Define a 3-D tensor:

```
a3dim = np.array([[[1,2],[3,4]],
                    [[5,6],[7,8]]
                    ])
print("a3dim Shape : ",a3dim.shape)

tf_t=tf.convert_to_tensor(a3dim,dtype=tf.float64)

print('tf_t : ',tf_t)
print('tf_t[0][0][0] : ',tf_t[0][0][0])
print('tf_t[1][1][1] : ',tf_t[1][1][1])
print('run(tf_t) : \n',tfs.run(tf_t))
```

The output is as follows:

```
a3dim Shape :  (2, 2, 2)
tf_t :  Tensor("Const_4:0", shape=(2, 2, 2), dtype=float64)
tf_t[0][0][0] :  Tensor("strided_slice_8:0", shape=(),
dtype=float64)
tf_t[1][1][1] :  Tensor("strided_slice_11:0", shape=(),
dtype=float64)
run(tf_t) :
 [[[ 1.    2.][ 3.    4.]]
  [[ 5.    6.][ 7.    8.]]]
```

Variables

In the previous sections, we learned how to define tensor objects of different types, such as constants, operations, and placeholders. The values of parameters need to be held in an updatable memory location while building and training models with TensorFlow. Such updatable memory locations for tensors are known as variables in TensorFlow.

To summarize this, TensorFlow variables are tensor objects in that their values can be modified during the execution of the program.

Although t f.Variable seems to be similar to t f.placeholder, they have certain differences. These are listed in the following table:

tf.placeholder	tf.Variable
tf.placeholder defines the input data that does not get updated over time	tf.Variable defines values that get updated over time
tf.placeholder does not need to be provided with an initial value at the time of definition	tf.Variable needs an initial value to be provided at the time of definition

In TensorFlow, a variable can be created with the API function t f.Variable(). Let's look at an example of using placeholders and variables and create the following model in TensorFlow:

$$y = W \times x + b$$

1. Define the model parameters w and b as variables with the initial values [.3] and [-0.3]:

```
w = tf.Variable([.3], tf.float32)
b = tf.Variable([-.3], tf.float32)
```

2. Define the input placeholder x and the output operation node y:

```
x = tf.placeholder(tf.float32)
y = w * x + b
```

3. Print the variables and placeholders w, v, x, and y:

```
print("w:",w)
print("x:",x)
print("b:",b)
print("y:",y)
```

The output depicts the type of nodes as Variable, Placeholder, or operation node, as follows:

```
w: <tf.Variable 'Variable:0' shape=(1,) dtype=float32_ref>
x: Tensor("Placeholder_2:0", dtype=float32)
b: <tf.Variable 'Variable_1:0' shape=(1,) dtype=float32_ref>
y: Tensor("add:0", dtype=float32)
```

The preceding output indicates that x is a Placeholder tensor, y is an operation tensor, and that w and b are variables with a shape of (1,) and a data type of float32.

The variables in a TensorFlow session have to be initialized before they can be used. We can either initialize a single variable by running its initializer operation or we can initialize all or a group of variables.

For example, to initialize the w variable, we can use the following code:

```
tfs.run(w.initializer)
```

TensorFlow provides a convenient function that can initialize all of the variables:

```
tfs.run(tf.global_variables_initializer())
```

 TensorFlow also provides the `tf.variables_initializer()` function so that you can initialize a specific set of variables.

The global convenience function for initializing these variables can be executed in an alternative way. Instead of executing inside the `run()` function of a session object, the run function of the object returned by the initializer function itself can be executed:

```
tf.global_variables_initializer().run()
```

After the variables have been initialized, execute the model to get the output for the input values of x = [1,2,3,4]:

```
print('run(y,{x:[1,2,3,4]}) : ',tfs.run(y,{x:[1,2,3,4]}))
```

The output is as follows:

```
run(y,{x:[1,2,3,4]}) :  [ 0.          0.30000001  0.60000002  0.90000004]
```

Tensors generated from library functions

TensorFlow provides various functions to generate tensors with pre-populated values. The generated values from these functions can be stored in a constant or variable tensor. Such generated values can also be provided to the tensor constructor at the time of initialization.

As an example, let's generate a 1-D tensor that's been pre-populated with 100 zeros:

```
a=tf.zeros((100,))
print(tfs.run(a))
```

Some of the TensorFlow library functions that populate these tensors with different values at the time of their definition are listed as follows:

- Populating all of the elements of a tensor with similar values: `tf.ones_like()`, `tf.ones()`, `tf.fill()`, `tf.zeros()`, and `tf.zeros_like()`
- Populating tensors with sequences: `tf.range()`, and `tf.lin_space()`
- Populating tensors with a probability distribution: `tf.random_uniform()`, `tf.random_normal()`, `tf.random_gamm a()`, and `tf.truncated_normal()`

Obtaining variables with the tf.get_variable()

If a variable is defined with a name that has already been used for another variable, then an exception is thrown by TensorFlow. The `tf.get_variable()` function makes it convenient and safe to create a variable in place of using the `tf.Variable()` function. The `tf.get_variable()` function returns a variable that has been defined with a given name. If the variable with the given name does not exist, then it will create the variable with the specified initializer and shape.

Consider the following example:

```
w = tf.get_variable(name='w',shape=[1],dtype=tf.float32,initializer=[.3])
b = tf.get_variable(name='b',shape=[1],dtype=tf.float32,initializer=[-.3])
```

The initializer can either be a list of values or another tensor. An initializer can also be one of the built-in initializers. Some of these are as follows:

- `tf.ones_initializer`
- `tf.constant_initializer`
- `tf.zeros_initializer`
- `tf.truncated_normal_initializer`
- `tf.random_normal_initializer`
- `tf.random_uniform_initializer`
- `tf.uniform_unit_scaling_initializer`
- `tf.orthogonal_initializer`

The `tf.get_variable()` function only returns the global variables when the code is run across multiple machines in distributed TensorFlow. The local variables can be retrieved by using the `tf.get_local_variable()` function.

 Sharing or reusing variables: Getting variables that have already been defined promotes reuse. However, an exception will be thrown if the reuse flags are not set by using `tf.variable_scope.reuse_variable()` or `tf.variable.scope(reuse=True)`.

Now that we have learned how to define tensors, constants, operations, placeholders, and variables, let's learn about the next level of abstraction in TensorFlow that combines these basic elements to form a basic unit of computation: the computation graph.

Computation graph

A **computation graph** is the basic unit of computation in TensorFlow. A computation graph consists of nodes and edges. Each node represents an instance of `tf.Operation`, while each edge represents an instance of `tf.Tensor` that gets transferred between the nodes.

A model in TensorFlow contains a computation graph. First, you must create the graph with the nodes representing variables, constants, placeholders, and operations, and then provide the graph to the TensorFlow execution engine. The TensorFlow execution engine finds the first set of nodes that it can execute. The execution of these nodes starts the execution of the nodes that follow the sequence of the computation graph.

Thus, TensorFlow-based programs are made up of performing two types of activities on computation graphs:

- Defining the computation graph
- Executing the computation graph

A TensorFlow program starts execution with a default graph. Unless another graph is explicitly specified, a new node gets implicitly added to the default graph. Explicit access to the default graph can be obtained using the following command:

```
graph = tf.get_default_graph()
```

For example, the following computation graph represents the addition of three inputs to produce the output, that is, $y = x_1 + x_2 + x_3$:

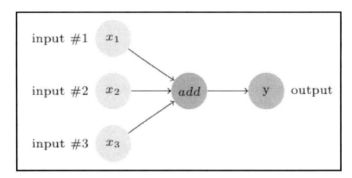

In TensorFlow, the add operation node in the preceding diagram would correspond to the code `y = tf.add( x1 + x2 + x3 )`.

The variables, constants, and placeholders get added to the graph as and when they are created. After defining the computation graph, a session object is instantiated that *executes* the operation objects and *evaluates* the tensor objects.

Let's define and execute a computation graph to calculate $y = w \times x + b$, just like we saw in the preceding example:

```
# Linear Model y = w * x + b
# Define the model parameters
w = tf.Variable([.3], tf.float32)
b = tf.Variable([-.3], tf.float32)
# Define model input and output
x = tf.placeholder(tf.float32)
y = w * x + b
output = 0

with tf.Session() as tfs:
    # initialize and print the variable y
    tf.global_variables_initializer().run()
    output = tfs.run(y,{x:[1,2,3,4]})
print('output : ',output)
```

Creating and using a session in the `with` block ensures that the session is automatically closed when the block is finished. Otherwise, the session has to be explicitly closed with the `tfs.close()` command, where `tfs` is the session name.

The order of execution and lazy loading

The nodes in a computation graph are executed in their order of dependency. If node x depends on node y, then x is executed before y when the execution of y is requested. A node is only executed if either the node itself or another node depending on it is invoked for execution. This execution philosophy is known as lazy loading. As the name implies, the node objects are not instantiated and initialized until they are actually required.

Often, it is necessary to control the order of the execution of the nodes in a computation graph. This can be done with the `tf.Graph.control_dependencies()` function. For example, if the graph has the nodes l, m, n, and o, and we want to execute n and o before l and m, then we would use the following code:

```
with graph_variable.control_dependencies([n,o]):
    # other statements here
```

This makes sure that any node in the preceding `with` block is executed after nodes n and o have been executed.

Executing graphs across compute devices – CPU and GPGPU

A graph can be partitioned into several parts, and each part can be placed and executed on different devices, such as a CPU or GPU. All of the devices that are available for graph execution can be listed with the following command:

```
from tensorflow.python.client import device_lib
print(device_lib.list_local_devices())
```

The output is listed as follows (the output for your machine will be different because this will depend on the available compute devices in your specific system):

```
[name: "/device:CPU:0"
device_type: "CPU"
memory_limit: 268435456
locality {
}
incarnation: 12900903776306102093
, name: "/device:GPU:0"
device_type: "GPU"
memory_limit: 611319808
locality {
  bus_id: 1
```

```
  }
incarnation: 2202031001192109390
physical_device_desc: "device: 0, name: Quadro P5000, pci bus id:
0000:01:00.0, compute capability: 6.1"
  ]
```

The devices in TensorFlow are identified with the
string /device:<device_type>:<device_idx>. In the last output, CPU and GPU denote
the device type, and 0 denotes the device index.

One thing to note about the last output is that it shows only one CPU, whereas our
computer has 8 CPUs. The reason for this is that TensorFlow implicitly distributes the code
across the CPU units and thus, by default, CPU:0 denotes all of the CPUs available to
TensorFlow. When TensorFlow starts executing graphs, it runs the independent paths
within each graph in a separate thread, with each thread running on a separate CPU. We
can restrict the number of threads used for this purpose by changing the number
of inter_op_parallelism_threads. Similarly, if, within an independent path, an
operation is capable of running on multiple threads, TensorFlow will launch that specific
operation on multiple threads. The number of threads in this pool can be changed by
setting the number of intra_op_parallelism_threads.

Placing graph nodes on specific compute devices

To enable the logging of variable placement by defining a config object, set
the log_device_placement property to true, and then pass this config object to the
session as follows:

```
tf.reset_default_graph()

# Define model parameters
w = tf.Variable([.3], tf.float32)
b = tf.Variable([-.3], tf.float32)
# Define model input and output
x = tf.placeholder(tf.float32)
y = w * x + b

config = tf.ConfigProto()
config.log_device_placement=True

with tf.Session(config=config) as tfs:
    # initialize and print the variable y
    tfs.run(global_variables_initializer())
    print('output',tfs.run(y,{x:[1,2,3,4]}))
```

The output from the console window of the Jupyter Notebook is listed as follows:

```
b: (VariableV2): /job:localhost/replica:0/task:0/device:GPU:0
b/read: (Identity): /job:localhost/replica:0/task:0/device:GPU:0
b/Assign: (Assign): /job:localhost/replica:0/task:0/device:GPU:0
w: (VariableV2): /job:localhost/replica:0/task:0/device:GPU:0
w/read: (Identity): /job:localhost/replica:0/task:0/device:GPU:0
mul: (Mul): /job:localhost/replica:0/task:0/device:GPU:0
add: (Add): /job:localhost/replica:0/task:0/device:GPU:0
w/Assign: (Assign): /job:localhost/replica:0/task:0/device:GPU:0
init: (NoOp): /job:localhost/replica:0/task:0/device:GPU:0
x: (Placeholder): /job:localhost/replica:0/task:0/device:GPU:0
b/initial_value: (Const): /job:localhost/replica:0/task:0/device:GPU:0
Const_1: (Const): /job:localhost/replica:0/task:0/device:GPU:0
w/initial_value: (Const): /job:localhost/replica:0/task:0/device:GPU:0
Const: (Const): /job:localhost/replica:0/task:0/device:GPU:0
```

Thus, by default, TensorFlow creates the variable and operations nodes on a device so that it can get the highest performance. These variables and operations can be placed on specific devices by using the `tf.device()` function. Let's place the graph on the CPU:

```
tf.reset_default_graph()

with tf.device('/device:CPU:0'):
    # Define model parameters
    w = tf.get_variable(name='w',initializer=[.3], dtype=tf.float32)
    b = tf.get_variable(name='b',initializer=[-.3], dtype=tf.float32)
    # Define model input and output
    x = tf.placeholder(name='x',dtype=tf.float32)
    y = w * x + b

config = tf.ConfigProto()
config.log_device_placement=True

with tf.Session(config=config) as tfs:
    # initialize and print the variable y
    tfs.run(tf.global_variables_initializer())
    print('output',tfs.run(y,{x:[1,2,3,4]}))
```

In the Jupyter console, we can see that the variables have been placed on the CPU and that execution also takes place on the CPU:

```
b: (VariableV2): /job:localhost/replica:0/task:0/device:CPU:0
b/read: (Identity): /job:localhost/replica:0/task:0/device:CPU:0
b/Assign: (Assign): /job:localhost/replica:0/task:0/device:CPU:0
w: (VariableV2): /job:localhost/replica:0/task:0/device:CPU:0
w/read: (Identity): /job:localhost/replica:0/task:0/device:CPU:0
mul: (Mul): /job:localhost/replica:0/task:0/device:CPU:0
```

```
add: (Add): /job:localhost/replica:0/task:0/device:CPU:0
w/Assign: (Assign): /job:localhost/replica:0/task:0/device:CPU:0
init: (NoOp): /job:localhost/replica:0/task:0/device:CPU:0
x: (Placeholder): /job:localhost/replica:0/task:0/device:CPU:0
b/initial_value: (Const): /job:localhost/replica:0/task:0/device:CPU:0
Const_1: (Const): /job:localhost/replica:0/task:0/device:CPU:0
w/initial_value: (Const): /job:localhost/replica:0/task:0/device:CPU:0
Const: (Const): /job:localhost/replica:0/task:0/device:CPU:0
```

Simple placement

TensorFlow follows the following rules for placing the variables on devices:

```
If the graph was previously run,
    then the node is left on the device where it was placed earlier
Else If the tf.device() block is used,
    then the node is placed on the specified device
Else If the GPU is present
    then the node is placed on the first available GPU
Else If the GPU is not present
    then the node is placed on the CPU
```

Dynamic placement

The `tf.device()` function can be provided with a function name in place of a device string. If a function name is provided, then the function has to return the device string. This way of providing a device string through a custom function allows complex algorithms to be used for placing the variables on different devices. For example, TensorFlow provides a round robin device setter function in `tf.train.replica_device_setter()`.

Soft placement

If a TensorFlow operation is placed on the GPU, then the execution engine must have the GPU implementation of that operation, known as the **kernel**. If the kernel is not present, then the placement results in a runtime error. Also, if the requested GPU device does not exist, then a runtime error is raised. The best way to handle such errors is to allow the operation to be placed on the CPU if requesting the GPU device results in an error. This can be achieved by setting the following `config` value:

```
config.allow_soft_placement = True
```

GPU memory handling

At the start of the TensorFlow session, by default, a session grabs all of the GPU memory, even if the operations and variables are placed only on one GPU in a multi-GPU system. If another session starts execution at the same time, it will receive an out-of-memory error. This can be solved in multiple ways:

- For multi-GPU systems, set the environment variable CUDA_VISIBLE_DEVICES=<list of device idx>:

  ```
  os.environ['CUDA_VISIBLE_DEVICES']='0'
  ```

  The code that's executed after this setting will be able to grab all of the memory of the visible GPU.

- For letting the session grab a part of the memory of the GPU, use the config option per_process_gpu_memory_fraction to allocate a percentage of the memory:

  ```
  config.gpu_options.per_process_gpu_memory_fraction = 0.5
  ```

  This will allocate 50% of the memory in all of the GPU devices.

- By combining both of the preceding strategies, you can make only a certain percentage, alongside just some of the GPU, visible to the process.
- Limit the TensorFlow process to grab only the minimum required memory at the start of the process. As the process executes further, set a config option to allow for the growth of this memory:

  ```
  config.gpu_options.allow_growth = True
  ```

  This option only allows for the allocated memory to grow, so the memory is never released back.

 To find out more about learning techniques for distributing computation across multiple compute devices, refer to our book, *Mastering TensorFlow*.

Multiple graphs

We can create our own graphs, which are separate from the default graph, and execute them in a session. However, creating and executing multiple graphs is not recommended, because of the following disadvantages:

- Creating and using multiple graphs in the same program would require multiple TensorFlow sessions, and each session would consume heavy resources
- Data cannot be directly passed in-between graphs

Hence, the recommended approach is to have multiple subgraphs in a single graph. In case we wish to use our own graph instead of the default graph, we can do so with the tf.graph() command. In the following example, we create our own graph, g, and execute it as the default graph:

```
g = tf.Graph()
output = 0

# Assume Linear Model y = w * x + b

with g.as_default():
 # Define model parameters
 w = tf.Variable([.3], tf.float32)
 b = tf.Variable([-.3], tf.float32)
 # Define model input and output
 x = tf.placeholder(tf.float32)
 y = w * x + b

with tf.Session(graph=g) as tfs:
 # initialize and print the variable y
 tf.global_variables_initializer().run()
 output = tfs.run(y,{x:[1,2,3,4]})

print('output : ',output)
```

Now, let's put this learning into practice and implement the classification of handwritten digital images with TensorFlow.

Machine learning, classification, and logistic regression

Let's now learn about machine learning, classification, and logistic regression.

Machine learning

Machine learning refers to the application of algorithms to make computers learn from data. The models that are learned by computers are used to make predictions and forecasts. Machine learning has been successfully applied in a variety of areas, such as natural language processing, self-driving vehicles, image and speech recognition, chatbots, and computer vision.

Machine learning algorithms are broadly categorized into three types:

- **Supervised learning**: In supervised learning, the machine learns the model from a training dataset that consists of features and labels. The supervised learning problems are generally of two types: *regression* and *classification*. Regression refers to predicting future values based on the model, while classification refers to predicting the categories of the input values.
- **Unsupervised learning**: In unsupervised learning, the machine learns the model from a training dataset that consists of features only. One of the most common types of unsupervised learning is known as **clustering**. Clustering refers to dividing the input data into multiple groups, thus producing clusters or segments.
- **Reinforcement learning**: In reinforcement learning, the agent starts with an initial model and then continuously learns the model based on the feedback from the environment. A reinforcement learning agent learns or updates the model by applying supervised or unsupervised learning techniques as part of the reinforcement learning algorithms.

These machine learning problems are abstracted to the following equation in one form or another:

$$y = f(x)$$

Here, y represents the *target* and x represents the *feature*. If x is a collection of features, it is also called a feature vector and denoted with X. The model is the function f that maps features to targets. Once the computer learns f, it can use the new values of x to predict the values of y.

The preceding simple equation can be rewritten in the context of linear models for machine learning as follows:

$$y = wx + b$$

Here, w is known as the weight and b is known as the bias. Thus, the machine learning problem now can be stated as a problem of finding w and b from the current values of X so that the equation can now be used to predict the values of y.

Regression analysis or regression modeling refers to the methods and techniques used to estimate relationships among variables. The variables that are used as input for regression models are called independent variables, predictors, or features, and the output variables from regression models are called dependent variables or targets. Regression models are defined as follows:

$$Y \approx f(X, \beta)$$

Where Y is the target variable, X is a vector of features, and β is a vector of parameters (w, b in the preceding equation).

Classification

Classification is one of the classical problems in machine learning.
Data under consideration could belong to one class or another, for example, if the images provided are data, they could be pictures of cats or dogs. Thus, the classes, in this case, are cats and dogs. Classification means identifying the label or class of the objects under consideration. Classification falls under the umbrella of supervised machine learning. In classification problems, a training dataset is provided that has features or inputs and their corresponding outputs or labels. Using this training dataset, a model is trained; in other words, the parameters of the model are computed. The trained model is then used on new data to find its correct labels.

Classification problems can be of two types: **binary class** or **multiclass**. Binary class means that the data is to be classified into two distinct and discrete labels; for example, the patient has cancer or the patient does not have cancer, and the images are of cats or dogs and so on. Multiclass means that the data is to be classified among multiple classes, for example, an email classification problem will divide emails into social media emails, work-related emails, personal emails, family-related emails, spam emails, shopping offer emails, and so on. Another example would be of pictures of digits; each picture could be labeled between 0 and 9, depending on what digit the picture represents. In this chapter, we will look at examples of both kinds of classification.

The most popular method for classification is logistic regression. Logistic regression is a probabilistic and linear classifier. The probability that the vector of input features belongs to a specific class can be described mathematically by the following equation:

$$P(Y = i|x, w, b) = \phi(z)$$

In the preceding equation, the following applies:

- Y represents the output
- i represents one of the classes
- x represents the inputs
- w represents the weights
- b represents the biases
- z represents the regression equation $z = w \times x + b$
- ϕ represents the smoothing function (or model, in our case)

The $\phi(z)$ function represents the probability that x belongs to class i when w and b are given. Thus, the model has to be trained to maximize the value of this probability.

Logistic regression for binary classification

For binary classification, the model function $\phi(z)$ is defined as the sigmoid function, which can be described as follows:

$$\phi(z) = \frac{1}{1 + e^{-z}} = \frac{1}{1 + e^{-(w \times x + b)}}$$

The sigmoid function transforms the y value to be between the range [0,1]. Thus, the value of $y=\phi(z)$ can be used to predict the class: if $y > 0.5$, then the object belongs to 1, otherwise the object belongs to 0.

The model training means to search for the parameters that minimize the loss function, which can either be the sum of squared errors or the sum of mean squared errors. For logistic regression, the likelihood is maximized as follows:

$$L(w) = P(y|x, w, b)$$

However, as it is easier to maximize the log-likelihood, we use the log-likelihood ($l(w)$) as the cost function. The loss function ($J(w)$) is written as -$l(w)$, and can be minimized by using optimization algorithms such as gradient descent.

The loss function for binary logistic regression is written mathematically as follows:

$$J(w) = -\sum_{i=1}^{n}[(y_i \times log(\phi(z_i))) + ((1 - y_i) \times (1 - log(\phi(z_i))))]$$

Here, $\phi(z)$ is the sigmoid function.

Logistic regression for multiclass classification

When more than two classes are involved, logistic regression is known as multinomial logistic regression. In multinomial logistic regression, instead of sigmoid, use the softmax function, which can be described mathematically as follows:

$$softmax\ \phi_i(z) = \frac{e_i^z}{\sum_j e_j^z} = \frac{e_i^{(w \times x + b)}}{\sum_j e_j^{(w \times x + b)}} =$$

The softmax function produces the probabilities for each class so that the probabilities vector adds up to *1*. At the time of inference, the class with the highest softmax value becomes the output or predicted class. The loss function, as we discussed earlier, is the negative log-likelihood function, -$l(w)$, that can be minimized by the optimizers, such as gradient descent.

The loss function for multinomial logistic regression is written formally as follows:

$$J(w) = -\sum_{i=1}^{n}[y_i \times log(\phi(z_i))]$$

Here, $\phi(z)$ is the softmax function.

We will implement this loss function in the next section. In the following section, we will dig into our example for multiclass classification with logistic regression in TensorFlow.

Logistic regression with TensorFlow

One of the most popular examples regarding multiclass classification is to label the images of handwritten digits. The classes, or labels, in this example are *{0,1,2,3,4,5,6,7,8,9}*. The dataset that we are going to use is popularly known as MNIST and is available from the following link: `http://yann.lecun.com/exdb/mnist/`. The MNIST dataset has 60,000 images for training and 10,000 images for testing. The images in the dataset appear as follows:

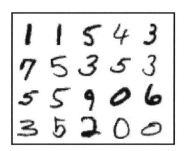

1. First, we must import `datasetslib`, a library that was written by us to help with examples in this book (available as a submodule of this book's GitHub repository):

```
DSLIB_HOME = '../datasetslib'
import sys
if not DSLIB_HOME in sys.path:
    sys.path.append(DSLIB_HOME)
%reload_ext autoreload
%autoreload 2
import datasetslib as dslib
```

```
from datasetslib.utils import imutil
from datasetslib.utils import nputil
from datasetslib.mnist import MNIST
```

2. Set the path to the `datasets` folder in our home directory, which is where we want all of the `datasets` to be stored:

```
import os
datasets_root = os.path.join(os.path.expanduser('~'),'datasets')
```

3. Get the MNIST data using our `datasetslib` and print the shapes to ensure that the data is loaded properly:

```
mnist=MNIST()

x_train,y_train,x_test,y_test=mnist.load_data()

mnist.y_onehot = True
mnist.x_layout = imutil.LAYOUT_NP
x_test = mnist.load_images(x_test)
y_test = nputil.onehot(y_test)

print('Loaded x and y')
print('Train: x:{}, y:{}'.format(len(x_train),y_train.shape))
print('Test: x:{}, y:{}'.format(x_test.shape,y_test.shape))
```

4. Define the hyperparameters for training the model:

```
learning_rate = 0.001
n_epochs = 5
mnist.batch_size = 100
```

5. Define the placeholders and parameters for our simple model:

```
# define input images
x = tf.placeholder(dtype=tf.float32, shape=[None,
mnist.n_features])
# define output labels
y = tf.placeholder(dtype=tf.float32, shape=[None, mnist.n_classes])

# model parameters
w = tf.Variable(tf.zeros([mnist.n_features, mnist.n_classes]))
b = tf.Variable(tf.zeros([mnist.n_classes]))
```

6. Define the model with `logits` and `y_hat`:

```
logits = tf.add(tf.matmul(x, w), b)
y_hat = tf.nn.softmax(logits)
```

7. Define the `loss` function:

```
epsilon = tf.keras.backend.epsilon()
y_hat_clipped = tf.clip_by_value(y_hat, epsilon, 1 - epsilon)
y_hat_log = tf.log(y_hat_clipped)
cross_entropy = -tf.reduce_sum(y * y_hat_log, axis=1)
loss_f = tf.reduce_mean(cross_entropy)
```

8. Define the `optimizer` function:

```
optimizer = tf.train.GradientDescentOptimizer
optimizer_f =
optimizer(learning_rate=learning_rate).minimize(loss_f)
```

9. Define the function to check the accuracy of the trained model:

```
predictions_check = tf.equal(tf.argmax(y_hat, 1), tf.argmax(y, 1))
accuracy_f = tf.reduce_mean(tf.cast(predictions_check, tf.float32))
```

10. Run the `training` loop for each epoch in a TensorFlow session:

```
n_batches = int(60000/mnist.batch_size)

with tf.Session() as tfs:
    tf.global_variables_initializer().run()
    for epoch in range(n_epochs):
        mnist.reset_index()
        for batch in range(n_batches):
            x_batch, y_batch = mnist.next_batch()
            feed_dict={x: x_batch, y: y_batch}
            batch_loss,_ = tfs.run([loss_f,
optimizer_f],feed_dict=feed_dict )
            #print('Batch loss:{}'.format(batch_loss))
```

11. Run the evaluation function for each epoch with the test data in the same TensorFlow session that was created previously:

```
feed_dict = {x: x_test, y: y_test}
accuracy_score = tfs.run(accuracy_f, feed_dict=feed_dict)
print('epoch {0:04d}   accuracy={1:.8f}'
        .format(epoch, accuracy_score))
```

We get the following output:

```
epoch 0000 accuracy=0.73280001 epoch 0001 accuracy=0.72869998 epoch 0002
accuracy=0.74550003 epoch 0003 accuracy=0.75260001 epoch 0004
accuracy=0.74299997
```

There you go. We just trained our very first logistic regression model using TensorFlow for classifying handwritten digit images and got 74.3% accuracy.

Now, let's see how writing the same model in Keras makes this process even easier.

Logistic regression with Keras

Keras is a high-level library that is available as part of TensorFlow. In this section, we will rebuild the same model we built earlier with TensorFlow core with Keras:

1. Keras takes data in a different format, and so we must first reformat the data using `datasetslib`:

   ```
   x_train_im = mnist.load_images(x_train)

   x_train_im, x_test_im = x_train_im / 255.0, x_test / 255.0
   ```

   In the preceding code, we are loading the training images in memory before both the training and test images are scaled, which we do by dividing them by `255`.

2. Then, we build the model:

   ```
   model = tf.keras.models.Sequential([
       tf.keras.layers.Flatten(),
       tf.keras.layers.Dense(10, activation=tf.nn.softmax)
   ])
   ```

3. Compile the model with the `sgd` optimizer. Set the categorical entropy as the `loss` function and the accuracy as a metric to test the model:

   ```
   model.compile(optimizer='sgd',
                 loss='sparse_categorical_crossentropy',
                 metrics=['accuracy'])
   ```

4. Train the model for 5 epochs with the training set of images and labels:

```
model.fit(x_train_im, y_train, epochs=5)

Epoch 1/5
60000/60000 [==============================] - 3s 45us/step - loss:
0.7874 - acc: 0.8095
Epoch 2/5
60000/60000 [==============================] - 3s 42us/step - loss:
0.4585 - acc: 0.8792
Epoch 3/5
60000/60000 [==============================] - 2s 42us/step - loss:
0.4049 - acc: 0.8909
Epoch 4/5
60000/60000 [==============================] - 3s 42us/step - loss:
0.3780 - acc: 0.8965
Epoch 5/5
60000/60000 [==============================] - 3s 42us/step - loss:
0.3610 - acc: 0.9012
10000/10000 [==============================] - 0s 24us/step
```

5. Evaluate the model with the test data:

```
model.evaluate(x_test_im, nputil.argmax(y_test))
```

We get the following evaluation scores as output:

```
[0.33530342621803283, 0.9097]
```

Wow! Using Keras, we can achieve higher accuracy. We achieved approximately 90% accuracy. This is because Keras internally sets many optimal values for us so that we can quickly start building models.

 To learn more about Keras and to look at more examples, refer to the book *Mastering TensorFlow,* from Packt Publications.

Summary

In this chapter, we briefly covered the TensorFlow library. We covered the TensorFlow data model elements, such as constants, variables, and placeholders, and how they can be used to build TensorFlow computation graphs. We learned how to create tensors from Python objects. Tensor objects can also be generated as specific values, sequences, or random valued distributions from various TensorFlow library functions.

We covered the TensorFlow programming model, which includes defining and executing computation graphs. These computation graphs have nodes and edges. The nodes represent operations and edges represent tensors that transfer data from one node to another. We covered how to create and execute graphs, the order of execution, and how to execute graphs on multiple compute devices, such as CPU and GPU.

We also learned about machine learning and implemented a classification algorithm to identify the handwritten digits dataset. The algorithm we implemented is known as multinomial logistic regression. We used both TensorFlow core and Keras to implement the logistic regression algorithm.

Starting from the next chapter, we will look at many projects that will be implemented using TensorFlow and Keras.

Questions

Enhance your understanding by practicing the following questions:

1. Modify the logistic regression model that was given in this chapter so that you can use different training rates and observe how it impacts training
2. Use different optimizer functions and observe the impact of different functions on training time and accuracy

Further reading

We suggest the reader learn more by reading the following materials:

- *Mastering TensorFlow* by Armando Fandango.
- TensorFlow tutorials at `https://www.tensorflow.org/tutorials/`.
- *TensorFlow 1.x Deep Learning Cookbook* by Antonio Gulli and Amita Kapoor

2
Using Machine Learning to Detect Exoplanets in Outer Space

In this chapter, we shall learn how to detect exoplanets in outer space using ensemble methods that are based on decision trees.

Decision trees are a family of non-parametric supervised learning methods. In a decision tree algorithm, the data is divided into two partitions by using a simple rule. The rule is applied again and again to further partition the data, thus forming a tree of decisions.

Ensemble methods combine the learning from multiple learning algorithms to improve predictions and reduce errors. These ensembles are differentiated on the basis of what kind of learners they use and how they structure those learns in the ensemble.

The two most popular ensemble methods based on decision trees are known as gradient boosted trees and random forests.

The following topics will be covered in this chapter:

- What is a decision tree?
- Why we need ensembles?
- Decision tree-based ensemble methods
  - Random forests
  - Gradient boosting
- Decision tree-based ensembles in TensorFlow
- Building a TensorFlow boosted tree model for exoplanet detection

The code from this chapter is available in Jupyter Notebook as ch-02_Detecting_Explonaets_in_Outer_Space.ipynb in the code bundle.

What is a decision tree?

Decision trees are a family of non-parametric supervised learning methods. In the decision tree algorithm, we start with the complete dataset and split it into two partitions based on a simple rule. The splitting continues until a specified criterion is met. The nodes at which the split is made are called interior nodes and the final endpoints are called terminal or leaf nodes.

As an example, let us look at the following tree:

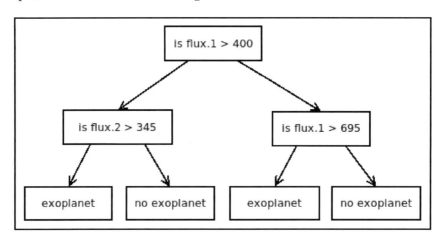

Here, we are assuming that the exoplanet data has only two properties: **flux.1** and **flux.2**. First, we make a decision if **flux.1 > 400** and then divide the data into two partitions. Then we divide the data again based on **flux.2** feature, and that division decides whether the planet is an exoplanet or not. How did we decide that condition **flux.1 > 400**? We did not. This was just to demonstrate a decision tree. During the training phase, that's what the model learns – the parameters of conditions that divide the data into partitions.

For classification problems, the decision tree has leaf nodes that shows the result as the discrete classification of the data and for regression problems, the leaf nodes show the results as a predicted number. Decision trees, thus, are also popularly known as **Classification and Regression Trees (CART)**.

Why do we need ensembles?

Decision trees are prone to overfitting training data and suffer from high variance, thus, providing poor predictions from new unseen data. However, using an ensemble of decision trees helps alleviate the shortcoming of using a single decision tree model. In an ensemble, many weak learners come together to create a strong learner.

Among the many ways that we can combine decision trees to make ensembles, the two methods that have been popular due to their performance for predictive modeling are:

- Gradient boosting (also known as gradient tree boosting)
- Random decision trees (also known as random forests)

Decision tree-based ensemble methods

In this section let us explore briefly two kinds of ensemble methods for decision trees: random forests and gradient boosting.

Random forests

Random forests is a technique where you construct multiple trees, and then use those trees to learn the classification and regression models, but the results are aggregated from the trees to produce a final result.

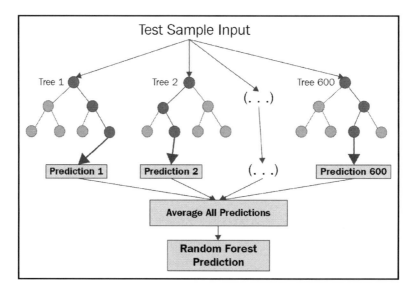

Random forests are an ensemble of random, uncorrelated, and fully-grown decision trees. The decision trees used in the random forest model are fully grown, thus, having low bias and high variance. The trees are uncorrelated in nature, which results in a maximum decrease in the variance. By uncorrelated, we imply that each decision tree in the random forest is given a randomly selected subset of features and a randomly selected subset of the dataset for the selected features.

The original paper describing random forests is available at the following link: `https://www.stat.berkeley.edu/~breiman/randomforest2001.pdf`.

The random forest technique does not reduce bias and as a result, has a slightly higher bias as compared to the individual trees in the ensemble.

Random forests were invented by Leo Breiman and have been trademarked by Leo Breiman and Adele Cutler. More information is available at the following link: `https://www.stat.berkeley.edu/~breiman/RandomForests`.

Intuitively, in the random forest model, a large number of decision trees are trained on different samples of data, that either fit or overfit. By averaging the individual decision trees, overfitting cancels out.

Random forests seem similar to bagging, aka bootstrap aggregating, but they are different. In bagging, a random sample with replacement is selected to train every tree in the ensemble. The tree is trained on all the features. In random forests, the features are also sampled randomly, and at each candidate that is split, a subset of features is used to train the model.

For predicting values in case of regression problems, the random forest model averages the predictions from individual decision trees. For predicting classes in case of a classification problem, the random forest model takes a majority vote from the results of individual decision trees.

An interesting explanation of random forests can be found at the following link: `https://machinelearning-blog.com/2018/02/06/the-random-forest-algorithm/`

Gradient boosting

Gradient boosted trees are an ensemble of shallow trees (or weak learners). The shallow decision trees could be as small as a tree with just two leaves (also known as decision stump). The boosting methods help in reducing bias mainly but also help reduce variance slightly.

Original papers by Breiman and Friedman who developed the idea of gradient boosting are available at following links:

- *Prediction Games and Arcing Algorithms* by Breiman, L at `https://www.stat.berkeley.edu/~breiman/games.pdf`
- *Arcing The Edge* by Breiman, L at `http://statistics.berkeley.edu/sites/default/files/tech-reports/486.pdf`
- *Greedy Function Approximation: A Gradient Boosting Machine* by Friedman, J. H. at `http://statweb.stanford.edu/~jhf/ftp/trebst.pdf`
- *Stochastic Gradient Boosting* by Friedman, J. H. at `https://statweb.stanford.edu/~jhf/ftp/stobst.pdf`

Intuitively, in the gradient boosting model, the decision trees in the ensemble are trained in several iterations as shown in the following image. A new decision tree is added at each iteration. Every additional decision tree is trained to improve the trained ensemble model in previous iterations. This is different from the random forest model where each decision tree is trained independently from the other decision trees in the ensemble.

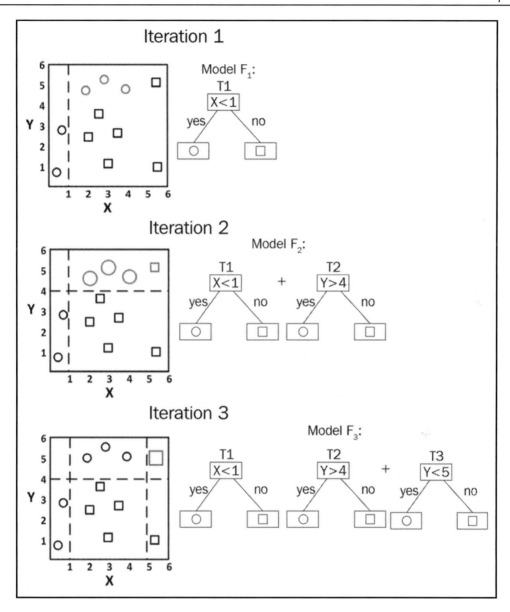

The gradient boosting model has lesser number of trees as compared to the random forests model but ends up with a very large number of hyperparameters that need to be tuned to get a decent gradient boosting model.

An interesting explanation of gradient boosting can be found at the following link: `http://blog.kaggle.com/2017/01/23/a-kaggle-master-explains-gradient-boosting/`.

Decision tree-based ensembles in TensorFlow

In this chapter, we shall use the gradient boosted trees and random forest implementation as pre-made estimators in TensorFlow from the Google TensorFlow team. Let us learn the details of their implementation in the upcoming sections.

TensorForest Estimator

TensorForest is a highly scalable implementation of random forests built by combining a variety of online HoeffdingTree algorithms with the extremely randomized approach.

Google published the details of the TensorForest implementation in the following paper: *TensorForest: Scalable Random Forests on TensorFlow* by Thomas Colthurst, D. Sculley, Gibert Hendry, Zack Nado, presented at Machine Learning Systems Workshop at the Conference on **Neural Information Processing Systems (NIPS)** 2016. The paper is available at the following link: `https://docs.google.com/viewer?a=v pid=sitessrcid= ZGVmYXVsdGRvbWFpbnxtbHN5c25pcHMyMDE2fGd4OjFlNTRiOWU2OGM2YzA4MjE.`

TensorForest estimators are used to implementing the following algorithm:

```
Initialize the variables and sets
    Tree = [root]
    Fertile = {root}
    Stats(root) = 0
    Splits[root] = []

Divide training data into batches.
For each batch of training data:

    Compute leaf assignment $l_i$ for each feature vector

    Update the leaf stats in Stats($l_i$)

    For each $l_i$ in Fertile set:
```

```
    if |Splits($l_i$)| < max_splits
        then add the split on a randomly selected feature to Splits($l_i$)
    else if $l_i$ is fertile and |Splits($l_i$)| = max_splits
        then update the split stats for $l_i$
Calculate the fertile leaves that are finished.
For every non-stale finished leaf:
    turn the leaf into an internal node with its best scoring split
    remove the leaf from Fertile
    add the leaf's two children to Tree as leaves
If |Fertile| < max_fertile
    Then add the max_fertile - |Fertile| leaves with
    the highest weighted leaf scores to Fertile and
    initialize their Splits and split statistics.
Until |Tree| = max_nodes or |Tree| stays the same for max_batches_to_grow
batches
```

More details of this algorithm implementation can be found in the TensorForest paper.

TensorFlow boosted trees estimator

TensorFlow Boosted Trees (TFBT) is an improved scalable ensemble model built on top of generic gradient boosting trees.

Google published the details of the TensorFlow boosted trees implementation in the following paper: *A scalable TensorFlow based framework for gradient boosting* by Natalia Ponomareva, Soroush Radpour, Gilbert Hendry, Salem Haykal, Thomas Colthurst, Petr Mitrichev, Alexander Grushetsky, presented at the European Conference on Machine Learning and Principles and Practice of Knowledge Discovery in Databases (ECML PKDD) 2017. The paper is available at the following link: http://ecmlpkdd2017.ijs.si/papers/paperID705.pdf.

The gradient boosting algorithm is implemented by various libraries such as `sklearn`, `MLLib`, and `XGBoost`. TensorFlow's implementation is different from these implementations as described in the following table extracted from the TFBT research paper:

Lib	D?	Losses	Regularization
scikit-learn	N	*R*: least squares, least absolute dev, huber and quantile. *C*: logistic, Max-Ent and exp	Depth limit, shrinkage, bagging, feature subsampling
GBM	N	*R*: least squares, least absolute dev, t-distribution, quantile, huber. *C*: logistic, Max-Ent, exp, poisson & right censored observations. Supports *ranking*	Shrinkage, bagging, depth limit, min # of examples per node.
MLLib	Y	*R*: least squared and least absolute dev. *C*: logistic.	Shrinkage, early stopping, depth limit, min # of examples per node, min gain, bagging.
Light GBM	Y	*R*: least squares, least absolute dev, huber, fair, poisson. *C*: logistic, Max-Ent. Supports *ranking*.	Dropout, shrinkage, # leafs limit, feature subsampling, bagging, L1 & L2
XGBoost	Y	*R*: least squares, poisson, gamma, tweedie regression. *C*: logistic, Max-Ent. Supports *ranking* and **custom**.	L1 & L2, shrinkage, feature subsampling, dropout, bagging, min child weight and gain, limit on depth and # of nodes, pruning.
TFBT	Y	Any twice differentiable loss from tf.contrib.losses and **custom** losses.	L1 & L2, tree complexity, shrinkage, line search for learning rate, dropout, feature subsampling and bagging, limit on depth and min node weight, pre- post- pruning.

D? is whether a library supports distributed mode. *R* stands for regression, *C* for classification.

TFBT Research Paper from Google

The TFBT model can be extended by writing custom loss functions in TensorFlow. The differentiation for these custom loss functions is automatically provided by TensorFlow.

Detecting exoplanets in outer space

For the project explained in this chapter, we use the *Kepler labeled time series data* from Kaggle: `https://www.kaggle.com/keplersmachines/kepler-labelled-time-series-data/home`. This dataset is derived mainly from the Campaign 3 observations of the mission by NASA's Kepler space telescope.

In the dataset, column 1 values are the labels and columns 2 to 3198 values are the flux values over time. The training set has 5087 data points, 37 confirmed exoplanets, and 5050 non-exoplanet stars. The test set has 570 data points, 5 confirmed exoplanets, and 565 non-exoplanet stars.

We will carry out the following steps to download, and then preprocess our data to create the train and test datasets:

1. Download the dataset using the Kaggle API. The following code will be used for the same:

```
armando@librenix:~/datasets/kaggle-kepler$ kaggle datasets download
-d keplersmachines/kepler-labelled-time-series-data

Downloading kepler-labelled-time-series-data.zip to
/mnt/disk1tb/datasets/kaggle-kepler
100%|████████████████████████████████████████| 57.4M/57.4M
[00:03<00:00, 18.3MB/s]
```

The folder contains the following two files:

```
exoTest.csv
exoTrain.csv
```

2. Link the folder `datasets` to our home folder so we can access it from the `~/datasets/kaggle-kepler` path and then we define the folder path and list the contents of the folder through the Notebook to confirm if we have access to the data files through the Notebook:

```
dsroot = os.path.join(os.path.expanduser('~'),'datasets','kaggle-
kepler')
os.listdir(dsroot)
```

We get the following output:

```
['exoTest.csv', 'kepler-labelled-time-series-data.zip',
'exoTrain.csv']
```

 The ZIP file is just a leftover of the download process because the Kaggle API begins by downloading the ZIP file and then proceeds to unzip the contents in the same folder.

3. We will then read the two `.csv` data files in the `pandas` DataFrames named `train` and `test` respectively:

```
import pandas as pd
train = pd.read_csv(os.path.join(dsroot,'exoTrain.csv'))
test = pd.read_csv(os.path.join(dsroot,'exoTest.csv'))
print('Training data\n',train.head())
print('Test data\n',test.head())
```

The first five lines of the `training` and `test data` look similar to the following:

```
Training data
      LABEL    FLUX.1    FLUX.2    FLUX.3   \
0        2     93.85     83.81     20.10
1        2    -38.88    -33.83    -58.54
2        2    532.64    535.92    513.73
3        2    326.52    347.39    302.35
4        2  -1107.21  -1112.59  -1118.95
     FLUX.4    FLUX.5    FLUX.6   FLUX.7    \
0    -26.98    -39.56   -124.71  -135.18
1    -40.09    -79.31    -72.81   -86.55
2    496.92    456.45    466.00   464.50
3    298.13    317.74    312.70   322.33
4  -1095.10  -1057.55  -1034.48  -998.34

    FLUX.8   FLUX.9       ...        FLUX.3188  \
0   -96.27   -79.89       ...           -78.07
1   -85.33   -83.97       ...            -3.28
2   486.39   436.56       ...           -71.69
3   311.31   312.42       ...             5.71
4 -1022.71  -989.57       ...          -594.37

   FLUX.3189  FLUX.3190  FLUX.3191   \
0    -102.15    -102.15      25.13
1     -32.21     -32.21     -24.89
2      13.31      13.31     -29.89
3      -3.73      -3.73      30.05
4    -401.66    -401.66    -357.24

   FLUX.3192  FLUX.3193  FLUX.3194
0      48.57      92.54      39.32
1      -4.86       0.76     -11.70
2     -20.88       5.06     -11.80
3      20.03     -12.67      -8.77
4    -443.76    -438.54    -399.71

   FLUX.3195  FLUX.3196  FLUX.3197
0      61.42       5.08     -39.54
```

```
1        6.46        16.00        19.93
2      -28.91       -70.02       -96.67
3      -17.31       -17.35        13.98
4     -384.65      -411.79      -510.54

[5 rows x 3198 columns]

Test data

    LABEL     FLUX.1     FLUX.2     FLUX.3    \
0      2     119.88     100.21      86.46
1      2    5736.59    5699.98    5717.16
2      2     844.48     817.49     770.07
3      2    -826.00    -827.31    -846.12
4      2     -39.57     -15.88      -9.16

      FLUX.4     FLUX.5     FLUX.6     FLUX.7   \
0      48.68      46.12      39.39      18.57
1    5692.73    5663.83    5631.16    5626.39
2     675.01     605.52     499.45     440.77
3    -836.03    -745.50    -784.69    -791.22
4      -6.37     -16.13     -24.05      -0.90

     FLUX.8     FLUX.9       ...      FLUX.3188   \
0      6.98       6.63       ...          14.52
1    5569.47    5550.44       ...        -581.91
2     362.95     207.27       ...          17.82
3    -746.50    -709.53       ...         122.34
4     -45.20      -5.04       ...         -37.87
     FLUX.3189   FLUX.3190   FLUX.3191    \
0       19.29       14.44       -1.62
1     -984.09    -1230.89    -1600.45
2      -51.66      -48.29      -59.99
3       93.03       93.03       68.81
4      -61.85      -27.15      -21.18

     FLUX.3192   FLUX.3193   FLUX.3194    \
0       13.33       45.50       31.93
1    -1824.53    -2061.17    -2265.98
2      -82.10     -174.54      -95.23
3        9.81       20.75       20.25
4      -33.76      -85.34      -81.46

     FLUX.3195   FLUX.3196   FLUX.3197
0       35.78      269.43       57.72
1    -2366.19    -2294.86    -2034.72
2     -162.68      -36.79       30.63
3     -120.81     -257.56     -215.41
```

```
4     -61.98     -69.34     -17.84

[5 rows x 3198 columns]
```

The training and test datasets have labels in the first column and 3197 features in the next columns. Now let us split the training and test data into labels and features with the following code:

```
x_train = train.drop('LABEL', axis=1)
y_train = train.LABEL-1 #subtract one because of TGBT
x_test = test.drop('LABEL', axis=1)
y_test = test.LABEL-1
```

In the preceding code, we subtract 1 from the labels, since the TFBT estimator assumes labels starting with numerical zero while the features in the datasets are numbers 1 and 2.

Now that we have the label and feature vectors for training and test data, let us build the boosted tree models.

Building a TFBT model for exoplanet detection

In this section, we shall build the gradient boosted trees model for detecting exoplanets using the Kepler dataset. Let us follow these steps in the Jupyter Notebook to build and train the exoplanet finder model:

1. We will save the names of all the features in a vector with the following code:

```
numeric_column_headers = x_train.columns.values.tolist()
```

2. We will then bucketize the feature columns into two buckets around the mean since the TFBT estimator only takes bucketed features with the following code:

```
bc_fn = tf.feature_column.bucketized_column
nc_fn = tf.feature_column.numeric_column
bucketized_features = [bc_fn(source_column=nc_fn(key=column),
                       boundaries=[x_train[column].mean()])
                 for column in numeric_column_headers]
```

3. Since we only have numeric bucketized features and no other kinds of features, we store them in the all_features variable with the following code:

```
all_features = bucketized_features
```

4. We will then define the batch size and create a function that will provide inputs from the label and feature vectors created from the training data. For creating this function we use a convenience function `tf.estimator.inputs.pandas_input_fn()` provided by TensorFlow. We will use the following code:

```
batch_size = 32
pi_fn = tf.estimator.inputs.pandas_input_fn
train_input_fn = pi_fn(x = x_train,
                       y = y_train,
                       batch_size = batch_size,
                       shuffle = True,
                       num_epochs = None)
```

5. Similarly, we will create another data input function that would be used to evaluate the model from the test features and label vectors and name it `eval_input_fn` using the following code:

```
eval_input_fn = pi_fn(x = x_test,
                      y = y_test,
                      batch_size = batch_size,
                      shuffle = False,
                      num_epochs = 1)
```

6. We will define the number of trees to be created as 100 and the number of steps to be used for training as 100. We also define the `BoostedTreeClassifier` as the `estimator` using the following code:

```
n_trees = 100
n_steps = 100

m_fn = tf.estimator.BoostedTreesClassifier
model = m_fn(feature_columns=all_features,
             n_trees = n_trees,
             n_batches_per_layer = batch_size,
             model_dir='./tfbtmodel')
```

Since we are doing classification, hence we use the `BoostedTreesClassifier`, for regression problems where a value needs to be predicted, TensorFlow also has an `estimator` named `BoostedTreesRegressor`.

One of the parameters provided to the `estimator` function is `model_dir` that defines where the trained model would be stored. The estimators are built such that they look for the model in that folder in further invocations for using them for inference and prediction. We name the folder as `tfbtmodel` to save the model.

 We have used the minimum number of models to define the `BoostedTreesClassifier`. Please look up the definition of this estimator in the TensorFlow API documentation to find various other parameters that can be provided to further customize the estimator.

The following output in the Jupyter Notebook describes the classifier estimator and its various settings:

```
INFO:tensorflow:Using default config.
INFO:tensorflow:Using config: {'_model_dir': './tfbtmodel',
'_tf_random_seed': None, '_save_summary_steps': 100,
'_save_checkpoints_steps': None, '_save_checkpoints_secs': 600,
'_session_config': None, '_keep_checkpoint_max': 5,
'_keep_checkpoint_every_n_hours': 10000, '_log_step_count_steps':
100, '_train_distribute': None, '_device_fn': None, '_service':
None, '_cluster_spec':
<tensorflow.python.training.server_lib.ClusterSpec object at
0x7fdd48c93b38>, '_task_type': 'worker', '_task_id': 0,
'_global_id_in_cluster': 0, '_master': '', '_evaluation_master':
'', '_is_chief': True, '_num_ps_replicas': 0,
'_num_worker_replicas': 1}
```

7. Post this, we will train the model using the `train_input_fn` function that provides the exoplanets input data using 100 steps with the following code:

```
model.train(input_fn=train_input_fn, steps=n_steps)
```

The Jupyter Notebook shows the following output to indicate the training in progress:

```
INFO:tensorflow:Calling model_fn.
INFO:tensorflow:Done calling model_fn.
INFO:tensorflow:Create CheckpointSaverHook.
WARNING:tensorflow:Issue encountered when serializing resources.
Type is unsupported, or the types of the items don't match field
type in CollectionDef. Note this is a warning and probably safe to
ignore.
'_Resource' object has no attribute 'name'
INFO:tensorflow:Graph was finalized.
INFO:tensorflow:Restoring parameters from
```

```
./tfbtmodel/model.ckpt-19201
INFO:tensorflow:Running local_init_op.
INFO:tensorflow:Done running local_init_op.
WARNING:tensorflow:Issue encountered when serializing resources.
Type is unsupported, or the types of the items don't match field
type in CollectionDef. Note this is a warning and probably safe to
ignore.
'_Resource' object has no attribute 'name'
INFO:tensorflow:Saving checkpoints for 19201 into
./tfbtmodel/model.ckpt.
WARNING:tensorflow:Issue encountered when serializing resources.
Type is unsupported, or the types of the items don't match field
type in CollectionDef. Note this is a warning and probably safe to
ignore.
'_Resource' object has no attribute 'name'
INFO:tensorflow:loss = 1.0475121e-05, step = 19201
INFO:tensorflow:Saving checkpoints for 19202 into
./tfbtmodel/model.ckpt.
WARNING:tensorflow:Issue encountered when serializing resources.
Type is unsupported, or the types of the items don't match field
type in CollectionDef. Note this is a warning and probably safe to
ignore.
'_Resource' object has no attribute 'name'
INFO:tensorflow:Loss for final step: 1.0475121e-05.
```

8. Use the `eval_input_fn` that provides batches from the `test` dataset to evaluate the model with the following code:

```
results = model.evaluate(input_fn=eval_input_fn)
```

The Jupyter Notebook shows the following output as the progress of the evaluation:

```
INFO:tensorflow:Calling model_fn.
WARNING:tensorflow:Trapezoidal rule is known to produce incorrect
PR-AUCs; please switch to "careful_interpolation" instead.
WARNING:tensorflow:Trapezoidal rule is known to produce incorrect
PR-AUCs; please switch to "careful_interpolation" instead.
INFO:tensorflow:Done calling model_fn.
INFO:tensorflow:Starting evaluation at 2018-09-07-04:23:31
INFO:tensorflow:Graph was finalized.
INFO:tensorflow:Restoring parameters from
./tfbtmodel/model.ckpt-19203
INFO:tensorflow:Running local_init_op.
INFO:tensorflow:Done running local_init_op.
INFO:tensorflow:Finished evaluation at 2018-09-07-04:23:50
INFO:tensorflow:Saving dict for global step 19203: accuracy =
0.99122804, accuracy_baseline = 0.99122804, auc = 0.49911517,
```

```
auc_precision_recall = 0.004386465, average_loss = 0.09851996,
global_step = 19203, label/mean = 0.00877193, loss = 0.09749381,
precision = 0.0, prediction/mean = 4.402521e-05, recall = 0.0
WARNING:tensorflow:Issue encountered when serializing resources.
Type is unsupported, or the types of the items don't match field
type in CollectionDef. Note this is a warning and probably safe to
ignore.
'_Resource' object has no attribute 'name'
INFO:tensorflow:Saving 'checkpoint_path' summary for global step
19203: ./tfbtmodel/model.ckpt-19203
```

Note that during the evaluation the estimator loads the parameters saved in the checkpoint file:

```
INFO:tensorflow:Restoring parameters from
./tfbtmodel/model.ckpt-19203
```

9. The results of the evaluation are stored in the `results` collection. Let us print each item in the `results` collection using the `for` loop in the following code:

```
for key,value in sorted(results.items()):
    print('{}: {}'.format(key, value))
```

The Notebook shows the following results:

```
accuracy: 0.9912280440330505
accuracy_baseline: 0.9912280440330505
auc: 0.4991151690483093
auc_precision_recall: 0.004386465065181255
average_loss: 0.0985199585556984
global_step: 19203
label/mean: 0.008771929889917374
loss: 0.09749381244182587
precision: 0.0
prediction/mean: 4.4025211536791176e-05
recall: 0.0
```

It is observed that we achieve an accuracy of almost 99% with the first model itself. This is because the estimators are prewritten with several optimizations and we did not need to set various values of hyperparameters ourselves. For some datasets, the default hyperparameter values in the estimators will work out of the box, but for other datasets, you will have to play with various inputs to the estimators.

Summary

In this chapter, we learned what a decision tree is and two broad classes of creating ensembles from the decision trees. The ensembles we took a look at were random forests and gradient boosting trees.

We also learned about the Kepler dataset from Kaggle competitions. We used the Kepler dataset to build an exoplanet detection model using TensorFlow's prebuilt estimator for gradient boosting trees known as the `BoostedTreesClassifier`. The `BoostedTreesClassifier` estimator is part of the machine learning toolkit recently released by the TensorFlow team. As for now, the TensorFlow team is working on releasing prebuilt estimators based on **support vector machine (SVM)** and extreme random forests as part of the `tf.estimators` API.

In the next chapter, we shall learn how to use TensorFlow in the browser using the `TensorFlow.js` API for sentiment analysis.

Questions

- How is gradient boosting different from random forests?
- How can you improve the performance of random forests?
- How can you improve the performance of gradient boosting trees?
- How to ensure that gradient boosting trees and random forests do not overfit?
- Modify the model in this chapter with different parameters such as the number of trees, batch size, number of epochs and number of steps and observe their effect on training time and different levels of accuracy.

Further reading

- https://www.tensorflow.org/tutorials/
- https://www.stat.berkeley.edu/~breiman/RandomForests
- https://www.stat.berkeley.edu/~breiman/randomforest2001.pdf
- https://machinelearning-blog.com/2018/02/06/the-random-forest-algorithm/
- http://blog.kaggle.com/2017/01/23/a-kaggle-master-explains-gradient-boosting/

- https://www.stat.berkeley.edu/~breiman/games.pdf
- http://statistics.berkeley.edu/sites/default/files/tech-reports/486.pdf
- http://statweb.stanford.edu/~jhf/ftp/trebst.pdf
- https://statweb.stanford.edu/~jhf/ftp/stobst.pdf
- https://docs.google.com/viewer?a=vpid=sitessrcid=ZGVmYXVsdGRvbWFpbnxtbHN5c25pcHMyMDE2fGd4OjFlNTRiOWU2OGM2YzA4MjE
- http://ecmlpkdd2017.ijs.si/papers/paperID705.pdf

Sentiment Analysis in Your Browser Using TensorFlow.js

3

Sentiment analysis is a popular problem in machine learning. People are constantly trying to understand the sentiment of a product or movie review. Currently, for sentiment analysis, we extract the text from a client/browser, pass it on to a server that runs a machine learning model to predict sentiment of the text, and the server then sends the result back to the client.

This is perfectly fine if we don't care about the latency in the system. However, there are many applications, such as stock trading, customer support conversations where it might be helpful to predict sentiment of the text with low latency. One obvious bottleneck in reducing latency is the server call.

If sentiment analysis could be achieved on the browser/client itself, we can get rid of the server call and can predict the sentiment in real time. Google recently released TensorFlow.js, which enables us to do the model training and inference on a browser/client.

Additionally, training the models on the client side opens up a world of opportunities. A brief summary of all the advantages of doing this are as follows:

- **Privacy**: Since data will never leave the client side, we are able to provide the magical experience of machine learning without compromising on data privacy
- **No hassle ML**: Since the code runs on a browser, the user doesn't need to install any libraries or dependencies
- **Latency**: Since there is no need to transfer data to servers for training/predictions, we can deploy ML models for low latency applications
- **Device agnostic**: A web page can be opened on any device (laptop, mobile. and so on) and so TensorFlow.js can take advantage of any hardware (GPU) or device sensors, such as accelerometers in mobile devices, to train ML models

Let's learn how to incorporate sentiment analysis in the browser using TensorFlow.js by covering the following topics:

- Understanding TensorFlow.js
- Understanding Adam Optimization
- Understanding Categorical Cross Entropy Loss
- Understanding Word Embeddings
- Setting up the sentiment analysis problem and building a model in Python
- Deploying the model using TensorFlow.js in a browser

Find the code for this chapter and Installation instructions are also present in a **README** file in repository for this project.

Understanding TensorFlow.js

TensorFlow recently open sourced TensorFlow.js. This is an open source library that helps us define and train deep learning models entirely on the browser using JavaScript as well as through a high-level layered API. We can use this to train deep learning models entirely on the client side. A server GPU is not required to train these models.

The following diagram illustrates the API overview of TensorFlow.js:

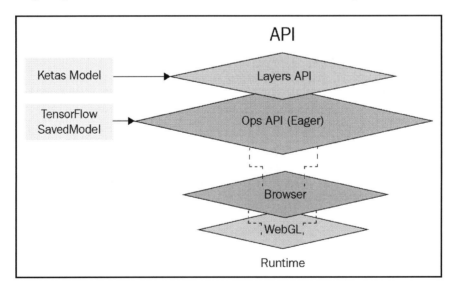

This is powered by **WebGL**. It also provides a high-level layered API. It has a support for **Eager** execution, too. You can achieve three things using TensorFlow.js:

- Load existing TensorFlow/Keras models for in browser predictions
- Retrain existing models using client data
- Define and train Deep Learning models from scratch on the **Browser**

Understanding Adam Optimization

Before we look at Adam optimization, let's try to first understand the concept of gradient descent.

Gradient descent is an iterative optimization algorithm to find the minimum of a function. An analogous example could be as follows: let's say we are stuck on somewhere in middle of a mountain and we want to reach the ground in fastest possible manner. As a first step, we will observe the slope of mountain in all directions around us and decide to take the the direction with steepest slope down.

We re-evaluate our choice of direction after every step we take. Also, the size of our walking also depends on the steepness of the downward slope. If the slope is very steep, we take bigger steps as it can help us to reach faster to the ground. This way after a few/large number of steps we can reach the ground safely. Similarly, in machine learning, we want to minimize some error/cost function by updating the weights of the algorithm. To find minimum of cost function using gradient, we update the weights of the algorithm proportional to the gradient in the direction of steepest descent. The proportionality constant is also known as Learning Rate in neural network literature.

However, in large scale machine learning, doing gradient descent optimization is pretty costly because we take only one step after a single pass on our entire training dataset. So, the time to converge to a minimum of cost function is huge if we were to take several thousand steps to converge.

A solution to this problem is Stochastic Gradient Descent (SGD), an approach to update weights of the algorithm after each training example and not wait for entire training dataset to pass through the algorithm for the update. We use the term, **stochastic** to denote the approximate nature of gradient as it is only computed after every training example. However, it is shown in the literature that after many iterations, SGD almost surely converges to the true local/global minimum of the function. Generally, in deep learning algorithms, we can observe that we tend to use mini-batch SGD where we update the weights after every mini batch and not after every training example.

Adam optimization is a variant of SGD where we maintain per parameter (weight) learning rate and update it based on the mean and variance of previous gradients of that parameter. Adam has been proven to be extremely good and fast for many deep learning problems. For more details on Adam optimization, please refer to the original paper (https://arxiv. org/abs/1412.6980).

Understanding categorical cross entropy loss

Cross entropy loss, or log loss, measures the performance of the classification model whose output is a probability between 0 and 1. Cross entropy increases as the predicted probability of a sample diverges from the actual value. Therefore, predicting a probability of 0.05 when the actual label has a value of 1 increases the cross entropy loss.

Mathematically, for a binary classification setting, cross entropy is defined as the following equation:

$$-(y_i \log(p_i) + (1 - y_i) \log(1 - p_i))$$

Here, y_i is the binary indicator (0 or 1) denoting the class for the sample i, p_i while denotes the predicted probability between 0 and 1 for that sample.

Alternatively, if there are more than two classes, we define a new term known as categorical cross entropy. It is calculated as a sum of separate loss for each class label per observation. Mathematically, it is given as the following equation:

$$-\Sigma_{c=1}^{M} y_{i,c} \log(p_{i,c})$$

Here, M denotes the number of classes, $y_{i,c}$ is a binary indicator (0 or 1) that indicates whether c is the correct class for the observation, i, and $p_{i,c}$ denotes the probability of observation i for class c.

In this chapter, as we perform binary classification on reviews, we will only use binary cross entropy as our classification loss.

Understanding word embeddings

Word embeddings refer to the class of feature learning techniques in **Natural Language Processing (NLP)** that are used to generate a real valued vector representation of a word, sentence, or document.

Many machine learning tasks today involve text. For example, Google's language translation or spam detection in Gmail both use text as input to their models to perform the tasks of translation and spam detection. However, modern day computers can only take real valued numbers as input and can't understand strings or text unless we encode them into numbers or vectors.

For example, let's consider a sentence, "*I like Football*", for which we want a representation of all of the words. A brute force method to generate the embeddings of the three words "*I*", "*like*", and "*Football*" is done through the one hot representation of words. In this case, the embeddings are given as follows:

- "I" = [1,0,0]
- "like" = [0,1,0]
- "Football" = [0,0,1]

The idea is to create a vector that has a dimension equal to the number of unique words in the sentence and to assign a 1 to the position where a word exists and zero everywhere else. There are two issues with this approach:

- The number of vector dimension scales with the number of words in the corpus. Let's say we have 100,000 unique words in a document. Therefore, we represent each word with a vector that has a dimension of 100,000. This increases the memory required to represent words, making our system inefficient.

- One hot representations like this fail to capture the similarity between words. For example, there are two words in a sentence, *"like"* and *"love"*. We know that *"like"* is more similar to *"love"* than it is to *"Football"*. However, in our current one hot representation, the dot product of any two vectors is zero. Mathematically, the dot product of *"like"* and *"Football"* is represented as follows:

    *"like" * "Football" = Transpose([0,1,0]) *[0,0,1] = 0*0 + 1*0 + 0*1 = 0*

    This is because we have a separate position in the vector for each word and only have 1 in that position.

For both spam detection and language translation problems, understanding the similarity between words is quite crucial. For this reason, there are several other ways (both supervised and unsupervised) in which we can learn about word embeddings.

You can learn more about how to use word embeddings with TensorFlow from this official tutorial. (`https://www.tensorflow.org/tutorials/representation/word2vec`)

This project uses the embedding layer from Keras to map the words in our movie reviews to real valued vector representations. In this project, we learn the vector representation of words in a supervised manner. Essentially, we initialize the word embeddings randomly and then use back propagation in neural networks to update the embeddings such that total network loss is minimized. Training them in a supervised manner helps to generate task specific embeddings. For example, we expect a similar representation of words such as *Awesome* and *Great* since they both signify a positive sentiment. Once we have encoded words in movie reviews, we can use them as input in our neural network layers.

Building the sentiment analysis model

In this section, we will learn how to build a sentiment analysis model from scratch using Keras. To perform sentiment analysis, we will use sentiment analysis data from the University of Michigan that is available at `https://www.kaggle.com/c/si650winter11/data`. This dataset contains 7,086 movie reviews with labels. Label 1 denotes a positive sentiment, while 0 denotes a negative sentiment. In the repository, the dataset is stored in the file named `sentiment.txt`.

Pre-processing data

Once you have installed the requisite packages (can be found in a `requirements.txt` file with the code) to run this project and read the data, the next step is to preprocess the data:

1. The first step is to get the tokens/word list from the reviews. Remove any punctuation and make sure that all of the tokens are in lowercase:

```
def get_processed_tokens(text):
    '''
    Gets Token List from a Review
    '''
    filtered_text = re.sub(r'[^a-zA-Z0-9\s]', '', text) #Removing
    Punctuations
```

```
filtered_text = filtered_text.split()
filtered_text = [token.lower() for token in filtered_text]
return filtered_text
```

For example, if we have an input `This is a GREAT movie!!!!,` our output should be `this is a great movie.`

2. Create a `token_idx` dictionary that maps tokens to integers to create embeddings. Note that the number of unique tokens (words) present in a dictionary can be very large, so we must filter out the ones that occur less than the threshold (the default value for this is 5 in the code) in the training set. This is because it is difficult to learn any relationship between movie sentiment and words that don't occur much in the dataset:

```
def tokenize_text(data_text, min_frequency =5):
    '''
    Tokenizes the reviews in the dataset. Filters non frequent
tokens
    '''
    review_tokens = [get_processed_tokens(review) for review in
                    data_text] # Tokenize the sentences
    token_list = [token for review in review_tokens for token in
review]
    #Convert to single list
    token_freq_dict = {token:token_list.count(token) for token in
set(token_list)} # Get the frequency count of tokens
    most_freq_tokens = [tokens for tokens in token_freq_dict if
    token_freq_dict[tokens] >= min_frequency]
    idx = range(len(most_freq_tokens))
    token_idx = dict(zip(most_freq_tokens, idx))
    return token_idx,len(most_freq_tokens)
```

3. Map each review in the dataset to a sequence of integers (based on the `token_idx` dictionary we created in the last step). However, before doing that, find the review with the largest number of tokens:

```
def get_max(data):
    '''
    Get max length of the token
    '''
    tokens_per_review = [len(txt.split()) for txt in data]
    return max(tokens_per_review)
```

4. To create the sequences that will be fed into the model to learn the embeddings, we must create a fixed-length sequence of (max_tokens) for each review in the dataset. We pre-pad the sequences with zeros if they are less than the maximum length to ensure that all of the sequences are of the same length. Pre-padding a sequence is preferred over post padding as it helps to achieve a more accurate result:

```
def create_sequences(data_text,token_idx,max_tokens):
    '''
    Create sequences appropriate for GRU input
    Input: reviews data, token dict, max_tokens
    Output: padded_sequences of shape (len(data_text), max_tokens)
    '''
    review_tokens = [get_processed_tokens(review) for review in
                  data_text] # Tokenize the sentences
    #Covert the tokens to their indexes
    review_token_idx = map( lambda review: [token_idx[k] for k in
review
                        if k in token_idx.keys() ],
review_tokens)
    padded_sequences =
pad_sequences(review_token_idx,maxlen=max_tokens)
    return np.array(padded_sequences)
```

Building the model

This model will consist of an embedding layer, followed by three layers of GRU and a fully connected layer with sigmoid activation. For the optimization and accuracy metric, we will use an Adam optimizer and binary_crossentropy, respectively:

1. The model is defined using the following parameters:

```
def define_model(num_tokens,max_tokens):
    '''
    Defines the model definition based on input parameters
    '''
    model = Sequential()
    model.add(Embedding(input_dim=num_tokens,
                    output_dim=EMBEDDING_SIZE,
                    input_length=max_tokens,
                    name='layer_embedding'))

    model.add(GRU(units=16, name = "gru_1",return_sequences=True))
    model.add(GRU(units=8, name = "gru_2",return_sequences=True))
    model.add(GRU(units=4, name= "gru_3"))
```

```
model.add(Dense(1, activation='sigmoid',name="dense_1"))
optimizer = Adam(lr=1e-3)
model.compile(loss='binary_crossentropy',
              optimizer=optimizer,
              metrics=['accuracy'])
print model.summary()
return model
```

2. Train the model with the following parameters:
   - Epochs = 15
   - Validation split = 0.05
   - Batch size = 32
   - Embedding Size = 8

```
def train_model(model,input_sequences,y_train):
    '''
    Train the model based on input parameters
    '''
    model.fit(input_sequences, y_train,
          validation_split=VAL_SPLIT, epochs=EPOCHS,
          batch_size=BATCH_SIZE)
    return model
```

3. Test the model trained on a few random review sentences to verify its performance:

Text	Predicted Score
Awesome movie	0.9957
Terrible Movie	0.0023
That movie really sucks	0.0021
I like that movie	0.9469

The predicted score is close to 1 for positive sentences and close to 0 for negative ones. This validates our random checks on the performance of our model.

 Note that the actual scores might vary a little if you train your model on different hardware types.

Running the model on a browser using TensorFlow.js

In this section, we are going to deploy the model on a browser.

The following steps demonstrate how to save the model:

1. Install TensorFlow.js, which will help us format our trained model in accordance with what can be consumed by the browser:

   ```
   pip install tensorflowjs
   ```

2. Save the model in the TensorFlow.js format:

   ```
   import tensorflowjs as tfjs
   tfjs.converters.save_keras_model(model, OUTPUT_DIR)
   ```

This will create a json file called `model.json`, which will contain the meta-variables and some other files, such as `group1-shard1of1`.

Good job! Deploying the model in the HTML file is a little trickier, however:

For running the code mentioned in the repository, please follow the `README.md` documentation carefully (note the troubleshooting part, if required) regarding the settings before running the `Run_On_Browser.html` file.

1. Incorporate TensorFlow.js in your JavaScript through script tags:

   ```
   <script
   src="https://cdn.jsdelivr.net/npm/@tensorflow/tfjs@0.8.0"></script>
   ```

2. Load the model and our `token_idx` dictionary. This will help us to load the relevant data before processing any review from the browser:

   ```
   async function createModel()
   {
   const model = await
   tf.loadModel('http://127.0.0.1:8000/model.json')
   return model
   }
   async function loadDict()
   {
    await $.ajax({
    url: 'http://127.0.0.1:8000/token_index.csv',
   ```

```
    dataType: 'text',
    crossDomain : true}).done(success);
}
function success(data)
{
    var wd_idx = new Object();
    lst = data.split(/\r?\n|\r/)
    for(var i = 0 ; i < lst.length ;i++){
        key = (lst[i]).split(',')[0]
        value = (lst[i]).split(',')[1]
        if(key == "")
            continue
        wd_idx[key] = parseInt(value)
    }
    word_index = wd_idx
}


async function init()
{
 word_index = undefined
 console.log('Start loading dictionary')
 await loadDict()
 //console.log(word_index)
 console.log('Finish loading dictionary')
 console.log('Start loading model')
 model = await createModel()
 console.log('Finish loading model')
}
```

3. Add some helper functions to process the review input from the browser. This includes processing text, mapping words to `token_idx`, and creating sequences for model predictions:

```
function process(txt)
{
 out = txt.replace(/[^a-zA-Z0-9\s]/, '')
 out = out.trim().split(/\s+/)
 for (var i = 0 ; i < out.length ; i++)
 out[i] = out[i].toLowerCase()
 return out
}

function create_sequences(txt)
{
 max_tokens = 40
 tokens = []
 words = process(txt)
```

```
seq = Array.from(Array(max_tokens), () => 0)
start = max_tokens-words.length
for(var i= 0 ; i< words.length ; i++)
{
    if (Object.keys(word_index).includes(words[i])){
        seq[i+start] = word_index[words[i]]
    }
}
return seq
}
```

4. Incorporate the predict function that processes the input sentence and uses the model's predict function to return a tensor with a predicted score, as shown in the previous section:

```
async function predict()
{
 txt = document.getElementById("userInput").value
 alert(txt);
 seq = create_sequences(txt)
 input = tf.tensor(seq)
 input = input.expandDims(0)
 pred = model.predict(input)
 document.getElementById("Sentiment").innerHTML = pred;

 pred.print()
}
```

5. To illustrate the entire process from a user's point of view, open the `Run_on_Browser.html` file. You will see something similar to what's shown in the following screenshot:

The left-hand side of the screenshot denotes the website's layout, while the right-hand side shows the console and outputs.

Note that we can load the dictionary and model beforehand to make the predictions faster.

6. Type a review into the box provided and click submit to see the model's predicted score. Try running the application with the `Awesome Movie` text:

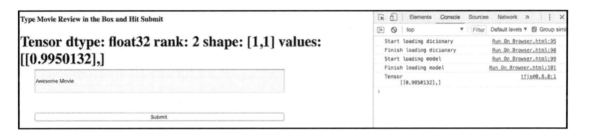

The predicted score is quite high, which indicates a positive sentiment. You can play around with different text to see the results.

Note that this is mainly for illustration purposes and that if you are up for it, you can improve the UI through JavaScript.

Summary

This chapter was a brief introduction to how to build an en- to-end system that trains a sentiment analysis model using Keras and deploys it in JavaScript using TensorFlow.js. The process of deploying the model in production is pretty seamless.

A potential next step would be to modify the JavaScript to predict sentiment as soon as a word is typed. As we mentioned previously, by deploying the model using TensorFlow.js, you can enable low- latency applications like real-time sentiment prediction without having to interact with the server.

Finally, we built a neural network in Python and deployed it in JavaScript. However, you can try building the entire model in JavaScript using TensorFlow.js.

In the next chapter, we will learn about Google's new library, TensorFlow Lite.

Questions

1. Can you evaluate the accuracy of the model if you use LSTM instead of GRUs?
2. What happens to the accuracy and training time if you increase Embedding Size?
3. Can you incorporate more layers in the model? What will happen to the training time?
4. Can you modify the code to train the model inside a browser instead of loading the trained model?

4
Digit Classification Using TensorFlow Lite

There has been a lot of progress in the field of **machine learning** (**ML**) in the last five years. These days, a variety of ML applications are being used in our daily lives and we don't even realize it. Since ML has taken the spotlight, it would be helpful if we could use it to run deep models on mobile devices, which is one of the most used devices in our daily life.

Innovation in mobile hardware, coupled with new software frameworks for deploying ML models on mobile devices, is proving to be one of the major accelerators for developing ML based applications on mobile or other edge devices like tablet..

In this chapter, we will learn about Google's new library, TensorFlow Lite, which can be used to deploy ML models on mobile devices. We will train a deep learning model on the MNIST digits dataset and look at how we can convert this model into a mobile-friendly format by understanding the following concepts:

- A brief introduction to TensorFlow Lite and its architecture
- Introduction to Classification model evaluation metrics
- Developing a deep learning model on the MNIST dataset
- Converting the trained model into a mobile-friendly format using TensorFlow Lite

 Note that this chapter will not discuss building an Android application to deploy these models since this has been extensively documented in Google's TensorFlow tutorials (https://www.tensorflow.org/lite/).

What is TensorFlow Lite?

Before we take a deep dive into TensorFlow Lite, let's try to understand what are the advantages of doing ML on edge devices like mobile/tablet and others.

- **Privacy**: If inference on a ML model can be performed on a device, user data doesn't need to leave the device, which helps in preserving the privacy of the user.
- **Offline predictions**: The device doesn't need to be connected to a network to make predictions on a ML model. This unlocks a lot of use cases in developing nations such as India where network connectivity is not so great.
- **Smart devices**: This can also enable the development of smart home devices such as microwaves and thermostats with on-device intelligence.
- **Power efficient**: An on-device ML can be more power-efficient as there is no need to transfer data back and forth to the server.
- **Sensor data utilization**: ML models can make use of rich sensor data since it is easily available on mobile.

However, mobile devices are not same as our desktops and laptops. There are different considerations when deploying the model on mobile or embedded devices such as:

- **Model size**: As we know, mobiles have limited memory and we can't store a memory-heavy model on a device. There are two ways of handling this:
  - We can round or quantize the weights of the model so that they require fewer floating-point representations. This is in line with our understanding that integers always require less memory to store than the floating point numbers.
  - Since we only use devices for inferences or predictions, we can strip out all the training operations in our Tensorflow graph which are not useful for making predictions.
- **Speed**: One of the important things for deploying models on mobile devices is the speed with which we can run an inference so that we gain a better user experience. Models have to be optimized in such a manner that they don't exceed the latency budget on the phone but are still fast.
- **Ease of deployment**: We need efficient frameworks/libraries so that deployment on mobile devices is very straightforward.

With these considerations in mind, Google has developed TensorFlow Lite, which is a lightweight version of original Tensorflow for deploying deep learning models on mobile and embedded devices.

To understand TensorFlow Lite, take a look at the following diagram, which shows its high-level architecture:

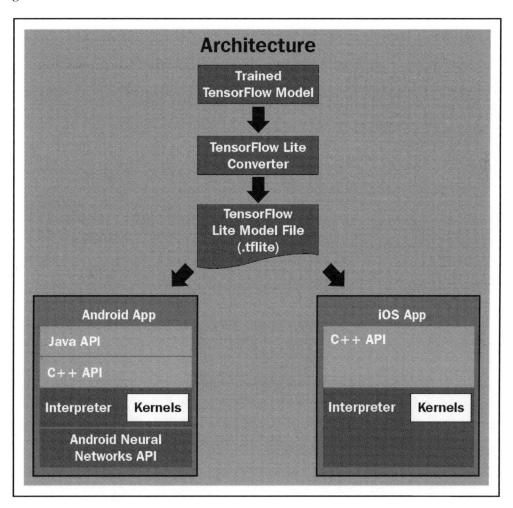

This architecture makes it evident that we need to convert a trained TF model into `.tflite` format. This format is different from usual TF models as it is optimized for inference on devices. We will learn about the conversion process in detail later in the chapter.

For now, let's try to understand the major features of using TF Lite format:

- The model is serialized and converted to a Flatbuffer format (`https://google.github.io/flatbuffers/`). Flatbuffers have the advantage that data can be directly accessed without parsing/unpacking of large files that contain weights.
- Weights and biases of the model are pre-fused into TF lite format.

TF lite is cross-platform and can be deployed on Android, iOS, Linux, and hardware devices such as Raspberry Pi.

It includes an on-device interpreter that has been optimized for faster execution on mobile. The core interpreter with all of the supported operations is around 400 KB, and 75 KB without the supported operations. This means that the model takes up little space on the device. Overall, the idea is to keep the parts of the model that are essential for inference and strip out all the other parts.

With innovation in hardware, many companies are also developing GPUs and Digital Signal Processors (DSPs) that are optimized for neural network inference. TF Lite provides the Android Neural Networks API, which can perform hardware acceleration on these devices.

Classification Model Evaluation Metrics

Just building a model does not suffice; we need to make sure that our model functions well and gives us a good and accurate output. To do this, we need to understand some classification metrics that will be used to evaluate the model throughout this book.

Let's begin by defining some building blocks of the metrics that will be used to evaluate the classification models. To do this, take a simple example of spam detection that is done by any online mailbox for reference. A spam email shall be considered to be of a positive class and the normal email to be of a negative class. We can summarize this spam detection model into four categories, which are illustrated in the following matrix:

True positives (TP)	False positives (FP)
Reality: Email is spam	Reality: Email is NOT spam
Model Prediction: Email is spam	Model Prediction: Email is spam
False negatives (FN)	**True negatives (TN)**
Reality: Email is spam	Reality: Email is NOT spam
Model Prediction: Email is NOT spam	Model Prediction: Email is NOT spam

This matrix is also commonly known as the **confusion matrix.**

The three major metrics that we will use to define classifier quality, primarily in an unbalanced dataset, are as follows:

- **Accuracy:** Accuracy is the most basic metric used for classification problems. It is defined as follows:

$$Accuracy = \frac{True\ Positives}{True\ Positives + False\ Positives + True\ Negatives + False\ Negatives}$$

- **Precision:** Precision tries to measure the true positives out of all predicted positives from the model. If your Gmail doesn't misclassify a lot of emails from your friends (or normal emails) and put them into spam, then it has very high precision. It is mathematically represented as follows:

$$Precision = \frac{True\ Positives}{True\ Positives + False\ Positives}$$

- **Recall:** Recall tries to measure the number of values classified as positive out of all real positives in the dataset. In simple terms, if your Gmail doesn't misclassify a lot of your spam emails as normal emails and sends them to your inbox, then it has very high recall:

$$Recall = \frac{True\ Positives}{True\ Positives + False\ Positives}$$

Ideally, we want a model with high precision and high recall. However, there is always a trade-off between high precision and high recall in machine learning.

Classifying digits using TensorFlow Lite

To complete this project, we will use the MNIST digit dataset, which is available in the TensorFlow datasets library (https://www.tensorflow.org/guide/datasets). It consists of images of handwritten digits from 0 to 9. The training dataset has 60,000 images and the testing set has 10,000 images. Some of the images in the dataset are as follows:

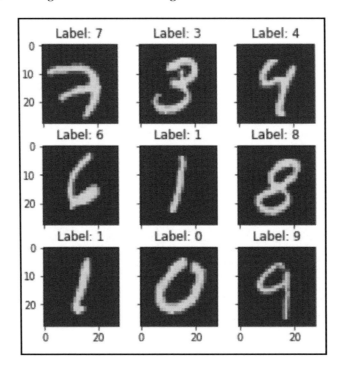

If we take a look at TensorFlow Lite tutorials, we will see that the focus is on using pre-trained models such as Mobilenet or retraining the existing ones. However, none of these tutorials talk about building new models, which is something we will be doing here.

 Note that we specifically choose a simple model because at the time of writing this book, TensorFlow Lite doesn't have adequate support for all types of complex models

We will use categorical cross entropy as the loss function for this classification problem. Categorical cross entropy was explained in detail in Chapter 3, *Sentiment Analysis in Your Browser Using TensorFlow.js*, of this book. In this chapter, we have 10 different digits in the dataset, so we will use the categorical cross entropy over 10 classes.

Pre-processing data and defining the model

We need to pre-process our data for making it ready to feed into our model, define our model, and create an evaluation metric:

1. Pre-process the data by ensuring the images are of shape 28x28x1 and converting the pixels into a float type variable for training. Also, here we define NUM_CLASSES = 10 as there are 10 different digits in the images.

```
x_train = x_train.reshape(x_train.shape[0], IMAGE_SIZE, IMAGE_SIZE,
1)
x_test = x_test.reshape(x_test.shape[0], IMAGE_SIZE, IMAGE_SIZE, 1)
x_train = x_train.astype('float32')
x_test = x_test.astype('float32')
Next, we normalize the image pixels by 255 as follows:
x_train /= 255
x_test /= 255
And finally, we convert the class labels to one hot for training as
follows:
y_train = keras.utils.to_categorical(y_train, NUM_CLASSES)
y_test = keras.utils.to_categorical(y_test, NUM_CLASSES)
```

2. Define the model as having two convolutional layers with the same filter sizes, two fully connected layers, two dropout layers with dropout probabilities of 0.25 and 0.5 respectively, a Rectified Linear (ReLU) after every fully connected or convolutional layer except the last one, and one max pool layer. Also we add a Softmax activation to convert the output of the model to probabilities for each of the 10 digits. Note that we use this model as it produces good results. You can try improving the model by adding more layers or trying different shapes of the existing layers.

```
model = Sequential()
model.add(Conv2D(32, kernel_size=(3, 3),
activation='relu',
input_shape=INPUT_SHAPE))
model.add(Conv2D(64, (3, 3), activation='relu'))
model.add(MaxPooling2D(pool_size=(2, 2)))
model.add(Dropout(0.25))
model.add(Flatten())
model.add(Dense(128, activation='relu'))
model.add(Dropout(0.5))
model.add(Dense(NUM_CLASSES))model.add(Activation('softmax', name =
'softmax_tensor'))
```

Note that we have named our output tensor `softmax_tensor`, which will come in pretty handy when we try to convert this model into a TensorFlow Lite format.

3. Further define the following parameters for the model:
   - Loss = Categorical Cross Entropy
   - Optimizer = AdaDelta. Adam optimizer, defined in `Chapter 3`, *Sentiment Analysis in Your Browser Using TensorFlow.js*, is an extension of AdaDelta. We use AdaDelta as it gives good result for this model. You can find more details about AdaDelta in the original paper (`https://arxiv.org/abs/1212.5701`).
   - Evaluation Metric = Classification Accuracy

Code for defining these is as follows:

```
model.compile(loss=keras.losses.categorical_crossentropy,

optimizer=keras.optimizers.Adadelta(),

metrics=['accuracy'])
```

4. Enable Tensorboard logging to visualize the model graph and training progress. Code is defined as follows:

```
tensorboard = TensorBoard(log_dir=MODEL_DIR)
```

5. Train the model using the following parameters:
   - Epochs = 12
   - Batch Size = 128:

```
self.model.fit(self.x_train, self.y_train,
batch_size=BATCH_SIZE,

epochs=EPOCHS,

verbose=1,

validation_data=(self.x_test, self.y_test),

callbacks = [self.tensorboard])

score = self.model.evaluate(self.x_test, self.y_test, verbose=0)
```

We achieved **99.24%** accuracy on the test dataset with just 12 epochs.

 Note that we use the `callbacks` parameter to log the training progress on TensorBoard.

Converting TensorFlow model to TensorFlow Lite

Now that we have trained the model in the usual way, let's look at how we can convert this model into a TensorFlow Lite format.

The general procedure for conversion is illustrated in the following diagram:

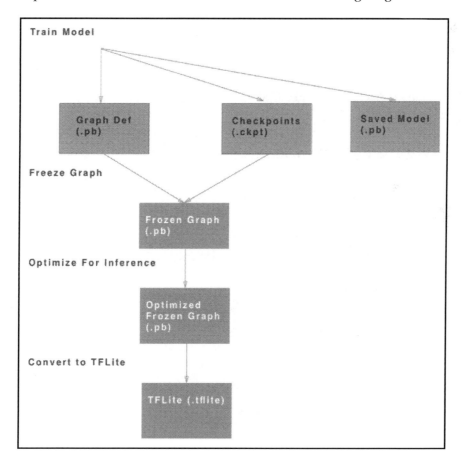

The procedure is simple: we take a trained model, freeze the graph, optimize it for inference/prediction, and convert it into `.tflite` format. Before going further, let's understand what we mean by Freeze Graph and Optimize For Inference:

- **Freeze Graph :** Freeze graph operation effectively freezes the weights of the model by converting all the of the TF Variables as Constants. As you can imagine, having all of the weights as constants can save space compared to keeping them as variables. As we only perform inference on mobile (and not training), we don't want to change the model weights anyway

- **Optimize For Inference**: Once the graph is frozen, we remove all the operations in the graph which are not useful for inference. For example, Dropout operation is used to train the model such that it doesn't overfit. However, there is absolutely no use of this operation during prediction on mobile.

For the rest of this section, we will heavily use TensorBoard visualization (`https://www.TensorFlow.org/guide/summaries_and_tensorboard`) for graph visualization. :

1. Once you have trained the model, you must have a file with the prefix `events.out.tfevents.` in your model folder. Go to the `logs` folder and type the following into terminal:

   ```
   tensorboard --logdir <model_folder>
   ```

   TensorBoard will start in port `6006` by default. Launch it by going to your browser and typing `localhost:6006` into the address bar. Once the Tensorboard opens, if you navigate to the Graphs tab at the top, you will be able to see the Tensorflow Graph of your model. In the following diagram, we illustrate the main graph, with annotations for the input tensor, output tensor, and training part of the graph. As we can see, we shouldn't keep anything from the training graph for inference/making predictions on mobile.

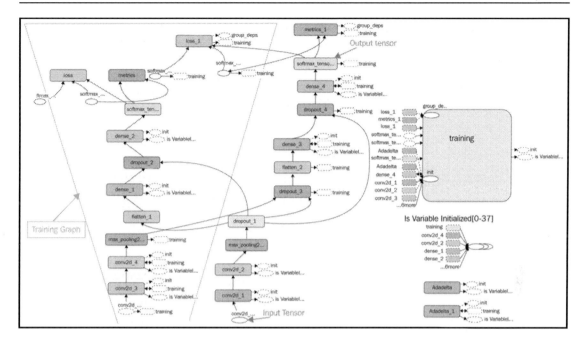

2. Next implement a function `freeze_sesssion` which takes TF session as input, converts all variables into constants, and returns the frozen graph. After executing this function, you will obtain a frozen graph file named `MNIST_model.pb` in the `<model_folder>/logs/freeze` folder.

```
from TensorFlow.python.framework.graph_util import
convert_variables_to_constants

def freeze_session(session, keep_var_names=None, output_names=None,
clear_devices=True):

graph = session.graph

with graph.as_default():

freeze_var_names = list(set(v.op.name for v in
tf.global_variables()).difference(keep_var_names or []))

output_names = output_names or []

output_names += [v.op.name for v in tf.global_variables()]

input_graph_def = graph.as_graph_def()

if clear_devices:
```

```
for node in input_graph_def.node:

node.device = ""

frozen_graph = convert_variables_to_constants(session,
input_graph_def,

output_names, freeze_var_names)

return frozen_graph
```

3. Now, here is where it gets really strange: you can't visualize the
   MNIST_model.pb file directly through TensorBoard. You need to write the graph
   in a format that TensorBoard can pick up. Execute the
   function pb_to_tensorboard mentioned below and you will see another file in
   <model_folder>/logs/freeze folder with prefix events.out.tfevents.

```
def pb_to_tensorboard(input_graph_dir,graph_type ="freeze"):

    file_name = ""

    if graph_type == "freeze":

        file_name = FREEZE_FILE_NAME

    elif graph_type == "optimize":

        file_name = OPTIMIZE_FILE_NAME

    with tf.Session() as sess:

        model_filename = input_graph_dir + "/" + file_name

        with gfile.FastGFile(model_filename, 'rb') as f:
            graph_def = tf.GraphDef()
            graph_def.ParseFromString(f.read())
    train_writer = tf.summary.FileWriter(input_graph_dir)

    train_writer.add_graph(sess.graph)
```

4. Next, start TensorBoard again with logdir as
   <model_folder>/logs/freeze and visualize the frozen graph. You will
   observe the you have stripped out most of the variables from the graph. The
   following diagram illustrates the frozen graph you will obtain:

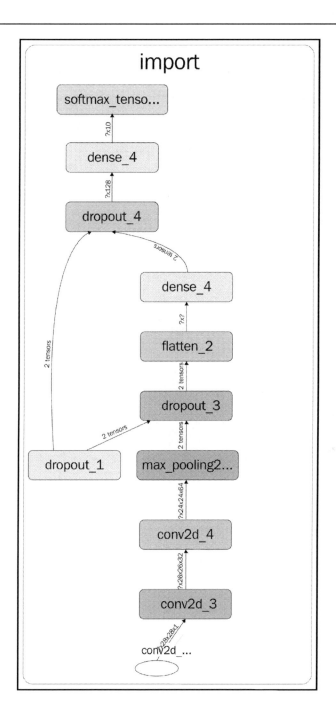

5. Next step is further trim to optimize it for inference. As explained before, we will remove Dropout variables from the graph as they are not useful for inference on mobile. However, there is no perfect way to remove those from the graph based on the existing TensorFlow functions/programs. The new improvements to TensorFlow Lite don't work for this example, which suggests that they are still under development. Instead, you will have to manually specify the operations you want to remove and connect the input of the Dropout operations to the operations after them in the graph. For example, in the frozen graph, let's say we want to remove the `dropout_3` operation. The following diagram shows the zoomed-in version of the frozen graph:

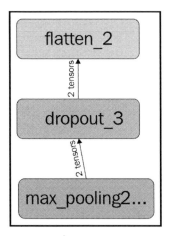

In such a case, you will have to connect the `max_pooling2` operation directly to the `flatten_2` operation, thereby skipping the `dropout_3` op in the graph.

Execute the function `optimize_graph` mentioned below to remove all of the dropout ops in the graph. It manually flushes out all the Dropout operations from the graph. This will result in a new file named `MNIST_optimized.pb` under the `<model_folder>/logs/optimized` folder.

```
def optimize_graph(input_dir, output_dir):
input_graph = os.path.join(input_dir, FREEZE_FILE_NAME)
output_graph = os.path.join(output_dir, OPTIMIZE_FILE_NAME)
input_graph_def = tf.GraphDef()
with tf.gfile.FastGFile(input_graph, "rb") as f:
input_graph_def.ParseFromString(f.read())
output_graph_def = strip(input_graph_def, u'dropout_1',
u'conv2d_2/bias', u'dense_1/kernel', u'training')
output_graph_def = strip(output_graph_def, u'dropout_3',
u'max_pooling2d_2/MaxPool', u'flatten_2/Shape',
u'training')
output_graph_def = strip(output_graph_def, u'dropout_4',
u'dense_3/Relu', u'dense_4/kernel', u'training')
output_graph_def = strip(output_graph_def, u'Adadelta_1',
u'softmax_tensor_1/Softmax',
u'training/Adadelta/Variable', u'training')
output_graph_def = strip(output_graph_def, u'training',
u'softmax_tensor_1/Softmax',
u'_', u'training')
with tf.gfile.GFile(output_graph, "wb") as f:
f.write(output_graph_def.SerializeToString())
```

6. Again, to visualize the graph in TensorBoard, you need to convert it using the function `pb_to_tensorboar` defined in step 3 so that it's TensorBoard-friendly and obtain a new file with the prefix `events.out.tfevents` in the same folder. The following figure illustrates the graph you will obtain after removing the Dropout operations.

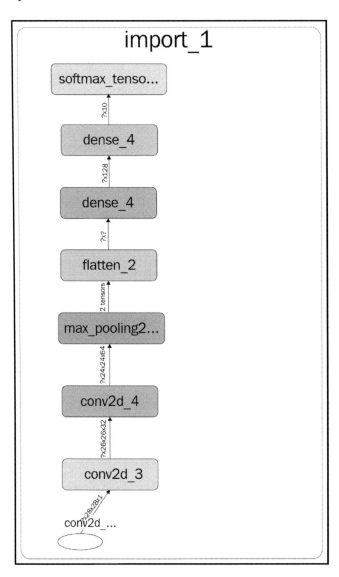

Note that getting rid of Dropout from the graph will not affect testing set accuracy as Dropout is not used for inference.

7. The last step in obtaining the model in a mobile-friendly format is to convert it into a `.tflite` file. For this step, you will use `toco` command, which stands for TensorFlow Lite Optimizing Converter (`https://www.tensorflow.org/lite/convert/`). The code is provided as follows:

```
toco \
--input_file=<model_folder>/logs/optimized/MNIST_optimized.pb\
--input_format=TensorFlow_GRAPHDEF \
--output_format=TFLITE \
--inference_type=FLOAT \
--input_type=FLOAT \
--input_arrays=conv2d_1_input \
--output_arrays=softmax_tensor_1/Softmax \
--input_shapes=1,28,28,1 \
--output_file=<model_folder>//mnist.tflite
```

This will produce a file named `mnist.tflite` in `<model_folder>`. Essentially, this step is trying to convert the optimized graph into a Flatbuffer for efficient on-device inference.

We will not cover deploying our project to the mobile device as its development is outside the scope of this book. However, feel free to take a look at TensorFlow Lite tutorials on how to deploy the TF Lite models Android (`https://www.tensorflow.org/lite/demo_android`) or iOS (`https://www.tensorflow.org/lite/demo_ios`).

Summary

Machine learning is at the edge of the next wave, where we try to make ML ubiquitous in our everyday life. It has several advantages such as offline access, data privacy, and so on.

In this chapter, we looked at a new library from Google known as TensorFlow Lite, which has been optimized for deploying ML models on mobile and embedded devices. We understood the architecture of TensorFlow Lite, which converts the trained TensorFlow model into `.tflite` format. This is designed for inference at fast speed and low memory on devices. TensorFlow Lite also supports multiple platforms, such as Android, iOS, Linux, and Raspberry Pi.

Next, we used the MNIST handwritten digit dataset to train a deep learning model. Subsequently, we followed the necessary steps to convert the trained model into `.tflite` format. The steps are as follows:

1. Froze the graph with variables converted to constants
2. Optimized the graph for inference by removing the unused ops like Dropout
3. Used **TensorFlow Optimization Converter Tool** (**toco**) to convert the optimized model to `.tflitte` format

At every step, we used TensorBoard to visualize the state of the graph.

This is a very exciting field that is continuing to evolve, both in terms of hardware and software. Once this technology reaches maturity, it will open up new use cases and business models across the world.

In the next chapter, we'll create a project that will help us convert text to speech.

Questions

The following are the questions:

1. How is TensorFlow Lite different from usual TensorFlow?
2. Can you try and if you can build the model on a movie review dataset in `Chapter 3`, *Sentiment Analysis in Your Browser Using TensorFlow.js*? Do you face some issues with Tensorflow Lite in that case?
3. Can you try Adam optimizer and see if it improves the performance of the model?
4. Can you think you operations other than Dropout which are also not important for inference on mobile?

5
Speech to Text and Topic Extraction Using NLP

Recognizing and understanding spoken language is a challenging problem due to the complexity and variety of speech data. There have been several different technologies deployed to recognize spoken words in the past. Most of those approaches were very limited in their scope, as they were unable to recognize a wide variety of words, accents, and tones, and aspects of spoken language, such as a pause between spoken words. Some of the prevalent modeling technique for speech recognition include **Hidden Markov Models (HMM)**, **Dynamic Time Warping (DTW)**, **Long Short-Term Memory Networks (LSTM)**, and **Connectionist Temporal Classification (CTC)**.

In this chapter, we shall learn about various options for speech to text and the prebuilt model from Google's TensorFlow team, using the Speech Commands Dataset. We shall cover the following topics:

- Speech to text frameworks and toolkits
- Google Speech Commands Dataset
- CNN based architecture for speech recognition
- A TensorFlow speech commands example

Download and follow the code for this chapter from `https://github.com/tensorflow/tensorflow/blob/master/tensorflow/examples/speech_commands/`.

Speech-to-text frameworks and toolkits

Many cloud-based AI providers offer speech to text as a service:

- Amazon's offering for speech recognition is known as **Amazon Transcribe**. Amazon Transcribe allows transcription of the audio files stored in Amazon S3 in four different formats: `.flac`, `.wav`, `.mp4`, and `.mp3`. It allows an audio file with a maximum of two hours in length and 1 GB in size. The results of the transcription are created as a JSON file in an Amazon S3 bucket.
- Google offers speech to text as part of its Google Cloud ML Services. Google Cloud Speech to Text supports `FLAC`, `Linear16`, `MULAW`, `AMR`, `AMR_WB`, and `OGG_OPUS` file formats.
- Microsoft offers a speech to text API as part of its Azure Cognitive Services platform, known as Speech Service SDK. The Speech Service SDK integrates with rest of the Microsoft APIs to transcribe recorded audio. It only allows the WAV or PCM file format with a single channel and sample rate of 6 kHz.
- IBM offers a speech to text API as part if its Watson platform. Watson Speech to Text supports eight audio formats: BASIC, FLAC, L16, MP3, MULAW, OGG, WAV, and WEBM. The maximum size and length of the audio files vary depending on the format used. The results of transcription are returned as a JSON file.

Apart from the support for various international spoken languages and an extensive global vocabulary, these cloud services support the following features to different extents:

- **Multichannel recognition**: Identifying multiple participants recorded in multiple channels
- **Speaker diarization**: Prediction of speech of a certain speaker
- **Custom models and model selection**: Plug in your own models and select from a plethora of pre-built models
- Inappropriate content filtering and noise filtering

There are also many open source toolkits for speech recognition, such as Kaldi.

Kaldi (`http:/kaldi-asr.org`) is a popular open source speech to text recognition library. It is written in C++ and is available from `https://github.com/kaldi-asr/kaldi`. Kaldi can be integrated into your applications using its C++ API. It also supports Android using NDK, clang++, and OpenBLAS.

Google Speech Commands Dataset

The Google Speech Commands Dataset was created by the TensorFlow and AIY teams to showcase the speech recognition example using the TensorFlow API. The dataset has 65,000 clips of one-second-long duration. Each clip contains one of the 30 different words spoken by thousands of different subjects.

 The Google Speech Commands Dataset is available from the following link: `http://download.tensorflow.org/data/speech_commands_v0.02.tar.gz`.

The clips were recorded in realistic environments with phones and laptops. The 35 words contained noise words and the ten command words most useful in a robotics environment, and are listed as follows:

- Yes
- No
- Up
- Down
- Left
- Right
- On
- Off
- Stop
- Go

More details on how the speech dataset is prepared can be found in the following links:

- `https://arxiv.org/pdf/1804.03209.pdf`
- `https://ai.googleblog.com/2017/08/launching-speech-commands-dataset.html`

With this dataset, thus the problem that shown in the example in this chapter is known as Keyword Spotting Task.

Neural network architecture

The network used for this example has three modules:

- A feature extraction module that processes the audio clips into feature vectors
- A deep neural network module that produces softmax probabilities for each word in the input frame of feature vectors
- A posterior handling module that combines the frame-level posterior scores into a single score for each keyword

Feature extraction module

In order to make the computation easy, the incoming audio signal is run through a voice-activity detection system and the signal is divided into speech and non-speech parts of the signals. The voice activity detector uses a 30-component diagonal covariance GMM model. The input to this model is 13-dimensional PLP features, their deltas, and double deltas. The output of GMM is passed to a State Machine that does temporal smoothing.

The output of this GMM-SM module is speech and non-speech parts of the signal.

The speech parts of the signal are further processed to generate the features. The acoustic features are generated based on 40-dimensional log-filterbank energies computed every 10 ms over a window of 25 ms. 10 Future and 30 Pas frames are added to the signal.

More details on feature extractor can be obtained from the original papers, links provided in the further readings section.

Deep neural network module

The DNN module is implemented with the Convolutional Neural Network (CNN) architecture. The code implements multiple variations of ConvNet, each variation producing different levels of accuracy and taking a different amount of time to train.

The code for building the model is provided in the `models.py` file. It allows the creation of four different models, depending on the parameter passed at the command line:

- `single_fc`: This model has only one fully connected layer.
- `conv`: This model is a full CNN architecture with two pairs of Convolution and MaxPool layers, followed by a fully connected layer.

- `low_latency_conv`: This model has one convolutional layer, followed by three fully connected layers. As the name suggests, it has a lesser number of parameters and computations compared with the `conv` architecture.

- `low_latency_svdf`: This model follows the architecture and layers from the paper titled *Compressing Deep Neural Networks using a Rank-Constrained Topology* available from `https://research.google.com/pubs/archive/43813.pdf`.

- `tiny_conv`: This model has only one convolutional and one fully connected layer.

The default architecture is `conv`, if the architecture is not passed from the command line. In our runs, the architectures showed the following accuracies for training, validation, and test sets when running the models with default accuracy and default number of steps of 18,000:

Architecture	Accuracy (in %)		
	Train set	Validation set	Test set
conv (default)	90	88.5	87.7
single_fc	50	48.5	48.2
low_latenxy_conv	22	21.6	23.6
low_latency_svdf	7	8.9	8.6
tiny_conv	55	65.7	65.4

Since the network architecture uses CNN layers that are more suitable for image data, the speech files are converted to a single-channel image by converting the audio signal of a short segment into vectors of frequency strengths.

As we can see from the preceding observations, the shortened architectures give lower accuracy for same hyper-parameters, but they run faster. Hence, they can be run for a higher number of epochs, or the learning rate could be increased to get higher accuracy.

Now let's see how to train and use this model.

Training the model

1. Move to the folder where you cloned the code from the repository, and train the model with the following command:

```
python tensorflow/examples/speech_commands/train.py
```

You will start seeing the output of the training as follows:

```
I tensorflow/core/platform/cpu_feature_guard.cc:141] Your CPU
supports instructions that this TensorFlow binary was not compiled
to use: SSE4.1 SSE4.2 AVX AVX2 FMA
I tensorflow/stream_executor/cuda/cuda_gpu_executor.cc:897]
successful NUMA node read from SysFS had negative value (-1), but
there must be at least one NUMA node, so returning NUMA node zero
I tensorflow/core/common_runtime/gpu/gpu_device.cc:1405] Found
device 0 with properties:
name: Quadro P5000 major: 6 minor: 1 memoryClockRate(GHz): 1.506
pciBusID: 0000:01:00.0
totalMemory: 15.90GiB freeMemory: 14.63GiB
I tensorflow/core/common_runtime/gpu/gpu_device.cc:1484] Adding
visible gpu devices: 0
I tensorflow/core/common_runtime/gpu/gpu_device.cc:965] Device
interconnect StreamExecutor with strength 1 edge matrix:
I tensorflow/core/common_runtime/gpu/gpu_device.cc:971] 0
I tensorflow/core/common_runtime/gpu/gpu_device.cc:984] 0: N
I tensorflow/core/common_runtime/gpu/gpu_device.cc:1097] Created
TensorFlow device (/job:localhost/replica:0/task:0/device:GPU:0
with 14168 MB memory) -> physical GPU (device: 0, name: Quadro
P5000, pci bus id: 0000:01:00.0, compute capability: 6.1)
```

2. Once the training iterations start, the code prints out the learning rate, along with accuracy and the cross entropy loss on the training set, as follows:

```
INFO:tensorflow:Training from step: 1
INFO:tensorflow:Step #1: rate 0.001000, accuracy 12.0%, cross
entropy 2.662751
INFO:tensorflow:Step #2: rate 0.001000, accuracy 6.0%, cross
entropy 2.572391
INFO:tensorflow:Step #3: rate 0.001000, accuracy 11.0%, cross
entropy 2.547692
INFO:tensorflow:Step #4: rate 0.001000, accuracy 8.0%, cross
entropy 2.615582
INFO:tensorflow:Step #5: rate 0.001000, accuracy 5.0%, cross
entropy 2.592372
```

3. The code also keeps saving the model every 100 steps, so that if training is interrupted, then it can be restarted from the latest checkpoint saved:

```
INFO:tensorflow:Saving to
"/tmp/speech_commands_train/conv.ckpt-100"
```

The training runs for several hours for 18,000 steps and at the end prints the final training learning rate, accuracy, loss, and confusion matrix as follows:

```
INFO:tensorflow:Step #18000: rate 0.000100, accuracy 90.0%, cross
entropy 0.420554
INFO:tensorflow:Confusion Matrix:
 [[368 2 0 0 1 0 0 0 0 0 0 0]
 [ 3 252 9 6 13 15 13 18 17 1 13 11]
 [ 0 1 370 12 2 2 7 2 0 0 0 1]
 [ 3 8 4 351 8 7 6 0 0 0 3 16]
 [ 3 4 0 0 324 1 3 0 1 5 7 2]
 [ 4 3 4 19 1 330 3 0 0 1 3 9]
 [ 2 2 12 2 4 0 321 7 0 0 2 0]
 [ 3 7 1 1 2 0 4 344 1 0 0 0]
 [ 5 10 0 0 0 9 1 1 0 334 3 0 0]
 [ 4 2 1 0 33 0 2 2 7 317 4 1]
 [ 5 2 0 0 15 0 1 1 0 2 323 1]
 [ 4 17 0 33 2 8 0 1 0 2 3 302]]
```

One observation from this output is that, although the code starts with a learning rate of 0.001, it reduces the learning rate to 0.001 towards the end. Since there are 12 command words, it also prints out a 12 x 12 confusion matrix.

The code also prints the accuracy and confusion matrix on the validation set as follows:

```
INFO:tensorflow:Step 18000: Validation accuracy = 88.5% (N=4445)
INFO:tensorflow:Saving to
"/tmp/speech_commands_train/conv.ckpt-18000"
INFO:tensorflow:set_size=4890
INFO:tensorflow:Confusion Matrix:
 [[404 2 0 0 0 0 0 0 0 0 2 0]
 [ 1 283 10 3 14 15 15 22 12 4 10 19]
 [ 0 7 394 4 1 3 9 0 0 0 1 0]
 [ 0 8 7 353 0 7 9 1 0 0 0 20]
 [ 2 4 1 0 397 6 2 0 1 6 5 1]
 [ 1 8 1 36 2 342 6 1 0 0 0 9]
 [ 1 2 14 1 4 0 386 4 0 0 0 0]
 [ 1 9 0 2 1 0 10 368 3 0 1 1]
 [ 2 13 0 0 7 10 1 0 345 15 3 0]
 [ 1 8 0 0 34 0 3 1 14 329 7 5]
 [ 0 1 1 0 11 3 0 0 1 2 387 5]
 [ 3 16 2 58 6 9 3 2 0 1 1 301]]
```

4. Finally, the code prints the test set accuracy as follows:

```
INFO:tensorflow:Final test accuracy = 87.7% (N=4890)
```

That's it. The model has been trained and can be exported for serving through TensorFlow, or embedding in another desktop, web, or mobile app.

Summary

In this chapter, we learned about a project for converting audio data to text. There are many open source SDKs and commercial paid cloud services that allow us to convert from audio recordings and files to text data. As an example project, we took Google's Speech Commands Dataset and TensorFlow's deep learning-based example to convert audio files to spoken words in order to recognize the commands.

In the next chapter, we continue this journey to build a project for predicting stock prices using Gaussian Processes, which is a popular algorithm for forecasting.

Questions

1. What is the interpretation of the confusion matrix provided at the end of the training?
2. Create a dataset of your own recorded voices with your friends and family members. Run the model on this data and observe what the accuracy is.
3. Retrain the model on your own dataset and check the accuracy for your own train, validation and test sets.
4. Experiment with different options from train.py and share your findings in a blog.
5. Add different architectures to the models.py file and see if you can create a better architecture for the speech dataset or your own recorded dataset.

Further reading

The following links are helpful in learning more about speech to text:

- `https://arxiv.org/pdf/1804.03209.pdf`
- `https://ai.googleblog.com/2017/08/launching-speech-commands-dataset.html`
- `https://research.google.com/pubs/archive/43813.pdf`
- `https://cloud.google.com/speech-to-text/docs/`
- `https://docs.aws.amazon.com/transcribe/latest/dg/what-is-transcribe.html`
- `https://docs.microsoft.com/en-us/azure/cognitive-services/speech-service/`
- `https://nlp.stanford.edu/projects/speech.shtml`

6
Predicting Stock Prices using Gaussian Process Regression

In this chapter, we will learn about a new model for forecasting known as **Gaussian processes**, popularly abbreviated as **GPs**, this is extremely popular in forecasting applications where we want to model non-linear functions with a few data points and also to quantify uncertainty in predictions.

We will use Gaussian processes to predict the stock prices of three major stocks, namely, Google, Netflix, and the **General Electric** (GE) company.

The rest of this chapter is divided into the following sections:

- Understanding Bayes' rule
- Bayesian inference
- Introducing Gaussian processes
- Understanding the stock market dataset
- Applying Gaussian processes to predict stock market prices

Understanding Bayes' rule

Let us begin by reviewing the Bayes' rule and it's associated terminology, before we start with our project.

Bayes' rule is used to describe the probability of an event, based on prior knowledge of conditions that might be related to the event. For example, let's say we want to predict the probability a person having diabetes. If we know the preliminary medical test results, we can hope to get a more accurate prediction than when we don't know results of the test. Let's put some numbers around this to understand mathematically:

- 1% of population has diabetes (and therefore 99% do not)
- Preliminary tests detect diabetes 80% of the time when it is there (therefore 20% of time we require advanced tests)
- 10% of time preliminary test detect diabetes even when it is not there (therefore 90% of time they give the correct result):

	Diabetes (1%)	No diabetes (99%)
Test Positive	80%	10%
Test Negative	20%	90%

So, if a person has diabetes, we will be looking at first column and he has 80% chance of being detected. And if a person doesn't have diabetes, we will be looking at second column and he has 10% chance of testing positive for diabetes from preliminary tests.

Now let's say a person was detected positively for diabetes from preliminary test. What are the chances that he actually has diabetes?

As it turns out, a renowned scientist Thomas Bayes' (171-1761) provided a mathematical framework to compute probability in the cases like above. His mathematical formula can be given as:

$$P(D|Positive) = \frac{P(Positive|D)P(D)}{P(Positive)}$$

Where:

- $P(D)$ denotes the probability of diabetes in a randomly selected person which is 1% in this case. $P(D)$ is also known as **prior** in Bayesian terminology which denotes our belief for an event without any additional information.
- $P(D|Positive)$ denotes the probability of a person having diabetes given that he was detected positive by preliminary search results. In Bayesian terminology, this is also known as **posterior** which denotes the updated probability of an event after having obtained additional information.
- $P(Positive|D)$ denotes the probability of getting a positive result in preliminary test given a person has diabetes. It is 80% in this case.

- $P(Positive)$ denotes the probability that a random person will be tested positive in preliminary test. This can also be written down as:

$$P(Positive) = P(Positive|D) * P(D) + P(Positive|NotD) * P(NotD)$$

$$P(Positive) = 0.8 * 0.1 + 0.2 * 0.9 = 0.26$$

Bayes' rule is used heavily to quantify uncertainty in predictions of machine learning systems.

Introducing Bayesian inference

Now that we know about the basics of Bayes' rule, let's try to understand the concept of Bayesian inference or modeling.

As we know, real-world environments are always dynamic, noisy, observation costly, and time-sensitive. When business decisions are based on forecasting in these environments, we want to not only produce better forecasts, but also quantify the uncertainty in these forecasts. For this reason, the theory of Bayesian inferences is extremely handy as it provides a principled approach to such problems.

For a typical time series model, we effectively carry out curve fitting based on y when given the x variable. This helps to fit a curve based on past observations. Let's try to understand its limitations. Consider the following example of temperature in a city:

Day	Temperature
May 1 10 AM	10.5 degrees Celsius
May 15 10 AM	17.5 degrees Celsius
May 30 10 AM	25 degrees Celsius

Using curve fitting, we obtain the following model:

$$Temp = 0.5 * Day + 10$$

However, this will imply that the temperature function is linear, and, on tenth day, we expect the temperature to be 15 degrees Celsius. It is common knowledge that the temperature of a city fluctuates a lot during a day and it depends on when we take the readings. Curve fitting defines one of the functions over a given set of readings.

This example leads us to the conclusion that there is a family of curves that can model the given observations. The idea of the distribution of curves that model the given observation is central to Bayesian inference or modeling. The question now is: what should be the process of choosing one function over this family of functions? Or whether we should, in fact, choose one?

One way to narrow down this family of functions is to short list a subset of them based on our prior knowledge about the problem. For example, we know that in May we don't expect temperatures to go below zero degrees Celsius. We can use this knowledge and discard all the functions which have points below zero degrees. Another popular way to think about this problem is to define a distribution over a function space based on our prior knowledge. Furthermore, the job of modeling, in this case, is to refine the distribution over possible functions based on the observed data points. Since these models don't have any defined parameters, they are popularly known as **Bayesian non-parametric models**.

Introducing Gaussian processes

The Gaussian process (GP) can be thought of as an alternative Bayesian approach to regression problems. They are also referred to as infinite dimensional Gaussian distributions. GP defines a priori over functions that can be converted into a posteriori once we have observed a few data points. Although it doesn't seem possible to define distributions over functions, it turns out that we only need to define distributions over a function's values at observed data points.

Formally, let's say that we observed a function, f, at n values $x_1, x_2, \ldots x_n$ as $f(x1), f(x2), \ldots f(n)$. The function is a GP if all of the values, $f(x1), f(x2), \ldots f(n)$, are jointly Gaussian, with a mean of $\mu(x)$ and a covariance of Σ_x given by $\Sigma_{ij} = k(x_i, x_j)$. Here, k the function defines how two variables are related to each other. We will discuss different kinds of kernels later in this section. The joint Gaussian distribution of many Gaussian variables is also known as Multivariate Gaussian.

From the previous temperature example, we can imagine that various functions can be fit to the given observations on temperature. Some functions are smoother than others. One way to capture smoothness is by using the covariance matrix. The covariance matrix ensures that two values (x_i, x_j) close in the input space produce closer values in the output space ($f(x_i), f(x_j)$).

Essentially, the problem we are trying to solve through GP is as follows: given a set of inputs, X, and its values, f, we are trying to estimate the distribution over outputs, f_*, for a new set of inputs, X_*. Mathematically, the quantity we are trying to estimate can be written as follows:

$$p(f_* | X, X_*, f)$$

To obtain this, we model f as a GP so that we know that both f and f_* are coming from a multivariate Gaussian with the following mean and covariance function:

$$\begin{pmatrix} f \\ f_* \end{pmatrix} \sim \mathcal{N}\left(\begin{pmatrix} \mu \\ \mu_* \end{pmatrix}, \begin{pmatrix} K & K_* \\ K_*^T & K_{**} \end{pmatrix} \right)$$

Where μ and μ_* represent the prior mean of the distribution of f and f_* over observed and unobserved function values, respectively, K represents the matrix obtained after applying the kernel function to each of the observed values, X.

Kernel function tries to map the similarity between two data points in the input space to the output space. Let's assume, there are two data points x_i and x_j with corresponding function values as $f(x_i)$ and $f(x_j)$. The Kernel function measures how the closeness between two points x_i and x_j in the input space maps to the similarity or correlation between their function values $f(x_i)$ and $f(x_j)$.

We apply this kernel function to all the pairs of observations in the dataset, thereby, creating a matrix of similarities known as Kernel/Covariance matrix (K). Assuming, there are 10 input data points, the kernel function will be applied to each pair of data points leading to a 10x10 Kernel Matrix (K). If the function values at two data points x_i and x_j is expected to be similar, kernel is expected to have high value at (i,j) in the matrix. We do a detailed discussion on different kernels in GPs in the next section.

In the equation, K_* represents the matrix obtained by applying the same kernel function to values in the training and testing dataset, and K_{**} is the matrix obtained by measuring the similarity between the input values in the test set.

At this point, we will assume that there is some linear algebra magic that can help us to achieve the conditional distribution of $p(f_* | X, X_*, f)$ from the joint distribution and obtain the following:

$$p(f_* | X, X_*, f) \sim N(\mu_*, \Sigma_*)$$

We are going to skip the derivations, but if you would like to know more, you can visit Rasmussen and Williams (`http://www.gaussianprocess.org/gpml/chapters/RW.pdf`).

With this analytical result, we have access to the entire distribution of function values over the testing dataset. Modeling the predictions as distributions also helps in quantifying the uncertainty surrounding the predictions, which is quite important in many time series applications.

Choosing kernels in GPs

In many applications, we find that the prior mean is always set to zero as it is simple, convenient and works well for many applications. However, choosing the appropriate kernels for the task is not always straightforward. As mentioned in the previous section, kernels effectively try to map the similarity between two input data points in the input space to the output (function) space. The only requirement for the kernel function (k) is that it should map any two input values x_i and x_j to a scalar such that Kernel Matrix (K) is a positive/semi-definite for it to be a valid covariance function.

For sake of brevity, we exclude explanation of fundamental concepts of Covariance matrices and how they are always positive semi-definite. We encourage the readers to refer to lecture notes from MIT (https://ocw.mit.edu/courses/electrical-engineering-and-computer-science/6-436j-fundamentals-of-probability-fall-2008/lecture-notes/MIT6_436JF08_lec15.pdf)

While a complete discussion of all of the types of kernels is beyond the scope of this chapter, we will discuss the two kernels used to build this project:

- **White noise kernel:** As the name suggests, the white noise kernel adds a white noise (of variance) to the existing covariance matrix. Mathematically, it is given as follows:

$$k(x_i, x_j) = \sigma^2 \delta(i, j)$$

  If there are many settings, the data points are not accurate and are corrupted by some random noise. Noise in the input data can be modeled by adding a white noise kernel to the covariance matrix.

- **Squared exponential (SE) kernel:** Given two scalars, x_i and x_j, the squared exponential kernel is given by the following equation:

$$k_{SE}(x_i, x_j) = \sigma^2 \exp\left[-\left(\frac{x_i - x_j}{l}\right)^2\right]$$

Here, σ is a scaling factor and l which is the smoothness parameter determines the smoothness of kernel function. It is quite a popular kernel because the functions drawn from the GP through this kernel are infinitely differentiable, which makes it suitable for many applications.

Here are some samples that have been drawn from a GP with an SE kernel that has σ fixed to 1:

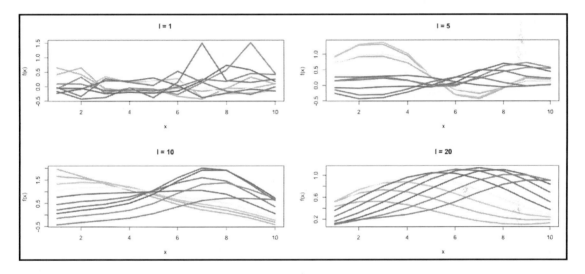

We can observe that the functions become smoother as l increases. For more information on different kinds of kernels, refer to *The Kernel Cookbook* (`https://www.cs.toronto.edu/~duvenaud/cookbook/`**https://www.cs.toronto.edu/~duvenaud/cookbook/**)

Choosing the hyper parameters of a kernel

So far, we have defined kernels with different parameters. For example, in a squared exponential kernel, we have the parameters σ and l. Let's denote the parameter set of any kernel as θ. The question now is, how do we estimate θ?

As mentioned previously, we model the distribution of the output of f function to be a random sample from a multivariate Gaussian distribution. In this manner, the marginal likelihood of observed data points is a multivariate Gaussian that's been conditioned on the input points X and the parameter θ. Thus, we can choose θ by maximizing the likelihood of the observed data points over this assumption.

Now that we have understood how GPs make predictions, let's see how we can make predictions on the stock market using GPs and potentially make some money.

Applying GPs to stock market prediction

In this project, we will try to predict the prices of three major stocks in the market. The dataset for this exercise can be downloaded from Yahoo Finance (`https://finance.yahoo.com`). We downloaded the entire stock history for three companies:

- Google (`https://finance.yahoo.com/quote/GOOG`)
- Netflix (`https://finance.yahoo.com/quote/NFLX`)
- General Electric company (`https://finance.yahoo.com/quote/GE`)

We choose three datasets to compare GP performance across different stocks. Feel free to try this for more stocks.

 All of these datasets are present in the GitHub repository. Thus, there is no need to download them again to run the code.

The CSV files in the dataset have multiple columns. They are as follows:

- **Date**: Calendar date when the price of the stock was measured.
- **Open**: The opening price of the day.
- **High:** The highest price of the day.
- **Low:** The lowest price of the day.
- **Close:** The closing price of the day.
- **Adj Close:** The adjusted closing price is the closing price of the stock that has been amended to include any dividends or other corporate actions before the following day's opening. This is our target variable or Y in the dataset.
- **Volume:** The volume denotes the number of shares traded during a day.

To begin our project, we will consider two forecasting problems each, for all three stock datasets:

- In the first problem, we will train on prices from the years 2008-2016 and predict for the entire year of 2017
- In the second problem, we will train on prices from the years 2008-2018 (up to the third quarter) and predict the fourth quarter of 2018

For predicting stock prices, we don't need to model the entire time series of a stock as a single time series, as in many classical methods (an example of this is regression). For GP, each time series is divided into several time series (one for each year) for every stock. Intuitively, this makes sense, as each stock follows a yearly cycle.

The time series of each year of a stock is an input to the model as a separate time series. Therefore, the forecasting problem becomes as follows: predict future prices of the stock given multiple yearly time series (one for each historical year) as the input. As GP models are distributions over functions, we want to predict the mean and uncertainty at each data point in the future.

Before modeling, we need to normalize the prices to be zero mean and unit standard deviation. This is a requirement in Gaussian processes because of the following:

- We assume the prior on the output distribution to be zero mean, so normalization is required to match our assumption.
- Many kernels for the covariance matrix have scale parameters in them. Normalizing the input helps us to get better estimates of kernel parameters.
- For obtaining the posterior distribution in Gaussian processes, we have to invert the covariance matrix. Normalization helps to avoid any kind of numerical issues with this procedure. Note that we haven't discussed the linear algebra of obtaining the posterior in detail in this chapter.

Once the data has been normalized, we can train our model and predict prices using Gaussian processes. For modeling, we use the plug, and play functions from the GPflow (https://github.com/GPflow/GPflow) library, which is a wrapper on top of TensorFlow for Gaussian processes.

The independent variable (X) in the prediction problem is comprised of two factors:

- The year
- The day of the year

The dependent variable (Y) in the problem is the normalized adjusted closing price for each day in a year as mentioned before.

Before training the model, we need to define the prior and kernel function for Gaussian Processes. For this problem, we use the standard zero mean prior. We use a kernel function for the covariance matrix that is generated as the sum of two kernels which are defined as follows:

- Squared exponential (or RBF, as mentioned in the GPflow package) kernel with `lengthscale` = 1 and `variance` = 63.
- White noise with initial `variance` to be very low, such as *1e-10*.

The idea behind choosing squared exponential is that it is infinitely differentiable and it's the easiest one to understand. White noise is used to account for any systemic noise we might observe in our target variables. While it may not be the best choice of kernels, it is good for understanding purposes. Feel free to experiment with other kernels and see whether they work well.

Creating a stock price prediction model

We will begin our project by processing the data present in the dataset:

1. Create a dataframe with yearly time series for each stock. Represent each year's stock price by an individual column in that dataframe. Restrict number of rows in the dataframe to 252 which is roughly the number of trading days in a year. Also add the fiscal quarter associated with each row of data as a separate column.

```
def get_prices_by_year(self):
    df = self.modify_first_year_data()
    for i in range(1, len(self.num_years)):
        df = pd.concat([df,
pd.DataFrame(self.get_year_data(year=self.num_years[i],
normalized=True))], axis=1)
    df = df[:self.num_days]
    quarter_col = []
    num_days_in_quarter = self.num_days // 4
    for j in range(0, len(self.quarter_names)):
quarter_col.extend([self.quarter_names[j]]*num_days_in_quarter)
    quarter_col = pd.DataFrame(quarter_col)
    df = pd.concat([df, quarter_col], axis=1)
    df.columns = self.num_years + ['Quarter']
    df.index.name = 'Day'
    df = self.fill_nans_with_mean(df)
    return df
```

Note that there are almost 252 trading days in a year, as stock markets are closed on weekends.

2. Even if there are more trading days in a particular year (like leap year), limit data to 252 days to ensure consistency across the years. In case the number of trading days is less than 252 in a particular year, extrapolate the data to 252 days by imputing the mean price of the year for missing days. Implement the following code to achieve this:

```
def fill_nans_with_mean(self, df):
    years = self.num_years[:-1]
    df_wo_last_year = df.loc[:,years]
    df_wo_last_year = df_wo_last_year.fillna(df_wo_last_year.mean())
    df_wo_last_year[self.num_years[-1]] = df[self.num_years[-1]]
    df= df_wo_last_year

    return df
```

3. For each year, normalize the prices to transform the yearly series to zero mean and unit standard deviation. Also, subtract the first day price from all of the data points in that year. This basically forces a yearly time series to start from zero, thereby avoiding any influence of previous year's prices on it.

```
def normalized_data_col(self, df):
    price_normalized = pd.DataFrame()
    date_list = list(df.Date)
    self.num_years = sorted(list(set([date_list[i].year for i in
range(0, len(date_list))])))
    for i in range(0, len(self.num_years)):
        prices_data = self.get_year_data(year=self.num_years[i],
normalized=False)
        prices_data = [(prices_data[i] - np.mean(prices_data)) /
np.std(prices_data) for i in range(0, len(prices_data))]
        prices_data = [(prices_data[i] - prices_data[0]) for i in
range(0, len(prices_data))]
        price_normalized = price_normalized.append(prices_data,
ignore_index=True)
    return price_normalized
```

 Please make sure to install this library as mentioned in the **README** file in the repository for this chapter, before executing the code.

4. As mentioned in the previous section, generate the covariance matrix as a sum of two kernels:

```
kernel = gpflow.kernels.RBF(2, lengthscales=1, variance=63) +
gpflow.kernels.White(2, variance=1e-10)
```

We use the SciPy optimizer in GPflow package to optimize hyper parameters using maximum likelihood estimation. Scipy is a standard optimizer from Python library Scipy. If you are not familiar with Scipy optimizer, please refer to the official page (`https://docs.scipy.org/doc/scipy/reference/generated/scipy.optimize.minimize.html`).

5. Implement the final wrapper function `make_gp_predictions` to train a GP model and make future price predictions. Following are the steps that the function implements:

   1. Takes the input of training data, start and end of training period and prediction year and quarter.
   2. Constructs 2 separate series using data from the start year of the training period, one for the independent variables (X) and one for the target (Y). Each element in series (X) represents each day of the year and consists of two independent variables, year and day of the year. For example, for start year 2008, X looks like [[2008,1], [2008,2],[2008,3].......[2008,252]].
   3. Appends the independent and target variables for each subsequent year to list X and Y respectively.
   4. If input `pred_quarters` is not None, predicts for the quarters specified instead of the entire year. For example, if `pred_quarters` is [4] and `pred_year` is 2018, the function will predict for Quarter 4 of 2018 using all the data till Quarter 3 of 2018.
   5. Defines the kernel function as mentioned before and trains the GP model using Scipy optimizer.
   6. Predicts the stock prices for the prediction period.

```
def make_gp_predictions(self, start_year, end_year, pred_year,
pred_quarters = []):
    start_year, end_year, pred_year= int(start_year),int(end_year),
int(pred_year)
    years_quarters = list(range(start_year, end_year + 1)) + ['Quarter']
    years_in_train = years_quarters[:-2]
    price_df =
self.preprocessed_data.prices_by_year[self.preprocessed_data.prices_by_year
.columns.intersection(years_quarters)]
    num_days_in_train = list(price_df.index.values)
```

```
#Generating X and Y for Training
first_year_prices = price_df[start_year]
if start_year == self.preprocessed_data.num_years[0]:
    first_year_prices = (first_year_prices[first_year_prices.iloc[:] !=
0])
    first_year_prices = (pd.Series([0.0],
index=[first_year_prices.index[0]-1])).append(first_year_prices)
first_year_days = list(first_year_prices.index.values)
first_year_X = np.array([[start_year, day] for day in first_year_days])
X = first_year_X
Target = np.array(first_year_prices)
for year in years_in_train[1:]:
    current_year_prices = list(price_df.loc[:, year])
    current_year_X = np.array([[year, day] for day in
num_days_in_train])
    X = np.append(X, current_year_X, axis=0)
    Target = np.append(Target, current_year_prices)
final_year_prices = price_df[end_year]
final_year_prices =
final_year_prices[final_year_prices.iloc[:].notnull()]
final_year_days = list(final_year_prices.index.values)
if pred_quarters is not None:
    length = 63 * (pred_quarters[0] - 1)
    final_year_days = final_year_days[:length]
    final_year_prices = final_year_prices[:length]
final_year_X = np.array([[end_year, day] for day in final_year_days])
X = np.append(X, final_year_X, axis=0)
Target = np.append(Target, final_year_prices)
if pred_quarters is not None:
    days_for_prediction = [day for day in
                            range(63 * (pred_quarters[0]-1), 63 *
pred_quarters[int(len(pred_quarters) != 1)])]
else:
    days_for_prediction = list(range(0,
self.preprocessed_data.num_days))
x_mesh = np.linspace(days_for_prediction[0], days_for_prediction[-1]
                        , 2000)
x_pred = ([[pred_year, x_mesh[i]] for i in range(len(x_mesh))])
X = X.astype(np.float64)
Target = np.expand_dims(Target, axis=1)
kernel = gpflow.kernels.RBF(2, lengthscales=1, variance=63) +
gpflow.kernels.White(2, variance=1e-10)
self.gp_model = gpflow.models.GPR(X, Target, kern=kernel)
gpflow.train.ScipyOptimizer().minimize(self.gp_model)
y_mean, y_var = self.gp_model.predict_y(x_pred)
return x_mesh, y_mean, y_var
```

Understanding the results obtained

Let's try to understand how good our predictions are for each of the stocks:

- **Netflix (NFLX)**: The following diagram illustrates the prices of the Netflix stock from **2002** through **2018**:

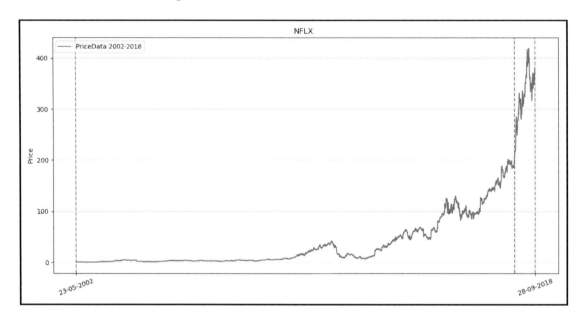

The price for the year **2018** is defined using the two vertical lines. It shows the growth in the price of the stock throughout the entire year.

As per the first problem case, we consider the period from **2008-2016** for training:

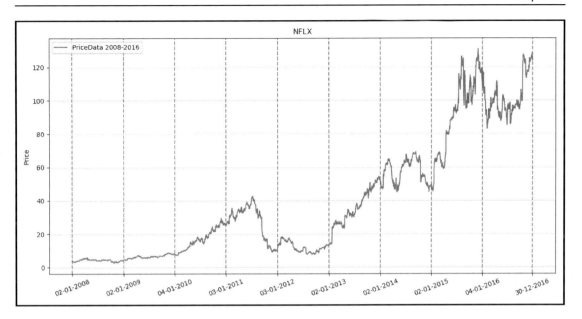

Normalizing the prices by each year for modeling gives us the following plot:

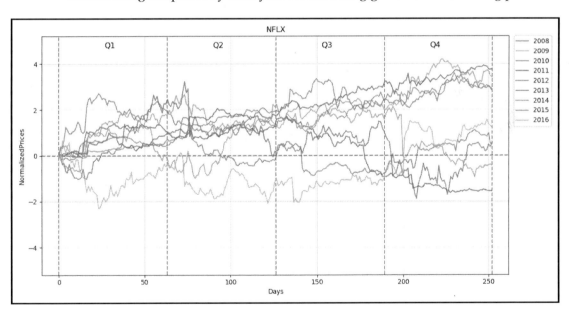

Predicting the prices of the stock for the whole year of **2017** with a **95% confidence interval** gives us the following plot:

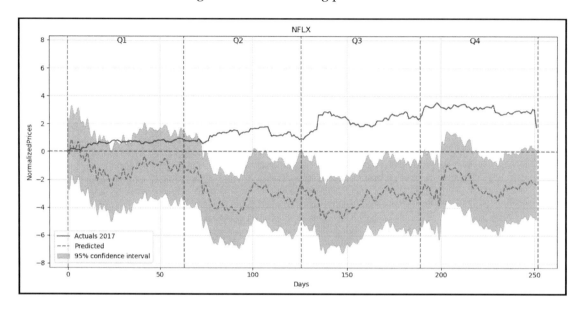

Comparing of the generated values with the actual values, it is clear that the model falters by predicting the value to be less than the actual value. However, the reason for this could be the highs and lows of the prices of Netflix in the year **2016**. These are not captured through the basic-level kernel used in this project.

For the second problem case, we consider the train period from **2008-2018**, including the first three quarters. The plot for the Netflix stock price during this period is as follows:

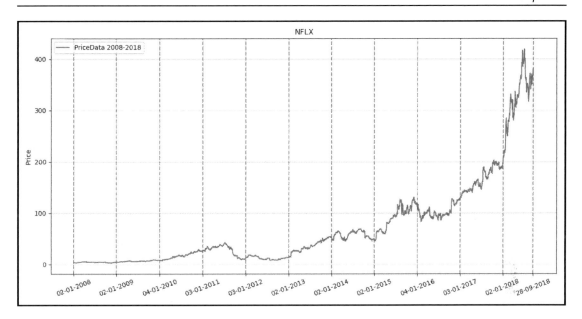

Using the normalized values, we achieve the following plot:

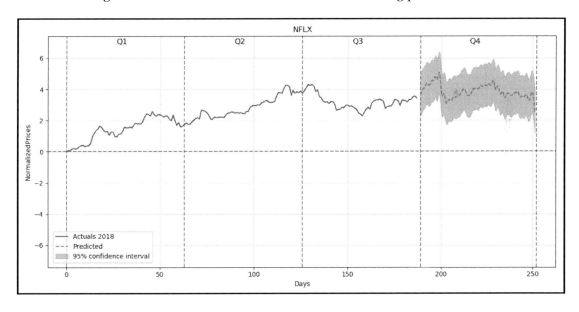

As we can see, the trend is very well captured in this prediction, along with uncertainty.

- **General Electric company** (**GE**): To understand the difference between the actual and the predicted prices, it is necessary to plot the graph that has the actual values. Here is the plot that illustrates the historical prices of GE stock:

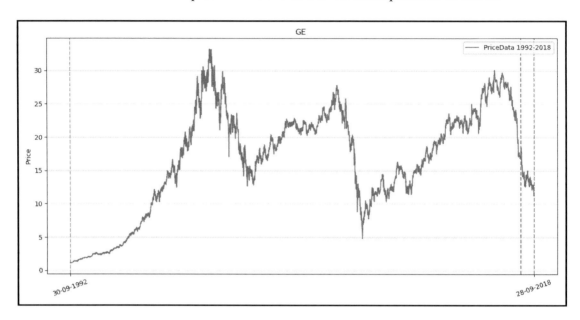

As mentioned previously, the dotted vertical lines represent the prices in the year **2018**.

As per our first problem case, we consider the period from **2008-2016** for training. The chart for that period is as follows:

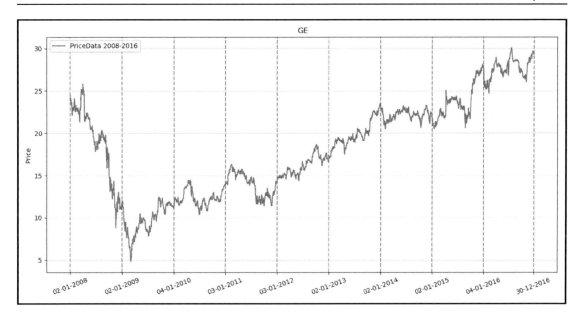

There was a huge dip in **2009**, but since then, the stock has been growing steadily.

Since we used normalized prices for every year for modeling purposes, let's look at the input data for our model:

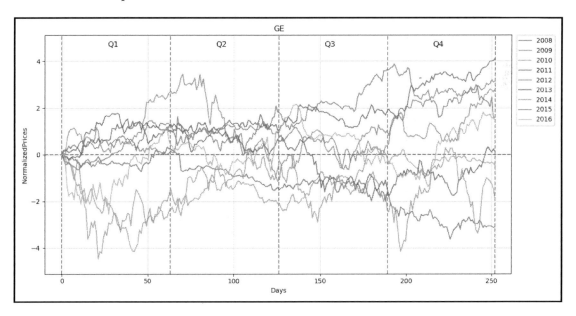

The predictions with normalized prices for the whole of **2017** with a **95% confidence interval** are as follows:

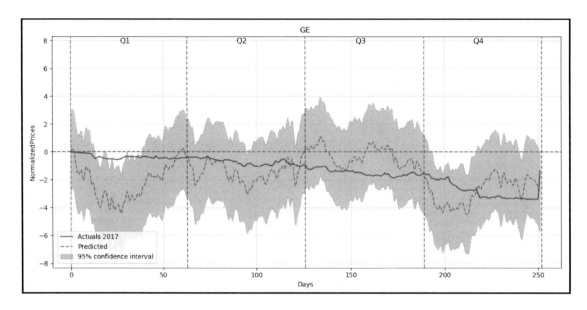

As we can see, the model has captured an accurate trend of the stock.

For the second prediction, we consider the train period from **2008-2018**, including the first three quarters of **2018**. The plot for the GE stock price during that period is as follows:

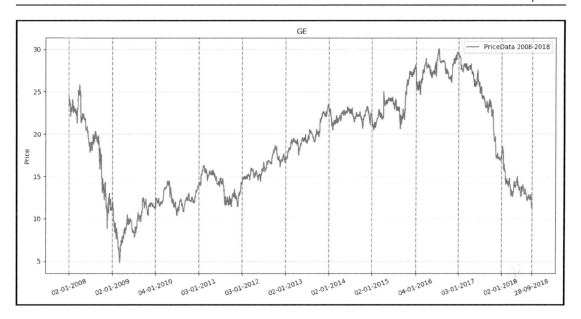

The predicted prices for that period with a **95% confidence interval** are as follows:

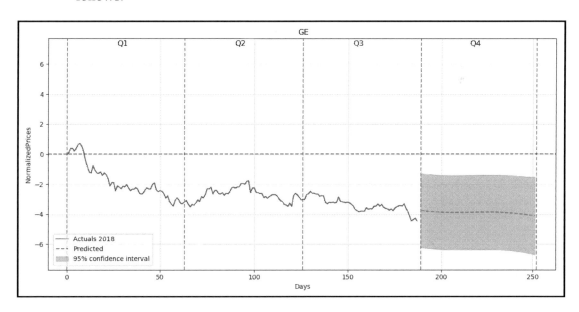

- **Google (GOOG):** The following chart illustrates the historical prices of Google stock:

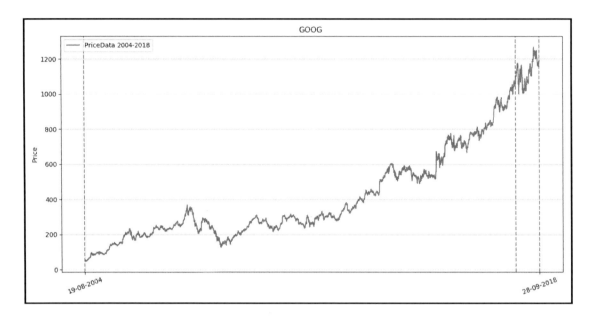

As specified previously, the dotted vertical lines represent the prices for **2018**.

As per the first problem case, the period from **2008-2016** is essential for training, so let's look at the chart for this period:

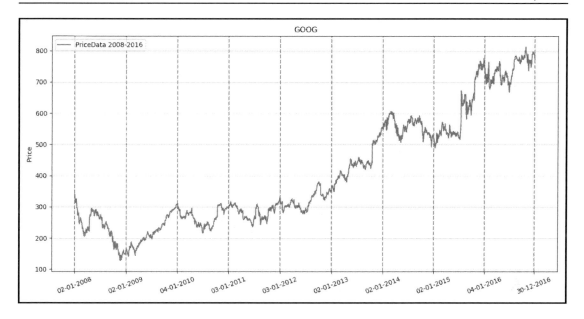

There was a huge dip in **2009** and since then, the stock has been growing steadily, except during **2015**.

Since we used normalized prices by year for modeling, let's look at the input data for our model:

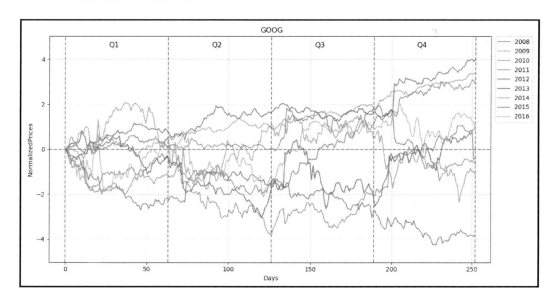

Predictions (normalized prices) for a complete year, **2017**, with a **95% confidence interval**, are as follows:

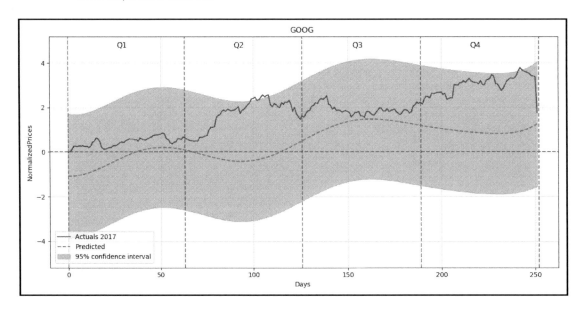

We were able to capture the overall upward trend of the price, but with very wide confidence bands.

For the next prediction, we considered the train period from **2008-2018**, including the first three quarters. A plot of the Google stock price during that period is as follows:

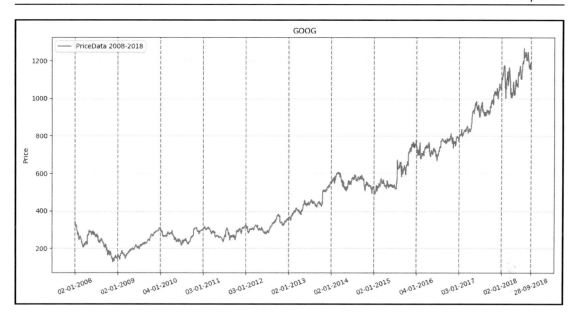

The predicted prices for that period with a **95% confidence interval** are as follows:

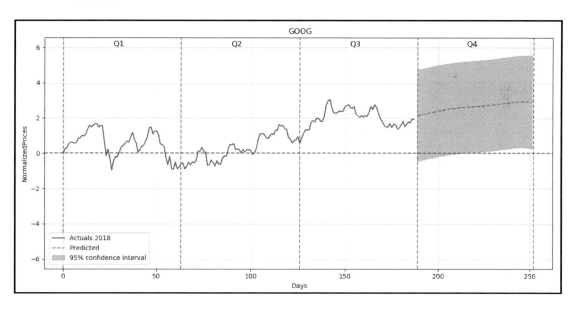

In 2018, the trend has been better captured overall.

Summary

In this chapter, we learned about a very popular Bayesian forecasting model known as the Gaussian process and used it to predict stock prices.

In the first part of this chapter, we looked at the forecasting problem by sampling an appropriate function from a multivariate Gaussian rather than use predicting point forecasts. We looked at a special kind of non-parametric Bayesian model named Gaussian processes.

Thereafter, we used GP to predict the prices of three stocks, namely Google, Netflix, and GE, for 2017 and Q4 2018. We observed that our predictions were mostly within a 95% confidence interval, but far from perfect.

Gaussian processes are used widely in applications where we need to model non-linear functions with uncertainty with very few data points. However, they sometimes fail to scale to very high dimensional problems in which other deep learning algorithms, such as LSTM, would perform better.

In the next chapter, we will take a closer look at an unsupervised approach to detecting credit card frauds using auto-encoders.

Questions

1. What are Gaussian processes?
2. Can you improve the predictions by trying out different kernels?
3. Can you apply GP model to other stocks in S&P 500 and compare its performance with the ones mentioned here?

7
Credit Card Fraud Detection using Autoencoders

The digital world is growing rapidly. We are used to performing many of our daily tasks online, such as booking cabs, shopping on e-commerce websites, and even recharging our phones. For the majority of these tasks, we are used to paying with credit cards. However, it is a known fact that a credit card can be compromised, which could result in a fraudulent transaction. The Nilson report estimates that for every $100 spent, seven cents are stolen. It estimates the total credit card fraud market to be around $30 billion.

Detecting whether a transaction is fraudulent or not is a very impactful data science problem. Every bank that issues credit cards invests in technology to detect fraud and take the appropriate actions immediately. There are lot of standard supervised learning techniques such as logistic regression, from random forest to classifying fraud.

In this chapter, we will take a closer look at an unsupervised approach to detecting credit card fraud using auto-encoders by exploring the following topics:

- Understanding auto-encoders
- Defining and training a fraud detection model
- Testing a fraud detection model

Understanding auto-encoders

Auto-encoders are a type of artificial neural network whose job is to learn a low-dimensional representation of input data using unsupervised learning. They are quite popular when it comes to dimensionality reduction of input and in generative models.

Essentially, an auto-encoder learns to compress data into a low-dimensional representation and then reconstructs that representation into something that matches the original data. This way, the low-dimensional representation ignores the noise, which is not helpful in reconstructing the original data.

As mentioned previously, they are also useful in generating models, particularly images. For example, if we feed the representation of *dog* and *flying*, it may attempt to generate an image of a *flying cat*, which it has not seen before.

Structurally, auto-encoders consist of two parts, the encoder and the decoder. The encoder generates the low-dimensional representation of inputs, and the decoder helps regenerate the input from the representation. Generally, the encoder and the decoder are feedforward neural networks with one or multiple hidden layers.

The following diagram illustrates the configuration of a typical auto-encoder:

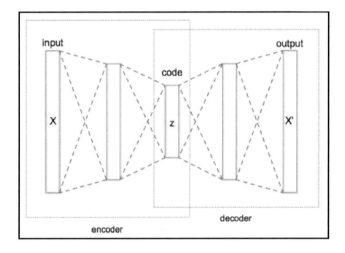

To define the encoder (ϕ) and the decoder (Ψ), an auto-encoder can be mathematically represented as follows:

$$
\begin{aligned}
&\phi : \mathcal{X} \to \mathcal{F} \\
&\psi : \mathcal{F} \to \mathcal{X} \\
&\phi, \psi = \arg\min_{\phi,\psi} \| X - (\psi \circ \phi) X \|^2
\end{aligned}
$$

As mentioned in the equation, the parameters of the encoder and the decoder are optimized in a way that minimizes a special kind of error, which is known as **reconstruction error.** Reconstruction error is the error between the reconstructed input and the original input.

Building a fraud detection model

For this project, we are going to use the credit card dataset from Kaggle (`https://www.kaggle.com/mlg-ulb/creditcardfraud`), Andrea Dal Pozzolo, Olivier Caelen, Reid A. Johnson and Gianluca Bontempi. Calibrating Probability with Undersampling for Unbalanced Classification. In Symposium on Computational Intelligence and Data Mining (CIDM), IEEE, 2015. It consists of credit card transaction data from two days, from European cardholders. The dataset is highly imbalanced and contains approximately 284,000 pieces of transaction data with 492 instances of fraud (0.172% of the total).

There are 31 numerical columns in the dataset. Two of them are time and amount. **Time** denotes the amount of time elapsed (in seconds) between each transaction and the first transaction in the dataset. **Amount** is the total amount regarding the transaction. For our model, we will eliminate the time column as it doesn't help with the accuracy of the model. The rest of the features (V1, V2 ... V28) are obtained from Principal Component Analysis (`https://ocw.mit.edu/courses/mathematics/18-650-statistics-for-applications-fall-2016/lecture-videos/lecture-19-video/`) of original features for confidential reasons. **Class** is the target variable, which indicates whether the transaction was fraudulent or not.

To pre-process the data, there is not much that needs to be done. This is mainly because a lot of the data is already cleaned up.

Usually, in a classical machine learning model such as logistic regression, we feed the data points of both negative and positive classes into the algorithm. However, since we are using auto-encoders, we will model it differently.

Essentially, our training set will consist of only non-fraudulent transaction data. The idea is that whenever we pass a fraudulent transaction through our trained model, it should detect it as an anomaly. We are framing this problem as anomaly detection rather than classification.

The model will consist of two fully connected encoder layers with 14 and seven neurons, respectively. There will be two decoder layers with seven and 29 neurons, respectively. Additionally, we will use L1 regularization during training.

Lastly, to define the model, we will use Keras with Tensorflow at the backend for training auto-encoders.

Regularization is a technique in machine learning that's used to reduce overfitting. Overfitting happens when the model learns a signal as well as noise in the training data and can't generalize well to unseen dataset. While there are many ways to avoid overfitting such as cross validation, sampling, and so on, regularization specifically adds a penalty to weights of the model so that we don't learn an overly complex model. L1 regularization adds an L1 norm penalty on all the weights of the model. This way, any weight that doesn't contribute to the accuracy is shrunk to zero.

Defining and training a fraud detection model

The following are the steps for defining and training the model:

1. Transform `'Amount'` by removing the mean and scaling it to the unit's variance:

```
def preprocess_data(data):
data = data.drop(['Time'], axis=1)
data['Amount'] =
StandardScaler().fit_transform(data['Amount'].values.reshape(-1,
1))
return
 data
```

Note that we use the `StandardScaler` utility from scikit-learn for this purpose.

2. To model our dataset, split it into train and test data, with train consisting of only non-fraudulent transaction and test consisting of both fraudulent and non-fraudulent transactions:

```
def get_train_and_test_data(processed_data):
X_train, X_test = train_test_split(processed_data, test_size=0.25,
random_state=RANDOM_SEED)
X_train = X_train[X_train.Class == 0]
X_train = X_train.drop(['Class'], axis=1)
y_test = X_test['Class']
X_test = X_test.drop(['Class'], axis=1)
X_train = X_train.values
```

```
X_test = X_test.values
return X_train, X_test,y_test
```

3. Define the model by using the following code:

```
def define_model(self):
dim_input = self.train_data.shape[1]
layer_input = Input(shape=(dim_input,))
layer_encoder = Dense(DIM_ENCODER, activation="tanh",
activity_regularizer=regularizers.l1(10e-5))(layer_input)
layer_encoder = Dense(int(DIM_ENCODER / 2),
activation="relu")(layer_encoder)
layer_decoder = Dense(int(DIM_ENCODER / 2),
activation='tanh')(layer_encoder)
layer_decoder = Dense(dim_input, activation='relu')(layer_decoder)
autoencoder = Model(inputs=layer_input, outputs=layer_decoder)
return autoencoder
```

4. Once the model is defined, train the model using Keras:

```
def train_model(self):
self.model.compile(optimizer=OPTIMIZER,
loss=LOSS,
metrics=[EVAL_METRIC])
checkpoint = ModelCheckpoint(filepath=os.path.join(MODEL_SAVE_DIR,
"trained_model.h5"),
verbose=0,
save_best_only=True)
log_tensorboard = TensorBoard(log_dir='./logs',
histogram_freq=0,
write_graph=True,
write_images=True)
history = self.model.fit(self.train_data, self.train_data,
epochs=EPOCHS,
batch_size=BATCH_SIZE,
shuffle=True,
validation_data=(self.test_data, self.test_data),
verbose=1,
callbacks=[checkpoint, log_tensorboard]).history
self.history = history
print("Training Done. Plotting Loss Curves")
self.plot_loss_curves()
```

5. Use the following parameters to find the output of the model:

    -   EPOCHS = 100.
    -   BATCH_SIZE = 32.
    -   OPTIMIZER = 'Adam'.
    -   LOSS = Mean squared error between reconstructed and original input.
    -   EVAL_METRIC = 'Accuracy'. This is the usual binary classification accuracy.

6. Store a `TensorBoard` file to visualize the graph or other variables on it. Also, store the best-performing model through the checkpoints provided by Keras. Generate the loss curves by epoch for the training and testing data:

```
def plot_loss_curves(self):
fig = plt.figure(num="Loss Curves")
fig.set_size_inches(12, 6)
plt.plot(self.history['loss'])
plt.plot(self.history['val_loss'])
plt.title('Loss By Epoch')
plt.ylabel('Loss')
plt.xlabel('Epoch Num')
plt.legend(['Train_Data', 'Test_Data'], loc='upper right');
plt.grid(True, alpha=.25)
plt.tight_layout()
image_name = 'Loss_Curves.png'
fig.savefig(os.path.join(PLOTS_DIR,image_name), dpi=fig.dpi)
plt.clf()
```

7. The following diagram illustrates the loss curves that are generated when the model is trained for 100 epochs:

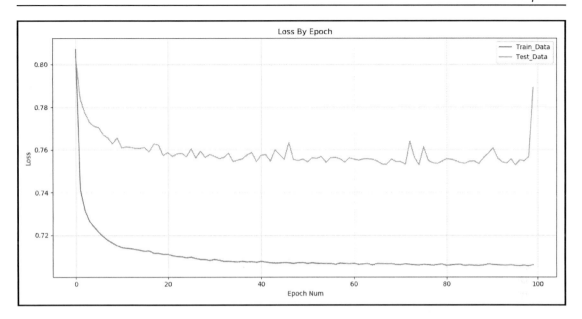

We can observe that for the training set, the loss or reconstruction error decreases at the start of the training and saturates toward the end. This saturation implies that the model has finished learning the weights.

Save the model with the lowest loss in the testing set.

Testing a fraud detection model

Once the training process is complete, break down the reconstruction error in the testing set by fraudulent and non-fraudulent (normal) transactions. Generate the reconstruction error by different classes of transactions:

```
def plot_reconstruction_error_by_class(self):
self.get_test_predictions()
mse = np.mean(np.power(self.test_data - self.test_predictions, 2), axis=1)
self.recon_error = pd.DataFrame({'recon_error': mse,
'true_class': self.y_test})
## Plotting the errors by class
# Normal Transactions
fig = plt.figure(num = "Recon Error with Normal Transactions")
fig.set_size_inches(12, 6)
```

```
ax = fig.add_subplot(111)
normal_error_df = self.recon_error[(self.recon_error['true_class'] == 0) &
(self.recon_error['recon_error'] < 50)]
_ = ax.hist(normal_error_df.recon_error.values, bins=20)
plt.xlabel("Recon Error Bins")
plt.ylabel("Num Samples")
plt.title("Recon Error with Normal Transactions")
plt.tight_layout()
image_name = "Recon_Error_with_Normal_Transactions.png"
fig.savefig(os.path.join(PLOTS_DIR, image_name), dpi=fig.dpi)
plt.clf()
```

The following diagrams illustrate the reconstruction error distribution of fraudulent and normal transactions in the testing set:

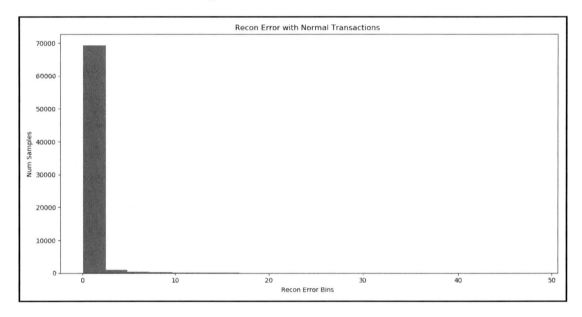

The next diagram is for fraud transactions:

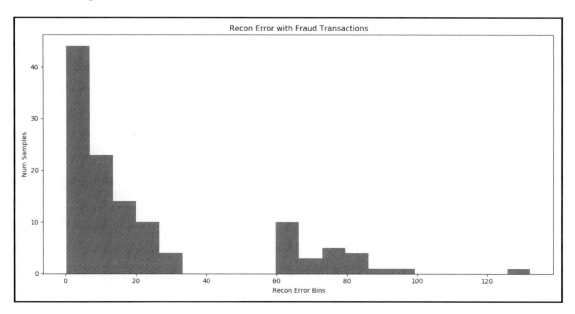

As we can see, the reconstruction error for normal transactions is very close to zero for most of the transactions. However, the reconstruction error with fraudulent transactions has a wide distribution, with the majority still being close to zero.

This suggests that a threshold on the reconstruction error can serve as a classification threshold on normal versus fraudulent transactions.

For evaluating the model, we will use the metrics Precision and Recall which were defined in Chapter 4, *Digit Classification Using TensorFlow Lite*, of the book. Firstly, let's look at the precision and recall at various thresholds of reconstruction error:

```
def get_precision_recall_curves(self):
precision, recall, threshold =
precision_recall_curve(self.recon_error.true_class,
self.recon_error.recon_error)
# Plotting the precision curve
fig = plt.figure(num ="Precision Curve")
fig.set_size_inches(12, 6)
plt.plot(threshold, precision[1:], 'g', label='Precision curve')
plt.title('Precision By Recon Error Threshold Values')
plt.xlabel('Threshold')
plt.ylabel('Precision')
plt.tight_layout()
image_name = 'Precision_Threshold_Curve.png'
```

```
fig.savefig(os.path.join(PLOTS_DIR, image_name), dpi=fig.dpi)
plt.clf()
plt.plot(threshold, recall[1:], 'g', label='Recall curve')
plt.title('Recall By Recon Error Threshold Values')
plt.xlabel('Threshold')
plt.ylabel('Recall')
plt.tight_layout()
image_name = 'Recall_Threshold_Curve.png'
fig.savefig(os.path.join(PLOTS_DIR, image_name), dpi=fig.dpi)
plt.clf()
```

The reconstruction error threshold for precision and recall are shown in the following graph:

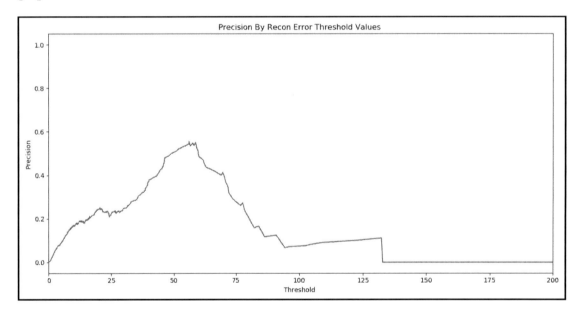

The diagram represents the error threshold for recall:

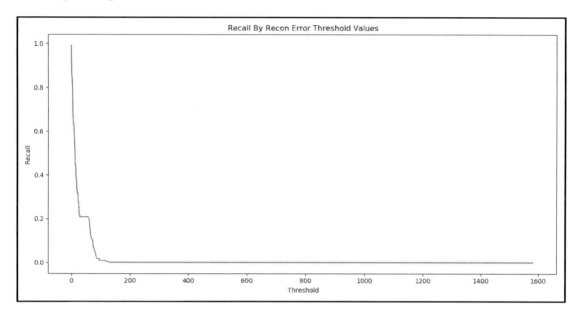

As we can see, recall decreases when there is an increase in reconstruction error, and vice versa for precision. There are a few dips due to the dataset.

There is one other thing that we need to keep in mind. As mentioned previously, there is always a trade-off between high precision and high recall in machine learning. We need to choose any one for our particular model.

Generally, businesses prefer a model with high precision or high recall. For fraud detection, we would like to have a model with high recall. This is essential as we can classify the majority of fraudulent transactions as fraud. One method to counter the loss of precision is to do a manual verification of transactions classified as fraud to determine whether they are actually fraudulent. This will help in ensuring a good experience for the end user.

Here is the code to generate a confusion matrix with `min_recall` = 80%:

```python
def get_confusion_matrix(self, min_recall = 0.8):
# Get the confusion matrix with min desired recall on the testing dataset
used.
precision, recall, threshold =
precision_recall_curve(self.recon_error.true_class,
self.recon_error.recon_error)
idx = filter(lambda x: x[1] > min_recall, enumerate(recall[1:]))[-1][0]
th = threshold[idx]
print ("Min recall is : %f, Threshold for recon error is: %f "
%(recall[idx+1], th))
# Get the confusion matrix
predicted_class = [1 if e > th else 0 for e in
self.recon_error.recon_error.values]
cnf_matrix = confusion_matrix(self.recon_error.true_class, predicted_class)
classes = ['Normal','Fraud']
fig = plt.figure(figsize=(12, 12))
plt.imshow(cnf_matrix, interpolation='nearest', cmap=plt.cm.Blues)
plt.title("Confusion Matrix")
plt.colorbar()
tick_marks = np.arange(len(classes))
plt.xticks(tick_marks, classes, rotation=45)
plt.yticks(tick_marks, classes)
fmt = 'd'
thresh = cnf_matrix.max() / 2.
for i, j in itertools.product(range(cnf_matrix.shape[0]),
range(cnf_matrix.shape[1])):
plt.text(j, i, format(cnf_matrix[i, j], fmt),
horizontalalignment="center",
color="white" if cnf_matrix[i, j] > thresh else "black")
plt.ylabel('True label')
plt.xlabel('Predicted label')
plt.tight_layout()
image_name = 'Confusion_Matrix_with_threshold_{}.png'.format(th)
fig.savefig(os.path.join(PLOTS_DIR, image_name), dpi=fig.dpi)
plt.clf()
```

The confusion matrix that's obtained from the preceding code is shown in the following diagram:

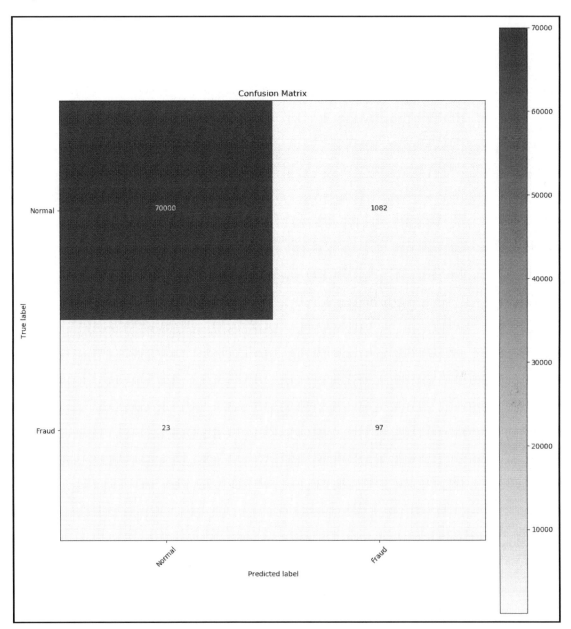

We can observe that out of 120 fraudulent transactions, 97 of them have been classified correctly. However, we have also classified 1,082 normal transaction as being fraudulent, which will have to go through a manual verification process to ensure a good experience for the end user.

As a note of caution, we should not assume that auto-encoders are helpful in all binary classification tasks and can achieve better performance than state-of-the-art classification models. The idea behind this project was to illustrate a different approach of using auto-encoders to perform classification tasks.

 Note that in this chapter, we have used the same validation and test set for illustrative purposes. Ideally, once we have defined the threshold on the reconstruction error, we should test the model on some unseen dataset to evaluate its performance in a better manner.

Summary

Credit card fraud are ubiquitous in nature. Every company in today's world is employing machine learning to combat payment fraud on their platform. In this chapter, we looked at the problem of classifying fraud using the credit card dataset from Kaggle.

We learned about auto-encoders as a dimensionality reduction technique. We understood that the auto-encoder architecture consists of two components: an encoder and a decoder. We model the parameters of a fully connected network using reconstruction loss.

Thereafter, we looked at the fraud classification problem through the lens of an anomaly detection problem. We trained the auto-encoder model using normal transactions. We then looked at the reconstruction error of the auto-encoder for both normal and fraudulent transactions, and observed that the reconstruction error has a wide distribution for fraudulent transactions. We then defined a threshold on reconstruction to classify the model and generated the confusion matrix.

In the next chapter, we will explore the concept of Bayesian neural networks, which combines the concepts of deep learning and Bayesian learning to model uncertainty in the prediction of deep neural networks.

Questions

The following are the questions:

- What is an auto-encoder?
- What are different components of an auto-encoder?
- What is the reconstruction loss?
- What is the precision and recall?

8
Generating Uncertainty in Traffic Signs Classifier Using Bayesian Neural Networks

As humans, we love the uncertainty that comes with predictions. For example, we always want to know what the chances are of it raining before we leave the house. However, with traditional deep learning, we only have a point prediction and no notion of uncertainty. Predictions from these networks are assumed to be accurate, which is not always the case. Ideally, we would like to know the level of confidence of predictions from neural networks before making a decision.

For example, having uncertainty in the model could have potentially avoided the following disastrous consequences:

- In May 2016, the Tesla Model S crashed in northern Florida into a truck that was turning left in front of it. According to the official Tesla blog (`https://www.tesla.com/en_GB/blog/tragic-loss`), *Neither Autopilot nor the driver noticed the white side of the tractor trailer against a brightly lit sky, so the brake was not applied.*
- In July 2015, two African Americans were classified as gorillas by Google's image classifier, raising concerns of racial discrimination. Here (`https://www.usatoday.com/story/tech/2015/07/01/google-apologizes-after-photos-identify-black-people-as-gorillas/29567465/`) is the press release.

The thing that is pretty clear from these examples is that quantifying uncertainty in predictions could have avoided these disasters. The question now is: If it's so obvious, why didn't Tesla or Google implement it in the first place?

Bayesian algorithms (like Gaussian processes) can quantify uncertainty, but cannot scale to large datasets such as images and videos, whereas deep learning is able to produce much better accuracy—except that it lacks any notion of uncertainty.

In this chapter, we will explore the concept of Bayesian neural networks, which combines the concepts of deep learning and Bayesian learning with model uncertainty in the predictions of deep neural networks. We will cover the following topics:

- Introduction to Bayesian deep learning
- What are Bayesian neural networks?
- Building a Bayesian neural network with the German Traffic Sign Image dataset

Understanding Bayesian deep learning

We've all understood the basics of Bayes' rule, as explained in Chapter 6, *Predicting Stock Prices using Gaussian Process Regression*.

For Bayesian machine learning, we use the same formula as Bayes' rule to learn model parameters (w) from the given data, X. The formula, then, looks like this:

$$P(w|X) = \frac{P(X|w)P(w)}{P(X)}$$

Here, $P(X)$ or the probability of observed data is also called evidence. This is always difficult to compute. One brute-force way is to integrate out $P(X|w)$ for all the values of model parameters, but this is obviously too expensive to evaluate. $P(w)$ is the prior on parameters, which is nothing but some randomly initialized value of parameters in most cases. Generally, we don't care about setting the priors perfectly as we expect the inference procedure to converge to the right value of parameters.

$P(X|w)$ is known as the likelihood of data, given the modeling parameters. Effectively, it shows how likely it is to obtain the given observations in the data when given the model parameters. We use likelihood as a measure to evaluate different models. The higher the likelihood, the better the model.

Finally, $P(w|X)$, a posterior, is what we want to calculate. It's a probability distribution over model parameters that's obtained from the given data. Once we obtain the uncertainty in model parameters, we can use them to quantify the uncertainty in model predictions.

Generally, in machine learning, we use **Maximum Likelihood estimation (MLE)** (`https://ocw.mit.edu/courses/mathematics/18-05-introduction-to-probability-and-statistics-spring-2014/readings/MIT18_05S14_Reading10b.pdf`) to get the estimates of model parameters. However, in the case of Bayesian deep learning, we estimate a posterior from the prior and the procedure is known as **Maximum a posteriori (MAP)** estimation (`https://ocw.mit.edu/courses/sloan-school-of-management/15-097-prediction-machine-learning-and-statistics-spring-2012/lecture-notes/MIT15_097S12_lec15.pdf`).

Bayes' rule in neural networks

Traditionally, neural networks produce a point estimate by optimizing weights and biases to minimize a loss function, such as the mean squared error in regression problems. As mentioned earlier, this is similar to finding parameters using the Maximum likelihood estimation criteria:

$$w^{MLE} = argmax_w \, logP(X|w)$$

Typically, we obtain the best parameters through backpropagation in neural networks. To avoid overfitting, we introduce a regularizer of L_2 norm over weights. If you are not aware of regularization, please refer to the following Andrew Ng video: `http://openclassroom.stanford.edu/MainFolder/CoursePage.php?course=MachineLearning`. It has been shown that L_2 normalization is equivalent to placing a normal prior on weights $P(w) \sim (0, I)$. With a prior on weights, the MLE estimation problem can be framed as a MAP estimation:

$$w^{MAP} = argmax_w \, logP(w|X)$$

Using Bayes' rule, the preceding equation can be written as follows:

$$w^{MAP} = argmax_w \, logP(X|w) + logP(w)$$

 The exact proof of equivalence of regularization to the Bayesian framework is outside the scope of this chapter. If you are interested, you can read more about it at the following MIT lecture: `http://www.mit.edu/~9.520/spring09/Classes/class15-bayes.pdf`.

From this, we can observe that traditional neural networks with regularization can be framed as a problem of inference using Bayes' rule. Bayesian neural networks aim to determine the posterior distribution using Monte Carlo or Variational inference techniques. In the rest of this chapter, we will look at how to build a Bayesian neural network using TensorFlow Probability.

Understanding TensorFlow probability, variational inference, and Monte Carlo methods

TensorFlow Probability (tfp in code – `https://www.tensorflow.org/probability/ overview#layer_2_model_building`) was recently released by Google to perform probabilistic reasoning in a scalable manner. It provides tools and functionalities to define distributions, build neural networks with prior on weights, and perform probabilistic inference tasks such as Monte Carlo or Variational Inference.

Let's take a look at some of the functions/utilities we will be using for building our model:

- **Tfp.distributions.categorical**: This is a standard categorical distribution that's characterized by probabilities or log-probabilities over K classes. In this project, we have Traffic Sign images from 43 different traffic signs. We will define a categorical distribution over 43 classes in this project.
- **Probabilistic layers**: Built on top of the TensorFlow layers implementation, probabilistic layers incorporate uncertainty over the functions they represent. Effectively, they incorporate uncertainty in the weights of the neural networks. They have the functionality to forward pass through the inputs by sampling from the posterior of weight distributions ($P(w|X)$). Specifically, we will use the Convolutional2DFlipout (`https://www.tensorflow.org/probability/ api_docs/python/tfp/layers/Convolution2DFlipout`) layer, which can compute the forward pass by sampling from the posterior of the weight parameters of the model.

- **Kullback-leibler (KL) divergence**: If we want to measure the difference between two numbers, we just subtract them. What if we want to obtain a difference between two probability distributions? What is the equivalent of subtraction in this case? Often in the case in probability and statistics, we will replace the observed data or complex distributions with a simpler, approximating distribution. KL Divergence helps us measure just how much information we lose when we choose an approximation. Essentially, it is a measure of one probability distribution from others. A KL divergence of 0 indicates that two distributions are identical. If you want to know more about the mathematics of KL divergence, please refer to a great explanation from MIT open courseware, which can be found at `https://ocw.mit.edu/courses/sloan-school-of-management/15-097-prediction-machine-learning-and-statistics-spring-2012/lecture-notes/MIT15_097S12_lec15.pdf`.

- **Variational inference**: Variational inference is a machine learning method that's used to approximate complex, intractable integrals in Bayesian learning through optimization.

As we know, our aim in Bayesian learning is to calculate the $P(w|X)$ posterior , given prior $P(w)$ and data X. A prerequisite for computing the posterior is the computation of distribution of X (data) in order to obtain $P(X)$, or *evidence*. As mentioned earlier, the distribution of X is intractable as it is too expensive to compute using a brute-force approach. To address this problem, we will use something called Variational Inference (VI). In VI, we define a family of distributions $Q(w; \lambda)$, parameterized by λ. The core idea is to optimize λ so that the approximate distribution is as close to the true posterior as possible. We measure the difference between two distributions using KL divergence. As it turns out, it is not easy to minimize the KL divergence. We can show you that this KL divergence is always positive and that it comprises two parts using the following mathematical formula:

$$KL(Q(w; \lambda), P(w|X)) = -ELBO + P(X)$$

Here, **ELBO** is **Evidence Lower Bound** (`https://www.cs.princeton.edu/courses/archive/fall11/cos597C/lectures/variational-inference-i.pdf`).

- **Monte Carlo method:** Monte Carlo methods are computational methods which rely on repeated random sampling to obtain the statistical behavior of some phenomenon (behavior). They are typically used to model uncertainties or generate what-if scenarios for business.

Let's say you commute by train every day to work. You are thinking about whether to take the company shuttle to the office instead. Now, there are many random variables associated with a bus ride, such as time of arrival, traffic, number of passengers boarding the bus, and so on.

One way that we can look at this what-if scenario is if we take the mean of these random variables and calculate the arrival time. However, that will be too naive as it doesn't take into account variance in these variables. Another way is to sample from these random variables (somehow, if you are able to do that!) and generate what-if scenarios of reaching the office.

To make a decision, you will need an acceptable criteron. For instance, if you observe that in 80% of these what-if scenarios you reach office on or before time, you can continue forward. This approach is also known as the Monte Carlo simulation.

In this project, we will model the weights of neural networks as random variables. To determine the final prediction, we will sample from the distributions of these weights repeatedly to obtain the distribution of predictions.

Note that we have skipped some mathematical details. Feel free to read more about Variational Inference (https://www.cs.princeton.edu/courses/archive/fall11/cos597C/lectures/variational-inference-i.pdf).

Building a Bayesian neural network

For this project, we will use the German Traffic Sign Dataset (http://benchmark.ini.rub.de/?section=gtsrbamp;subsection=dataset) to build a Bayesian neural network. The training dataset contains 26,640 images in 43 classes. Similarly, the testing dataset contains 12,630 images.

Please read the README.md file in this book's repository before executing the code to install the appropriate dependencies and for instructions on how to run the code.

The following is an image that's present in this dataset:

You can see that there are different kinds of traffic sign depicted by different classes in the dataset.

We begin by pre-processing our dataset and making it conform to the requirements of the learning algorithm. This is done by reshaping the images to a uniform size via histogram equalization, which is used to enhance contrast, and cropping them to only focus on the traffic signs in the image. Also, we convert the images to grayscale as traffic signs are identified by shape and not color in the image.

For modeling, we define a standard Lenet model (`http://yann.lecun.com/exdb/lenet/`), which was developed by Yann Lecun. Lenet is one of the first convolutional neural networks that was designed. It is small and easy to understand, yet large enough to provide interesting results.

A standard Lenet model has the following properties:

- Three convolutional layers with increasing filter sizes
- Four fully connected layers
- No dropout layers
- **Rectified linear** (**ReLU**) after every fully connected or convolutional layer
- Max pooling after every convolutional layer

We train this model to minimize the negative of ELBO loss that is defined in the *Understanding TensorFlow Probability, Variational Inference, and Monte Carlo methods* section of this chapter. Specifically, we define ELBO loss as a combination of two terms:

- Expected log likelihood or cross entropy that can be estimated through the Monte Carlo method
- KL divergence

Once the model is trained, we evaluate the predictions on the hold-out dataset. One of the major differences in Bayesian neural network evaluation is that there is no single set of parameters (weights of the model) that we can obtain from training. Instead, we obtain a distribution of all the parameters. For evaluation, we will have to sample values from the distribution of each parameter to obtain the accuracy on the testing set. We will sample the parameters of the model multiple times to obtain a confidence interval on our predictions.

Lastly, we will show some uncertainty in our predictions in sample images from the testing dataset and also plot the distribution of the weight parameters we obtain.

Defining, training, and testing the model

Download both the training and testing datasets from `http://benchmark.ini.rub.de/?section=gtsrbamp;subsection=dataset`. Let's look at the steps to build the project after you have downloaded the dataset:

1. Begin by transforming the images present in the dataset using histogram equalization. This is essential as each image in the dataset may have a different scale of illumination. You can see from the following two images how images of the same traffic sign have very different illumination. Histogram equalization helps to normalize these differences and makes the training data more consistent:

Once we have performed the equalization, crop the image to focus on just the sign, and resize the image to 32 x 32 as desired by our learning algorithm:

Note that we use 32 x 32 as the shape of images for training as it is big enough to preserve the nuances of the image for detection and small enough to train the model faster.

```
def normalize_and_reshape_img(img):
# Histogram normalization in v channel
hsv = color.rgb2hsv(img)
hsv[:, :, 2] = exposure.equalize_hist(hsv[:, :, 2])
img = color.hsv2rgb(hsv)
# Crop of the centre
min_side = min(img.shape[:-1])
```

```
centre = img.shape[0] // 2, img.shape[1] // 2
img = img[centre[0] - min_side // 2:centre[0] + min_side // 2,
centre[1] - min_side // 2:centre[1] + min_side // 2,
:]
# Rescale to the desired size
img = transform.resize(img, (IMG_SIZE, IMG_SIZE))
return
    img
```

2. Create dictionaries with label and image information for the train/test dataset and store them as pickle files so that we don't have to run the pre-processing code every time we run the model. This means that we essentially pre-process the transformed data to create our train and test datasets:

```
def preprocess_and_save_data(data_type ='train'):
'''
Preprocesses image data and saves the image features and labels as
pickle files to be used for the model
:param data_type: data_type is 'train' or 'test'
:return: None
'''
if data_type =='train':
root_dir = os.path.join(DATA_DIR, 'GTSRB/Final_Training/Images/')
imgs = []
labels = []
all_img_paths = glob.glob(os.path.join(root_dir, '*/*.ppm'))
np.random.shuffle(all_img_paths)
for img_path in all_img_paths:
img = normalize_and_reshape_img(io.imread(img_path))
label = get_class(img_path)
imgs.append(img)
labels.append(label)
X_train = np.array(imgs, dtype='float32')
# Make one hot targets
Y_train = np.array(labels, dtype = 'uint8')
train_data = {"features": X_train, "labels": Y_train}
if not os.path.exists(os.path.join(DATA_DIR,"Preprocessed_Data")):
os.makedirs(os.path.join(DATA_DIR,"Preprocessed_Data"))
pickle.dump(train_data,open(os.path.join(DATA_DIR,"Preprocessed_Dat
a","preprocessed_train.p"),"wb"))
return train_data
elif data_type == 'test':
# Reading the test file
test = pd.read_csv(os.path.join(DATA_DIR, "GTSRB", 'GT-
final_test.csv'), sep=';')
X_test = []
y_test = []
i = 0
```

```
for file_name, class_id in zip(list(test['Filename']),
list(test['ClassId'])):
img_path = os.path.join(DATA_DIR, 'GTSRB/Final_Test/Images/',
file_name)
X_test.append(normalize_and_reshape_img(io.imread(img_path)))
y_test.append(class_id)
test_data = {"features": np.array(X_test,dtype ='float32'),
"labels": np.array(y_test,dtype = 'uint8')}
if not os.path.exists(os.path.join(DATA_DIR,"Preprocessed_Data")):
os.makedirs(os.path.join(DATA_DIR,"Preprocessed_Data"))
pickle.dump(test_data,open(os.path.join(DATA_DIR,"Preprocessed_Data
","preprocessed_test.p"),"wb"))
return test_data
```

 We will use grayscale images in our project as our task throughout this project is to classify traffic sign images into one of the 43 classes and provide a measure of uncertainty in our classification. We do not care about the color of the image.

3. Define the model using the LeNet architecture in Keras. Finally, we will assign the 43 sized vector of outputs from the LeNet model into a categorical distribution function (`tfd.categorical`) from TensorFlow probability. This will help us generating the uncertainty in predictions afterwards:

```
with tf.name_scope("BNN", values=[images]):
model = tf.keras.Sequential([
tfp.layers.Convolution2DFlipout(10,
kernel_size=5,
padding="VALID",
activation=tf.nn.relu),
tf.keras.layers.MaxPooling2D(pool_size=[3, 3],
strides=[1, 1],
padding="VALID"),
tfp.layers.Convolution2DFlipout(15,
kernel_size=3,
padding="VALID",
activation=tf.nn.relu),
tf.keras.layers.MaxPooling2D(pool_size=[2, 2],
strides=[2, 2],
padding="VALID"),
tfp.layers.Convolution2DFlipout(30,
kernel_size=3,
padding="VALID",
activation=tf.nn.relu),
tf.keras.layers.MaxPooling2D(pool_size=[2, 2],
strides=[2, 2],
padding="VALID"),
```

```
tf.keras.layers.Flatten(),
tfp.layers.DenseFlipout(400, activation=tf.nn.relu),
tfp.layers.DenseFlipout(120, activation = tf.nn.relu),
tfp.layers.DenseFlipout(84, activation=tf.nn.relu),
tfp.layers.DenseFlipout(43) ])
logits = model(images)
targets_distribution = tfd.Categorical(logits=logits)
```

4. We define the loss to minimize the KL divergence up to ELBO. Compute the
   ELBO loss that is defined in the *Understanding TensorFlow Probability, Variational
   Inference, and Monte Carlo methods* section of this chapter. As you can see, we use
   the `model.losses` attribute to compute the KL divergence. This is because
   the `losses` attribute of a TensorFlow Keras Layer represents a side-effect
   computation such as regularizer penalties. Unlike regularizer penalties on
   specific TensorFlow variables, here the `losses` represent the KL divergence
   computation:

```
# Compute the -ELBO as the loss, averaged over the batch size.
neg_log_likelihood = -
  tf.reduce_mean(targets_distribution.log_prob(targets))
kl = sum(model.losses) / X_train.shape[0]
    elbo_loss = neg_log_likelihood + kl
```

5. Use the Adam optimizer, as defined in Chapter 3, *Sentiment Analysis in your
   browser using TensorFlow.js,* to optimize the ELBO loss:

```
with tf.name_scope("train"):
optimizer = tf.train.AdamOptimizer(learning_rate=LEARNING_RATE)
train_op = optimizer.minimize(elbo_loss)
```

Note that we are using the Adam optimizer because it generally performs
better than other optimizers with default parameters.

6. Train the model with the following parameters:
   - Epochs = 1,000
   - Batch size = 128
   - Learning rate = 0.001:

```
with tf.Session() as sess:
sess.run(init_op)
# Run the training loop.
train_handle = sess.run(train_iterator.string_handle())
test_handle = sess.run(test_iterator.string_handle())
```

```
for step in range(EPOCHS):
    _ = sess.run([train_op, accuracy_update_op],
feed_dict={iter_handle: train_handle})
    if step % 5== 0:
loss_value, accuracy_value = sess.run(
        [elbo_loss, accuracy], feed_dict={iter_handle: train_handle})
print("Epoch: {:>3d} Loss: {:.3f} Accuracy: {:.3f}".format(
step, loss_value, accuracy_value))
```

7. Once the model is trained, each weight in the Bayesian neural network will have a distribution and not a fixed value. Sample each weight multiple times (50, in the code) and obtain different predictions for each sample. Sampling, although useful, is expensive. Therefore, we should only use Bayesian neural networks where we require some measure of uncertainty in our predictions. Here is the code for Monte Carlo sampling:

```
#Sampling from the posterior and obtaining mean probability for
held out dataset
probs = np.asarray([sess.run((targets_distribution.probs),
        feed_dict={iter_handle: test_handle})
for _ in range(NUM_MONTE_CARLO)])
```

8. Once you have the samples, obtain the mean probability for each image in the test dataset and compute the mean accuracy like in usual machine learning classifiers.

    The mean accuracy we obtain for this dataset is ~ 89% for 1,000 Epochs. You can tune the parameters further or create a deeper model to obtain better accuracy. Here is the code for getting the mean accuracy:

```
mean_probs = np.mean(probs, axis=0)
# Get the average accuracy
Y_pred = np.argmax(mean_probs, axis=1)
print("Overall Accuracy in predicting the test data = percent",
round((Y_pred == y_test).mean() * 100,2))
```

9. The next step is to calculate the distribution of accuracy for each Monte Carlo sample of each test image. For that, compute the predicted class and compare it with the test label. The predicted class can be obtained by assigning the label to the class with the maximum probability for a given network parameter sample. This way, you can get the range of accuracies and can also plot those accuracies on a histogram. Here is the code for obtaining accuracy and generating a histogram:

```
test_acc_dist = []
for prob in probs:
y_test_pred = np.argmax(prob, axis=1).astype(np.float32)
```

```
accuracy = (y_test_pred == y_test).mean() * 100
test_acc_dist.append(accuracy)
plt.hist(test_acc_dist)
plt.title("Histogram of prediction accuracies on test dataset")
plt.xlabel("Accuracy")
plt.ylabel("Frequency")
save_dir = os.path.join(DATA_DIR, "..", "Plots")
plt.savefig(os.path.join(save_dir,
"Test_Dataset_Prediction_Accuracy.png"))
```

The histogram that's generated will look something like the following:

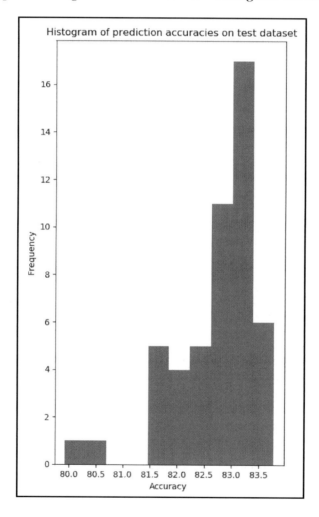

As you can see, we have a distribution of accuracies. This distribution can help us obtain the confidence interval over the accuracy of our model on the test dataset.

 Note that the plot might look differently when you run the code, since it is obtained through random sampling.

10. Take a few images from the test dataset and see their predictions for different samples in Monte Carlo. Use the following function `plot_heldout_prediction` to generate the histogram of predictions from different samples in Monte Carlo:

```
def plot_heldout_prediction(input_vals, probs , fname, title=""):
save_dir = os.path.join(DATA_DIR, "..", "Plots")
fig = figure.Figure(figsize=(1, 1))
canvas = backend_agg.FigureCanvasAgg(fig)
ax = fig.add_subplot(1,1,1)
ax.imshow(input_vals.reshape((IMG_SIZE,IMG_SIZE)),
interpolation="None")
canvas.print_figure(os.path.join(save_dir, fname + "_image.png"),
format="png")
fig = figure.Figure(figsize=(10, 5))
canvas = backend_agg.FigureCanvasAgg(fig)
ax = fig.add_subplot(1,1,1)
#Predictions
y_pred_list = list(np.argmax(probs,axis=1).astype(np.int32))
bin_range = [x for x in range(43)]
ax.hist(y_pred_list,bins = bin_range)
ax.set_xticks(bin_range)
ax.set_title("Histogram of predicted class: " + title)
ax.set_xlabel("Class")
ax.set_ylabel("Frequency")
fig.tight_layout()
save_dir = os.path.join(DATA_DIR, "..", "Plots")
canvas.print_figure(os.path.join(save_dir, fname +
"_predicted_class.png"), format="png")
print("saved {}".format(fname))
```

Let's look at some of the images and their predictions:

For the preceding image, all of the predictions belonged to the correct class 02, as shown in the following diagram:

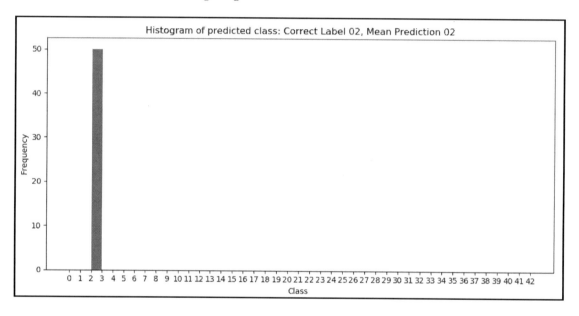

In the following two cases, although our mean prediction was correct, some samples in Monte Carlo predicted the wrong class. You can imagine how quantifying uncertainty in such cases can make a self-driving car make better decisions on the road.

Case 1:

In the preceding image, some of the Monte Carlo predictions belonged to the wrong class, as shown in the following diagram:

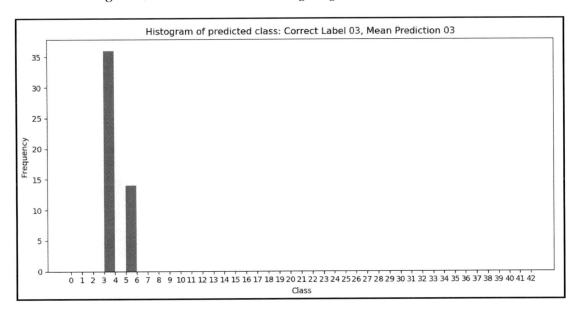

Case 2:

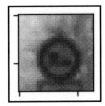

In the preceding image, some of the Monte Carlo predictions belonged to the wrong class, as shown in the following diagram:

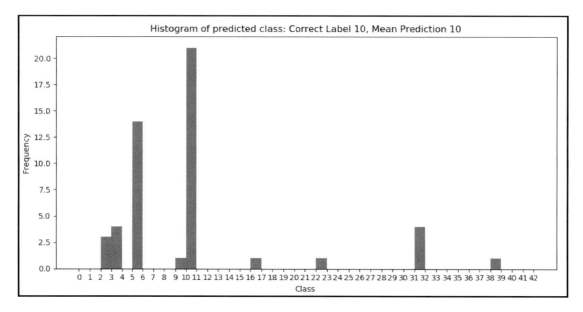

Case 3:

In the following case, average prediction is incorrect, but some samples were correctly predicted:

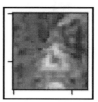

For the preceding image, we obtained the following histogram:

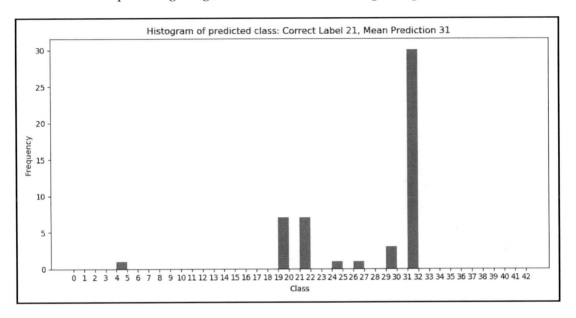

Case 4:

Obviously, we will get cases where we didn't predict correctly for any sample:

For this image, we obtained the following histogram:

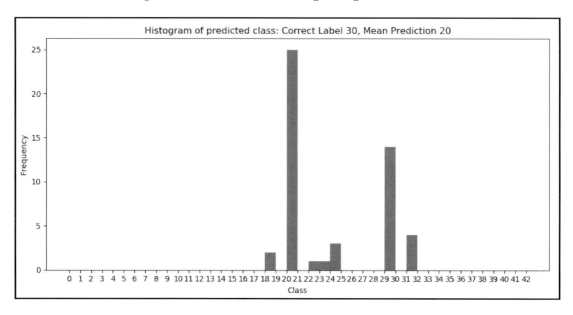

11. Finally, visualize the posterior of weights in the network. In the following plot we are showing both the posterior mean and standard deviation of the different weights in the network:

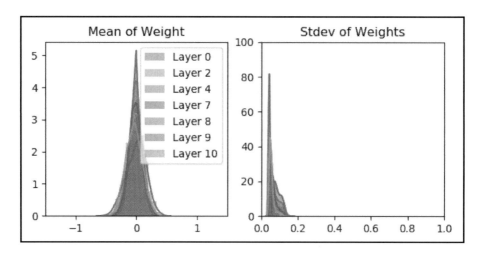

Having a distribution on weights enables us to develop predictions for the same image, which is extremely useful in developing a confidence interval around our predictions.

Summary

Neural networks, as we know, are great for point predictions, but can't help us identify the uncertainty in their predictions. On the other hand, Bayesian learning is great for quantifying uncertainty, but doesn't scale well in multiple dimensions or problems with big unstructured datasets such as images.

In this chapter, we looked at how we can combine neural networks with Bayesian learning using Bayesian neural networks.

We used the dataset of German Traffic Signs to develop a Bayesian neural network classifier using Google's recently released tool: TensorFlow probability. TF probability provides high-level APIs and functions to perform Bayesian modeling and inference.

We trained the Lenet model on the dataset. Finally, we used Monte Carlo to sample from the posterior of the parameters of the network to obtain predictions for each sample of the test dataset to quantify uncertainty.

However, we have only scratched the surface in terms of the complexity of Bayesian neural networks. If we want to develop safe AI, then understanding uncertainty in our predictions is of the utmost importance.

In the next chapter, we will learn about a new concept in machine learning known as autoencoders. We will look at how to detect credit card fraud using them.

Questions

1. What is TensorFlow probability?
2. What is Variational inference and why is it important?
3. What is KL divergence?
4. What do we mean by prior and posterior on the weights of neural networks?

9

Generating Matching Shoe Bags from Shoe Images Using DiscoGANs

Human beings are quite smart when it comes to understanding the relationship between different domains. For example, we can easily understand the relationship between a Spanish sentence and its translated version in English. We can even guess which color tie to wear to match a certain kind of suit. While it seems easy for humans, this is not a straightforward process for machines.

The task of style transfer across different domains for machines can be framed as a conditional image generation problem. Given an image from one domain, can we learn to map to an image from a different domain.

While there have been many approaches to achieve this using pairwise labeled data from two different domains, these approaches are fraught with problems. The major issue with these approaches is obtaining the pairwise labeled data, which is both an expensive and time-consuming process.

In this chapter, we will learn about an approach for learning style transfer without explicitly providing pairwise labeled data to the algorithm. This approach, known as DiscoGANs, is highlighted in the recently released paper by Kim et. al named *Learning to Discover Cross-Domain Relations with Generative Adversarial Networks* (`https://arxiv.org/pdf/1703.05192.pdf`). Specifically, we will try to generate matching shoes from shoe bag images.

The remainder of this chapter is organized as follows:

- Introduction to **Generative Adversarial Networks (GANs)**
- What are DiscoGANs?
- How to generate matching shoes from shoe bag images and vice versa

Understanding generative models

An unsupervised learning model that learns the underlying data distribution of the training set and generates new data that may or may not have variations is commonly known as a **generative model**. Knowing the true underlying distribution might not always be a possibility, hence the neural network trains on a function that tries to be as close a match as possible to the true distribution.

The most common methods used to train generative models are as follows:

- **Variational autoencoders:** A high dimensional input image is encoded by an auto-encoder to create a lower dimensional representation. During this process, it is of the utmost importance to preserve the underlying data distribution. This encoder can only be used to map to the input image using a decoder and cannot introduce any variability to generate similar images. The VAE introduces variability by generating constrained latent vectors that still follow the underlying distribution. Though VAEs help in creating probabilistic graphical models, the generated images tend to be slightly blurry.

- **PixelRNN/PixelCNN:** These auto-regressive models are used to train networks that model the conditional distribution of a successive individual pixel, given previous pixels starting from the top left. RNNs move horizontally and vertically over any image. The training for PixelRNNs is a stable and simple process with better log likelihoods than other models, but they are time consuming and relatively inefficient.

- **Generative adversarial networks:** Generative adversarial networks were first published in the 2014 paper by *Goodfellow et al.* (https://arxiv.org/abs/1406. 2661). These can be thought of as a competition framework with two adversaries called the generator and the discriminator. These are nothing but two differentiable functions in the form of neural networks. The generator takes a randomly generated input known as a latent sample and produces an image. The overall objective of the generator is to generate an image that is as close as possible to the real input image (such as MNIST digits) and give it as an input to the discriminator.

  The discriminator is essentially a classifier that's trained to distinguish between real images (original MNIST digits) and fake images (output of the generator). Ideally, after being trained, the generator should adapt its parameters and capture the underlying training data distribution and fool the discriminator about its input being a real image.

Let's consider an analogy that is inspired by the real world. Imagine that GANs work like the relationship between a forger making counterfeit currency and the police identifying and discarding that forged currency. The aim of the forger is to try and pass off the fake currency as real currency in the market. This is analogous to what a generator tries to do. The police try and inspect every currency note it can, accepting the original notes and scrapping the fake ones. The police know of the details of the original currency and compare it to the properties of the currency in question in order to make a decision regarding its authenticity. If there is a match, the currency is retained; otherwise, it is scrapped. This is in line with the work of a discriminator.

Training GANs

The following diagram illustrates the basic architecture of GANs:

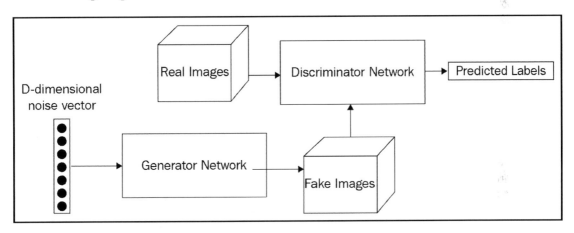

A random input is used to generate a sample of data. For example, a generator, $G(z)$, uses a prior distribution, $p(z)$, to achieve an input, z. Using z, it then generates some data. This output is fed as input to the discriminator neural network, $D(x)$. It takes an input x from $p_{data}(x)$, where $p_{data}(x)$ is our real data distribution. $D(x)$ then solves a binary classification problem using the `sigmoid` function, which gives us an output in the range of 0 to 1.

GANS are trained to be part of a competition between the generator and discriminator. The objective function can be represented mathematically as follows:

$$\min_{\theta_g} \max_{\theta_d} \left[\mathbb{E}_{x \sim p_{data}} \log D_{\theta_d}(x) + \mathbb{E}_{z \sim p(z)} \log \left(1 - D_{\theta_d} \left(G_{\theta_d}(z) \right) \right) \right]$$

In this, the following applies:

- Θ_d denotes the parameters of the discriminator
- θ_g denotes the parameters of the generator
- p_{data} denotes the underlying distribution of training data
- $D_{\theta_d}(x)$ denotes the discriminator operation over input images x
- $G_{\theta_g}(z)$ denotes the generator operation over latent sample z
- $D_{\theta_d}\left(G_{\theta_g}(z) \right)$ denotes the discriminator output for generated fake data $G(z)$

In the objective function, the first term from the left represents the cross entropy of the discriminator's output from a real distribution (p_{data}). The second term from the left is the cross entropy between the random distribution (p_z) and one minus the prediction of the discriminator on the output of the generator that was generated using random sample z from p_z. The discriminator tries to maximize both terms to classify the images as real and fake, respectively. On the other hand, the generator tries to fool the discriminator by minimizing this objective.

In order to train GANs, gradient-based optimization algorithms, such as stochastic gradient descent, are used. Algorithmically, it flows as follows:

1. First, sample *m* noise samples and *m* real data samples.
2. Freeze the generator, that is, set the training as false so that the generator network only does a forward pass without any back propagation. Train the discriminator on this data.
3. Sample different *m* noise samples.
4. Freeze the discriminator and train the generator on this data.
5. Iterate through the preceding steps.

Formally, the pseudocode is as follows.

In this example, we are performing mini-batch stochastic gradient descent training of generative adversarial nets. The number of steps to apply to the discriminator, k, is a hyper parameter. We used $k=1$, the least expensive option, in our experiment:

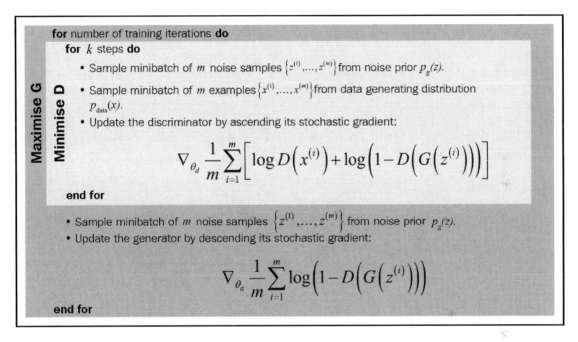

Pseudocode for GAN training. With k=1, this equates to training D, then G, one after the other. Adapted from Goodfellow et al. 2014

The gradient-based updates can use any standard gradient-based learning rule. We used momentum in our experiment.

Applications

Some of the applications of GANs include converting monochrome or black and white images into colored images, filling additional details in an image, such as the insertion of objects into a partial image or into an image with only edges, and constructing images representing what somebody would look like when they are older given an image of their present self.

Challenges

Though GANs generate one of the sharpest images from a given piece of input data, their optimization is difficult to achieve due to unstable training dynamics. They also suffer from other challenges, such as mode collapse and bad initialization. Mode collapse is a phenomena where, if the data is multimodal, the generator is never incentivized to cover both modes, which leads to lower variability among generated samples and, hence, lower utility of GANs. If all generated samples start to become identical, it leads to complete collapse. In cases where most of the samples show some commonality, there is partial collapse of the model. At the core of this, GANs work on an objective function that aims to achieve optimization of min-max, but if the initial parameters end up being inefficient, then it becomes an oscillating process with no true optimization. In addition to this, there are issues such as GANs failing to differentiate the count of particular objects that should occur at a location. For example, GANs have no idea that there can't be more than two eyes and can generate images of human faces with 3 eyes. There are also issues with GANs being unable to adapt to a 3D perspective, such as front and posterior view. This gives a flat 2D image instead of depth for a 3D object.

Different variants of GANs have evolved over time. Some of them are as follows:

- **Deep convolutional GANs (DCGANs)** were one of the first major improvements on the GAN architecture. It is made up of convolutional layers that avoid the use of max pooling or fully connected layers. The convolutional stride and transposed convolution for downsampling and upsampling is majorly used by this. It also uses ReLU activation in the generator and LeakyReLU in the discriminator.
- **InfoGANs** are another variant of GANs that try and encode meaningful features of the image (for example, rotation) in parts of the noise vector, z.
- **Conditional GANs (cGANs)** use extra conditional information that describes some aspect of the data as input to the generator and discriminator. For example, if we are dealing with vehicles, the condition could describe attributes such as four-wheeled or two-wheeled. This helps generate better samples and additional features. In this chapter, we will mainly focus on DiscoGANs, which are described in the following section.

Understanding DiscoGANs

In this section, we are mainly going to take a closer look at Discovery GANS, which are popularly known as **DiscoGANs**.

Before going further, let's try to understand reconstruction loss in machine learning, since this is one of the concepts that this chapter is majorly dependent on. When learning about the representation of an unstructured data type such as an image/text, we want our model to encode the data in such a manner that when it's decoded, the underlying image/text can be generated back. To incorporate this condition in the model explicitly, we use a reconstruction loss (essentially the Euclidean distance between the reconstructed and original image) in training the model.

Style transfer has been one of the most prominent use cases of GANs. Style transfer basically refers to the problem where, if you are given an image/data in one domain, is it possible to successfully generate an image/data in another domain. This problem has become quite famous among several researchers.

You can read more about style transfer problems from the paper Neural Style Transfer: A Review (`https://arxiv.org/abs/1705.04058`) by Jing et. al. However, most of the work is done by using an explicitly paired dataset that's generated by humans or other algorithms. This puts limitations on these approaches, since paired data is seldom available and is too costly to generate.

DiscoGANs, on the other hand, propose a method of learning cross-domain relations without the explicit need for paired datasets. This method takes an image from one domain and generates the corresponding image from the other domain. Let's say we are trying to transfer an image from Domain A to Domain B. During the learning process, we force the generated image to be the image-based representation of the image from Domain A through a reconstruction loss and to be as close to the image in Domain B as possible through a GAN loss, as mentioned earlier. Essentially, this approach tends to generate a bijective (one-to-one) mapping between two domains, rather than a many-to-one or one-to-many mapping.

Fundamental units of a DiscoGAN

As mentioned previously, normal GANs have a generator and a discriminator. Let's try to understand the building blocks of DiscoGANs and then proceed to understand how to combine them so that we can learn about cross-domain relationships. These are as follows:

- **Generator:** In the original GANs, the generator would take an input vector z randomly sampled from, say, Gaussian distribution, and generate fake images. In this case, however, since we are looking to transfer images from one domain to another, we replace the input vector z with an image. Here are the parameters of the generator function:

Parameters	Value
Input image size	64x64x3
Output image size	64x64x3
# Convolutional layers	4
# Conv transpose/Deconv layers	4
Normalizer function	Batch Normalization
Activation function	LeakyReLU

Before specifying the structure of each particular layer, let's try to understand a few of the terms that were mentioned in the parameters.

- **Transposed convolution:** As we mentioned previously, generators are used to generate images from the input vector. In our case, the input image is first convolved by 4 convolutional layers, which produce an embedding. Generating an image from the embedding involves upsampling from a low resolution to a higher resolution.

General ways of upsampling include manual feature engineering to interpolate lower dimensional images. A better approach could be to employ Transposed Convolution, also known as the **fractional stride convolution/deconvolution**. It doesn't employ any predefined interpolation method. Let's say that we have a 4x4 matrix that is convolved with a 3x3 filter (stride 1 and no padding); this will result in a matrix of size 2x2. As you can see, we downsampled the original image from 4x4 to 2x2. The process of going from 2x2 back to 4x4 can be achieved through transposed convolution.

From an implementation perspective, the built-in function in TensorFlow for defining convolutional layers can be used directly with the `num_outputs` value, which can be changed to perform upsampling.

- **Batch normalization**: This method is used to counter the internal covariance shift that happens in deep neural networks.

A covariance shift can be defined as when the model is able to predict when the distribution of inputs changes. Let's say we train a model to detect black and white images of dogs. During the inference phase, if we supply colored images of dogs to the model, it will not perform well. This is because the model learned the parameters based on black and white images, which are not suitable for predicting colored images.

Deep neural networks experience what is known as an internal covariance shift, since changes in the parameters of an internal layer change the distribution of input in the next layer. To fix this issue, we normalize the output of each batch by using its mean and variance, and pass on a weighted combination of mean and variance to the next layer. Due to the weighted combination, batch normalization adds two extra parameters in each layer of the neural network.

Batch normalization helps speed up training and tends to reduce overfitting because of its regularization effects.

In this model, we use batch normalization in all of the convolutional and convolutional transpose layers, except the first and the last layers.

- **Leaky ReLU: ReLU**, or **rectified linear units,** are quite popular in the deep learning domain today as activation functions. ReLU units in deep neural networks can be fragile at times since they can cause neurons to die or never get activated again at any data point. The following diagram illustrates the ReLU function:

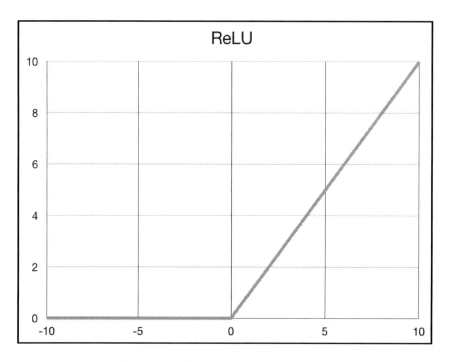

Leaky ReLU is used to try and fix this problem. They have small negative values instead of zeros for negative input values. This avoids the dying issue with regard to neurons. The following diagram illustrates a sample Leaky ReLU function:

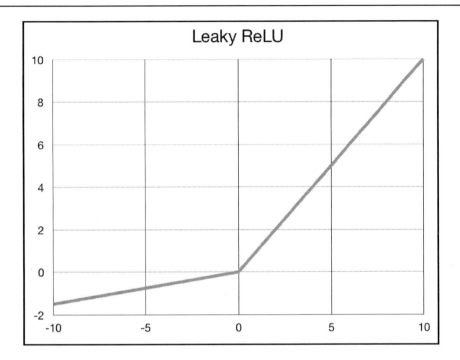

- **Discriminator**: In the GANs that we described previously, the generator takes an input vector that's been randomly sampled from, say, a Gaussian distribution, and generates fake images. In this case, however, since we are looking to transfer images from one domain to another, we replace the input vector with an image.

The parameters of the discriminator from an architectural standpoint are as follows:

- **Layers:** The discriminator is made up of 5 convolutional layers, each stacked on top of the other, and then followed by two fully connected layers.
- **Activation:** Leaky ReLU activation is used for all layers except the last fully connected layer. The last layer uses `sigmoid` to predict the probability of a sample.
- **Normalizer:** This performs batch normalization, except on the first and last layers of the network.
- **Stride:** A stride length of 2 is used for all of the convolutional layers.

DiscoGAN modeling

For each mapping, that is, **handbags** (denoted by **b**) to **shoes** (denoted by **s**), or vice versa, we add two generators. Let's say, for the mapping **b** to **s**, the first generator maps the input image from domain **b** to **s**, while the second generator reconstructs the image from domain **s** to domain **b**. Intuitively, we need a second generator to achieve the objective (one-to-one) mapping we talked about in the previous sections. Mathematically, this can be represented as follows:

$$G_{bs}\left(x_b\right) = x_s$$

$$G_{sb}\left(x_s\right) = x_b$$

While modeling, since this is a very hard constraint to satisfy, we add a reconstruction loss. Reconstruction loss is given as follows:

$$L_{CONST_b} = d\left(G_{sb}\left(x_s, x_b\right)\right)$$

Now, the usual GAN loss that is required to generate fake images of another domain is given by the following equation:

$$L_{GAN_s} = -E_{x_b \sim P_b}\left[D_s\left(G_{bs}\left(x_b\right)\right)\right]$$

For each mapping, the generator receives two losses:

- The reconstruction loss, which tries to see how well we can map the generated image to its original domain
- The usual GAN loss, which is for the task of fooling the discriminator

In this case, the discriminator is the usual discriminator, with the loss that we mentioned in the section of *Training GANs*. Let's denote it by using L_{D_b}.

The total generator and discriminator loss is given by the following equation:

$$L_G = \left(L_{GAN_s} + L_{GAN_b}\right) + L_{CONST_b} + L_{CONST_s}$$

$$L_D = L_{D_s} + L_{D_b}$$

Building a DiscoGAN model

The base datasets in this problem are obtained from the edges2handbags (https://people.eecs.berkeley.edu/~tinghuiz/projects/pix2pix/datasets/edges2handbags.tar.gz) and edges2shoes (https://people.eecs.berkeley.edu/~tinghuiz/projects/pix2pix/datasets/edges2shoes.tar.gz) datasets. Each image that's present in these datasets contain two sub-images. One is the colored image of the object, while the other is the image of the edges of the corresponding color image.

Follow the steps to build a DiscoGAN model:

1. First, resize and crop the images in this dataset to obtain the handbag and shoe images:

```python
def extract_files(data_dir, type = 'bags'):
    '''
  :param data_dir: Input directory
  :param type: bags or shoes
    :return: saves the cropped files to the bags to shoes directory
    '''

    input_file_dir = os.path.join(os.getcwd(), data_dir, "train")
    result_dir = os.path.join(os.getcwd(), type)
    if not os.path.exists(result_dir):
        os.makedirs(result_dir)

    file_names= os.listdir(input_file_dir)
    for file in file_names:
        input_image = Image.open(os.path.join(input_file_dir, file))
        input_image = input_image.resize([128, 64])
        input_image = input_image.crop([64, 0, 128, 64])  # Cropping
only the colored image. Excluding the edge image
        input_image.save(os.path.join(result_dir, file))
```

2. Save the images in the corresponding folders of bags and shoes. Some of the sample images are shown as follows:

Shoes   Bags

3. Implement the `generator` function with 4 convolutional layers followed by 4 convolutional transpose (or deconv) layers. The kernel size used in this scenario is 4, while the `stride` is 2 and 1 for the convolutional and deconv layers, respectively. Leaky Relu is used as activation function in all the layers. Code for the function is as follows:

```
def generator(x, initializer, scope_name =
'generator',reuse=False):
    with tf.variable_scope(scope_name) as scope:
        if reuse:
            scope.reuse_variables()
        conv1 = tf.contrib.layers.conv2d(inputs=x, num_outputs=32,
kernel_size=4, stride=2, padding="SAME",reuse=reuse,
activation_fn=tf.nn.leaky_relu, weights_initializer=initializer,
                                    scope="disc_conv1")  # 32 x
32 x 32
        conv2 = tf.contrib.layers.conv2d(inputs=conv1,
num_outputs=64, kernel_size=4, stride=2, padding="SAME",
                                    reuse=reuse,
activation_fn=tf.nn.leaky_relu,
normalizer_fn=tf.contrib.layers.batch_norm,
weights_initializer=initializer, scope="disc_conv2")  # 16 x 16 x
64
        conv3 = tf.contrib.layers.conv2d(inputs=conv2,
num_outputs=128, kernel_size=4, stride=2, padding="SAME",
                                    reuse=reuse,
activation_fn=tf.nn.leaky_relu,
normalizer_fn=tf.contrib.layers.batch_norm,
weights_initializer=initializer, scope="disc_conv3")  # 8 x 8 x 128
        conv4 = tf.contrib.layers.conv2d(inputs=conv3,
num_outputs=256, kernel_size=4, stride=2, padding="SAME",
                                    reuse=reuse,
activation_fn=tf.nn.leaky_relu,
normalizer_fn=tf.contrib.layers.batch_norm,
weights_initializer=initializer, scope="disc_conv4")  # 4 x 4 x 256

        deconv1 = tf.contrib.layers.conv2d(conv4, num_outputs=4 *
128, kernel_size=4, stride=1, padding="SAME",
activation_fn=tf.nn.relu,
normalizer_fn=tf.contrib.layers.batch_norm,
weights_initializer=initializer, scope="gen_conv1")
        deconv1 = tf.reshape(deconv1, shape=[tf.shape(x)[0], 8, 8,
128])

        deconv2 = tf.contrib.layers.conv2d(deconv1, num_outputs=4 *
64, kernel_size=4, stride=1, padding="SAME",
activation_fn=tf.nn.relu,
```

```
    normalizer_fn=tf.contrib.layers.batch_norm,
    weights_initializer=initializer, scope="gen_conv2")
        deconv2 = tf.reshape(deconv2, shape=[tf.shape(x)[0], 16, 16,
    64])

        deconv3 = tf.contrib.layers.conv2d(deconv2, num_outputs=4 *
    32, kernel_size=4, stride=1, padding="SAME",
    activation_fn=tf.nn.relu,
    normalizer_fn=tf.contrib.layers.batch_norm,
    weights_initializer=initializer, scope="gen_conv3")
        deconv3 = tf.reshape(deconv3, shape=[tf.shape(x)[0], 32, 32,
    32])

        deconv4 = tf.contrib.layers.conv2d(deconv3, num_outputs=4 *
    16, kernel_size=4, stride=1, padding="SAME",
    activation_fn=tf.nn.relu,
    normalizer_fn=tf.contrib.layers.batch_norm,
    weights_initializer=initializer, scope="gen_conv4")
        deconv4 = tf.reshape(deconv4, shape=[tf.shape(x)[0], 64, 64,
    16])

        recon = tf.contrib.layers.conv2d(deconv4, num_outputs=3,
    kernel_size=4, stride=1, padding="SAME", \
    activation_fn=tf.nn.relu, scope="gen_conv5")

        return recon
```

4. Define the discriminator using the parameters that we mentioned previously in section *Fundamental Units of a DiscoGAN*:

```
    def discriminator(x, initializer, scope_name ='discriminator',
    reuse=False):
        with tf.variable_scope(scope_name) as scope:
            if reuse:
                scope.reuse_variables()
            conv1 = tf.contrib.layers.conv2d(inputs=x, num_outputs=32,
    kernel_size=4, stride=2, padding="SAME",
                                            reuse=reuse,
    activation_fn=tf.nn.leaky_relu, weights_initializer=initializer,
                                            scope="disc_conv1")  # 32 x
    32 x 32
            conv2 = tf.contrib.layers.conv2d(inputs=conv1,
    num_outputs=64, kernel_size=4, stride=2, padding="SAME",
                                            reuse=reuse,
    activation_fn=tf.nn.leaky_relu,
    normalizer_fn=tf.contrib.layers.batch_norm,
    weights_initializer=initializer, scope="disc_conv2")  # 16 x 16 x
    64
```

```
      conv3 = tf.contrib.layers.conv2d(inputs=conv2,
num_outputs=128, kernel_size=4, stride=2, padding="SAME",
                                     reuse=reuse,
activation_fn=tf.nn.leaky_relu,
normalizer_fn=tf.contrib.layers.batch_norm,
weights_initializer=initializer, scope="disc_conv3")  # 8 x 8 x 128
      conv4 = tf.contrib.layers.conv2d(inputs=conv3,
num_outputs=256, kernel_size=4, stride=2, padding="SAME",
                                     reuse=reuse,
activation_fn=tf.nn.leaky_relu,
normalizer_fn=tf.contrib.layers.batch_norm,
weights_initializer=initializer, scope="disc_conv4")  # 4 x 4 x 256
      conv5 = tf.contrib.layers.conv2d(inputs=conv4,
num_outputs=512, kernel_size=4, stride=2, padding="SAME",
                                     reuse=reuse,
activation_fn=tf.nn.leaky_relu,
normalizer_fn=tf.contrib.layers.batch_norm,
weights_initializer=initializer, scope="disc_conv5")  # 2 x 2 x 512
      fc1 = tf.reshape(conv5, shape=[tf.shape(x)[0], 2 * 2 * 512])
      fc1 = tf.contrib.layers.fully_connected(inputs=fc1,
num_outputs=512, reuse=reuse, activation_fn=tf.nn.leaky_relu,
normalizer_fn=tf.contrib.layers.batch_norm,
weights_initializer=initializer, scope="disc_fc1")
      fc2 = tf.contrib.layers.fully_connected(inputs=fc1,
num_outputs=1, reuse=reuse, activation_fn=tf.nn.sigmoid,
weights_initializer=initializer, scope="disc_fc2")
      return fc2
```

5. Use the following `define_network` function, which defines the two generators and two discriminator for each domain. In the function, the definition of `generator` and `discriminator` remains the same as what we defined by using functions in the previous step. However, for DiscoGANs, the function defines one `generator` that generates fake images in another domain, and one `generator` that does the reconstruction. Also, the `discriminators` are defined for both real and fake images in each domain. Code the function is as follows:

```
def define_network(self):
    # generators
    # This one is used to generate fake data
    self.gen_b_fake = generator(self.X_shoes,
self.initializer,scope_name="generator_sb")
    self.gen_s_fake =   generator(self.X_bags,
self.initializer,scope_name="generator_bs")
    # Reconstruction generators
    # Note that parameters are being used from previous layers
    self.gen_recon_s = generator(self.gen_b_fake,
```

```
    self.initializer,scope_name="generator_sb",  reuse=True)
        self.gen_recon_b = generator(self.gen_s_fake,  self.initializer,
    scope_name="generator_bs", reuse=True)
        # discriminator for Shoes
        self.disc_s_real = discriminator(self.X_shoes,self.initializer,
    scope_name="discriminator_s")
        self.disc_s_fake =
    discriminator(self.gen_s_fake,self.initializer,
    scope_name="discriminator_s", reuse=True)
        # discriminator for Bags
        self.disc_b_real =
    discriminator(self.X_bags,self.initializer,scope_name="discriminato
    r_b")
        self.disc_b_fake = discriminator(self.gen_b_fake,
    self.initializer, reuse=True,scope_name="discriminator_b")
```

6. Let's define the `loss` function that we defined previously in *DiscoGAN modeling* section. Following function `define_loss` defines the reconstruction loss based on the Euclidean distance between the reconstructed and original image. To generate the GAN and discriminator loss, the function uses the cross entropy function:

```
def define_loss(self):
    # Reconstruction loss for generators
    self.const_loss_s =
tf.reduce_mean(tf.losses.mean_squared_error(self.gen_recon_s,
self.X_shoes))
    self.const_loss_b =
tf.reduce_mean(tf.losses.mean_squared_error(self.gen_recon_b,
self.X_bags))
    # generator loss for GANs
    self.gen_s_loss = tf.reduce_mean(
tf.nn.sigmoid_cross_entropy_with_logits(logits=self.disc_s_fake,
labels=tf.ones_like(self.disc_s_fake)))
    self.gen_b_loss = tf.reduce_mean(
tf.nn.sigmoid_cross_entropy_with_logits(logits=self.disc_b_fake,
labels=tf.ones_like(self.disc_b_fake)))
    # Total generator Loss
    self.gen_loss =  (self.const_loss_b + self.const_loss_s)  +
self.gen_s_loss + self.gen_b_loss
    # Cross Entropy loss for discriminators for shoes and bags
    # Shoes
    self.disc_s_real_loss = tf.reduce_mean(
tf.nn.sigmoid_cross_entropy_with_logits(logits=self.disc_s_real,
labels=tf.ones_like(self.disc_s_real)))
    self.disc_s_fake_loss = tf.reduce_mean(
tf.nn.sigmoid_cross_entropy_with_logits(logits=self.disc_s_fake,
```

```
labels=tf.zeros_like(self.disc_s_fake)))
   self.disc_s_loss = self.disc_s_real_loss + self.disc_s_fake_loss
# Combined
   # Bags
   self.disc_b_real_loss = tf.reduce_mean(
tf.nn.sigmoid_cross_entropy_with_logits(logits=self.disc_b_real,
labels=tf.ones_like(self.disc_b_real)))
   self.disc_b_fake_loss = tf.reduce_mean(
tf.nn.sigmoid_cross_entropy_with_logits(logits=self.disc_b_fake,
labels=tf.zeros_like(self.disc_b_fake)))
   self.disc_b_loss = self.disc_b_real_loss + self.disc_b_fake_loss
   # Total discriminator Loss
   self.disc_loss = self.disc_b_loss + self.disc_s_loss
```

7. Use the `AdamOptimizer` that was defined in Chapter 3, *Sentiment Analysis in Your Browser Using TensorFlow.js,* of the book and implement the following `define_optimizer` function as follows:

```
def define_optimizer(self):
   self.disc_optimizer =
tf.train.AdamOptimizer(LEARNING_RATE).minimize(self.disc_loss,
var_list=self.disc_params)
   self.gen_optimizer =
tf.train.AdamOptimizer(LEARNING_RATE).minimize(self.gen_loss,
var_list=self.gen_params)
```

8. For debugging, write the summary into a logging file. While you can add anything to the summary, the function `summary_` below adds all of the losses just to observe the curves on how various losses change over time. Code for the function is as follows:

```
def summary_(self):
   # Store the losses
   tf.summary.scalar("gen_loss", self.gen_loss)
   tf.summary.scalar("gen_s_loss", self.gen_s_loss)
   tf.summary.scalar("gen_b_loss", self.gen_b_loss)
   tf.summary.scalar("const_loss_s", self.const_loss_s)
   tf.summary.scalar("const_loss_b", self.const_loss_b)
   tf.summary.scalar("disc_loss", self.disc_loss)
   tf.summary.scalar("disc_b_loss", self.disc_b_loss)
   tf.summary.scalar("disc_s_loss", self.disc_s_loss)

   # Histograms for all vars
   for var in tf.trainable_variables():
       tf.summary.histogram(var.name, var)

   self.summary_ = tf.summary.merge_all()
```

9. Define the following parameters for training the model:

- Batch Size: 256
- Learning rate: 0.0002
- Epochs = 100,000 (use more if you are not getting the desired result)

10. Use the following code to train the model. Here is the brief explanation of what it does:

   1. For each Epoch, the code obtains the mini batch images of both shoes and bags. It passes the mini batch through the model to update the discriminator loss first.
   2. Samples a mini batch again for both shoes and bags and updates the generator loss keeping discriminator parameters fixed.
   3. For every 10 epochs, it writes a summary to Tensorboard.
   4. For every 1000 epochs, it randomly samples 1 image from both bags and shoes dataset and saves the reconstructed and fake images for visualization purposes
   5. Also, for every 1000 epochs, it saves the model which can be helpful if you want to restore training at some point.

```
print ("Starting Training")
for global_step in range(start_epoch,EPOCHS):
    shoe_batch = get_next_batch(BATCH_SIZE,"shoes")
    bag_batch = get_next_batch(BATCH_SIZE,"bags")
    feed_dict_batch = {model.X_bags: bag_batch, model.X_shoes: shoe_batch}
    op_list = [model.disc_optimizer, model.gen_optimizer, model.disc_loss,
model.gen_loss, model.summary_]
    _, _, disc_loss, gen_loss, summary_ = sess.run(op_list,
feed_dict=feed_dict_batch)
    shoe_batch = get_next_batch(BATCH_SIZE, "shoes")
    bag_batch = get_next_batch(BATCH_SIZE, "bags")
    feed_dict_batch = {model.X_bags: bag_batch, model.X_shoes: shoe_batch}
    _, gen_loss = sess.run([model.gen_optimizer, model.gen_loss],
feed_dict=feed_dict_batch)
    if global_step%10 ==0:
        train_writer.add_summary(summary_,global_step)
    if global_step%100 == 0:
        print("EPOCH:" + str(global_step) + "\tgenerator Loss: " +
str(gen_loss) + "\tdiscriminator Loss: " + str(disc_loss))
    if global_step % 1000 == 0:
        shoe_sample = get_next_batch(1, "shoes")
        bag_sample = get_next_batch(1, "bags")
        ops = [model.gen_s_fake, model.gen_b_fake, model.gen_recon_s,
```

```
model.gen_recon_b]
    gen_s_fake, gen_b_fake, gen_recon_s, gen_recon_b = sess.run(ops,
feed_dict={model.X_shoes: shoe_sample, model.X_bags: bag_sample})
    save_image(global_step, gen_s_fake, str("gen_s_fake_") +
str(global_step))
    save_image(global_step,gen_b_fake, str("gen_b_fake_") +
str(global_step))
    save_image(global_step, gen_recon_s, str("gen_recon_s_") +
str(global_step))
    save_image(global_step, gen_recon_b, str("gen_recon_b_") +
str(global_step))
  if global_step % 1000 == 0:
    if not os.path.exists("./model"):
      os.makedirs("./model")
    saver.save(sess, "./model" + '/model-' + str(global_step) + '.ckpt')
    print("Saved Model")
print ("Starting Training")
for global_step in range(start_epoch,EPOCHS):
  shoe_batch = get_next_batch(BATCH_SIZE,"shoes")
  bag_batch = get_next_batch(BATCH_SIZE,"bags")
  feed_dict_batch = {model.X_bags: bag_batch, model.X_shoes: shoe_batch}
  op_list = [model.disc_optimizer, model.gen_optimizer, model.disc_loss,
model.gen_loss, model.summary_]
  _, _, disc_loss, gen_loss, summary_ = sess.run(op_list,
feed_dict=feed_dict_batch)
  shoe_batch = get_next_batch(BATCH_SIZE, "shoes")
  bag_batch = get_next_batch(BATCH_SIZE, "bags")
  feed_dict_batch = {model.X_bags: bag_batch, model.X_shoes: shoe_batch}
  _, gen_loss = sess.run([model.gen_optimizer, model.gen_loss],
feed_dict=feed_dict_batch)
  if global_step%10 ==0:
    train_writer.add_summary(summary_,global_step)
  if global_step%100 == 0:
    print("EPOCH:" + str(global_step) + "\tgenerator Loss: " +
str(gen_loss) + "\tdiscriminator Loss: " + str(disc_loss))
  if global_step % 1000 == 0:
    shoe_sample = get_next_batch(1, "shoes")
    bag_sample = get_next_batch(1, "bags")
    ops = [model.gen_s_fake, model.gen_b_fake, model.gen_recon_s,
model.gen_recon_b]
    gen_s_fake, gen_b_fake, gen_recon_s, gen_recon_b = sess.run(ops,
feed_dict={model.X_shoes: shoe_sample, model.X_bags: bag_sample})
    save_image(global_step, gen_s_fake, str("gen_s_fake_") +
str(global_step))
    save_image(global_step,gen_b_fake, str("gen_b_fake_") +
str(global_step))
    save_image(global_step, gen_recon_s, str("gen_recon_s_") +
str(global_step))
```

```
          save_image(global_step, gen_recon_b, str("gen_recon_b_") +
str(global_step))
    if global_step % 1000 == 0:
        if not os.path.exists("./model"):
            os.makedirs("./model")
        saver.save(sess, "./model" + '/model-' + str(global_step) + '.ckpt')

    print("Saved Model")
```

> We carried out the training on one GTX 1080 graphics card, which took a significant amount of time. Highly recommended to use a GPU with better processing than GTX 1080 if possible.

Summary

In this chapter, we first looked at what GANs are. They are a new kind of generative model that helps us to generate new images.

We also touched upon other kinds of generative models, such as Variational Auto-encoders and PixelRNN, to get an overview of different kinds of generative models. We also talked about different kinds of GANs to discuss the progress that had been made in this space since the first paper on GANs was published in 2014.

Then, we learned about DiscoGANs, a new type of GAN that can help us to learn about cross- domain relationships. Specifically, in this chapter, our focus was on building a model to generate handbag images from shoes and vice versa.

Finally, we learned about the architecture of DiscoGANs and how they differ from usual GANs.

In the next chapter, we will learn how to implement capsule networks on the Fashion MNIST dataset.

Questions

- Can you change the training parameters like learning rate, batch size and observe the changes in quality of the reconstructed and fake images?
- Can you visualize the stored summary in Tensorboard to understand the learning process?
- Can you think of other datasets which can be used for Style transfer?

10
Classifying Clothing Images using Capsule Networks

In this chapter, we will learn how to implement capsule networks on the Fashion MNIST dataset. This chapter will cover the inner workings of capsule networks and explain how to implement them in TensorFlow. You will also learn how to evaluate and optimize the model.

We have chosen capsule networks because they have the ability to preserve the spatial relationships of images. Capsule networks were introduced by Geoff Hinton, et al. They published a paper in 2017 that can be found at `https://arxiv.org/abs/1710.09829`. Capsule networks gained immense popularity within the deep learning community as a new type of neural network.

By the end of this chapter, we will be able to classify clothing using capsule networks after going through the following:

- Understanding the importance of capsule networks
- A brief understanding of capsules
- The routing by agreement algorithm
- The implementation of the CapsNet architecture for classifying Fashion-MNIST images
- The limitations of capsule networks

Understanding the importance of capsule networks

Convolutional neural networks (**CNNs**) form the backbone of all the major breakthroughs in image detection today. CNNs work by detecting the basic features that are present in the lower layers of the network and then proceed to detect the higher level features present in the higher layers of the network. This setup does not contain a pose (translational and rotational) relationship between the lower-level features that make up any complex object.

Imagine trying to identify a face. In this case, just having eyes, nose, and ears in an image can lead a CNN to conclude that it's a face without caring about the relative orientation of the concerned objects. To explain this further, if an image has a nose above the eyes, CNNs still can detect that it's an image. CNNs take care of this problem by using *max pooling*, which helps increase the *field of view* for the higher layers. However, this operation is not a perfect solution as we tend to lose valuable information in the image by using it.

As a matter of fact, Hinton himself states the following:

> *"The pooling operation used in convolutional neural networks is a big mistake and the fact that it works so well is a disaster."*

In the paper, Hinton tries to provide an intuition on solving this problem using the inverse graphics approach. For graphics in computers, an image is constructed by using an internal representation of the objects present in the image. This is done using arrays and matrices. This internal representation helps preserve the shape, the orientation, and the object's relative position when compared to all other objects in the image. The software takes this internal representation and publishes the image on the screen using a process known as **rendering**.

Hinton specifies that the human brain does some sort of inverse graphics. We see an image through our eyes, and then brain our dissects the image and constructs a hierarchical representation of different objects in the image before trying to match them to the existing patterns that we have seen. An interesting observation to note is that humans can identify objects in an image, irrespective of their viewing angle.

He then proceeds to argue that in order to perform classification, it is necessary to preserve the relative orientation and position of different objects in the image (this helps mimic the human capability, as we discussed previously). It's quite intuitive that once we have these relationships built into the representation using the model, it is very easy for a model to detect an object when it views it from various angles. Let's imagine the case of viewing the Taj Mahal (the famous monument in India). Our eyes can identify the Taj Mahal from various angles. However, if you present the same images to a CNN, it might fail to detect the Taj Mahal from different viewpoints. This is because CNNs don't have an understanding of 3D space like our brains do. This is the reason capsule network theory is quite important.

One of the major concerns here is this: *How do we incorporate these hierarchical relationships into the deep neural networks?* The relationship between different objects in an image is modeled by something called a **pose**, which is basically rotation and translation. This is specific to the graphics of a computer. We will look at how these relationships are modeled in capsule networks in the subsequent sections.

Understanding capsules

In traditional CNNs, we define different filters that run over the entire image. The 2D matrices produced by each filter are stacked on top of one another to constitute the output of a convolutional layer. Subsequently, we perform the max pooling operation to find the invariance in activities. Invariance here implies that the output is robust to small changes in the input as the max pooling operation always picks up the max activity. As mentioned previously, max pooling results in the valuable loss of information and is unable to represent the relative orientation of different objects to others in the image.

Capsules, on the other hand, encode all of the information of the objects they are detecting in a vector form as opposed to a scalar output by a neuron. These vectors have the following properties:

- The length of the vector indicates the probability of an object in the image.
- Different elements of the vector encode different properties of the object. These properties include various kinds of instantiation parameters such as pose (position, size, orientation), hue, thickness, and so on.

With this representation, if the detected object moves in the image, the length of the vector remains the same. However, the orientation or values of different elements in the vector representation will change. Let's take the previous example of viewing the Taj Mahal again. Even if we were to move (or change the orientation) of the Taj Mahal in the image, the capsule representation should be able to detect the object in the image.

How do capsules work?

Before looking at how capsules work, let's try to revisit how neurons function. A neuron receives scalar inputs from the previous layer's neurons, multiplies them by the corresponding weights, and sums the outputs. This summed output is passed through some non-linearity (such as ReLU) that outputs a new scalar, which is passed on to next layer's neurons.

In contrast to this, capsules take a vector as an input, as well as output a vector. The following diagram illustrates the process of computing the output of a capsule:

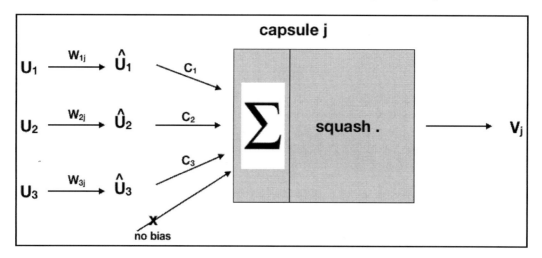

Let's look at each step in detail:

1. **Capsule j** (at the higher levels) receives the vector inputs from the lower layers as $\mathbf{u_1}$, $\mathbf{u_2}$, $\mathbf{u_3}$, and so on. As discussed earlier, each input vector encodes both the probability of an object detected at the lower layer and also its orientation parameters. These input vectors are multiplied by weight matrices, $\mathbf{W_{ij}}$, which try to model the relationship between lower layer objects and higher layer objects. In the case of detecting the Taj Mahal, you can think of this as a relationship between edges that are detected at the lower layers and the pillars of the Taj Mahal at the higher layers. The output of this multiplication is the predicted vector of the higher level object (in this case, the pillar) based on the detected objects in the lower layer. Therefore, $\hat{u}_i$ denotes the position of a pillar of the Taj Mahal based on the detected vertical edge, $\hat{u}_2$ can denote the position of the pillar based on the detected horizontal edge, and so on. Intuitively, if all of the predicted vectors point to the same object with a similar orientation, then that object must be present in the image:

$$\hat{u}_{j|i} = W_{ij}u_i$$

2. Next, these predicted vectors are multiplied by scalar weights (c_is), which help in routing the predicted vectors to the right capsules in the higher layer. We then sum the weighted vectors that are obtained through this multiplication. This step will feel familiar to traditional neural networks, which multiply the scalar inputs by weights before providing them to the input of higher-level neurons. In such cases, the weights are determined by a back propagation algorithm. However, in the case of capsule networks, they are determined by the dynamic routing algorithm, which we will discuss in detail in the next section. The formula is given as follows:

$$s_j = \Sigma_i c_{ij}\hat{u}_{j|i}$$

3. We mentioned a new word in the previous formula, known as **squashing**. This is
the non-linearity that is used in capsule networks. You can think of this as a
counterpart to the non-linearity we use in traditional neural networks.
Essentially, squashing tries to reduce the vector to less than a unit norm to
facilitate the interpretation of the length of the vector as probability:

$$\mathbf{v_j} = \frac{||s_j||^2}{1 + ||s_j||^2} \frac{s_j}{||s_j||}$$

Here, $\mathbf{v_j}$ is the output of the **j** layer capsule.

The implementation of the squashing function in the code is done as follows:

```
def squash(vectors, name=None):
    """
    Squashing Function as implemented in the paper
    :parameter vectors: vector input that needs to be squashed
    :parameter name: Name of the tensor on the graph
    :return: a tensor with same shape as vectors but squashed as mentioned in
    the paper
    """
    with tf.name_scope(name, default_name="squash_op"):
    s_squared_norm = tf.reduce_sum(tf.square(vectors), axis=-2, keepdims=True)
    scale = s_squared_norm / (1. + s_squared_norm) / tf.sqrt(s_squared_norm +
    tf.keras.backend.epsilon())
    return scale*vectors
```

The dynamic routing algorithm

As mentioned earlier, it is necessary for the capsule in the lower layer to decide how to
send its output to the higher-level capsules. This is achieved through the novel concept of
the dynamic routing algorithm, which was introduced in the paper (https://arxiv.org/
pdf/1710.09829.pdf). The key idea behind this algorithm is that the lower layer capsule
will send their output to the higher-level capsules that *match* the input.

This is achieved through the weights (c_{ij}) mentioned in the last section. These weights multiply the outputs from the lower layer capsule **i** before pushing them as the input to the higher level capsule **j**. Some of the properties of these weights are as follows:

- c_{ij}s are non-negative in nature and are determined by the dynamic-routing algorithm
- The number of weights in the lower layer capsule is equal to the number of higher-level capsules
- The sum of the weights of each lower layer capsule **i** amounts to 1

Implement the iterative routing algorithm using the following code:

```
def routing(u):
    """
    This function performs the routing algorithm as mentioned in the paper
    :parameter u: Input tensor with [batch_size, num_caps_input_layer=1152,
1, caps_dim_input_layer=8, 1] shape.
                    NCAPS_CAPS1: num capsules in the PrimaryCaps layer 1
                    CAPS_DIM_CAPS2: dimensions of output vectors of Primary
caps layer 1

    :return: "v_j" vector (tensor) in Digitcaps Layer
                    Shape:[batch_size, NCAPS_CAPS1=10, CAPS_DIM_CAPS2=16, 1]
    """
    #local variable b_ij: [batch_size, num_caps_input_layer=1152,
                    num_caps_output_layer=10, 1, 1]
    #num_caps_output_layer: number of capsules in Digicaps layer 1+1
    b_ij = tf.zeros([BATCH_SIZE, NCAPS_CAPS1, NCAPS_CAPS2, 1, 1],
dtype=np.float32, name="b_ij")

    # Preparing the input Tensor for total number of DigitCaps capsule for
multiplication with W
    u = tf.tile(u, [1, 1, b_ij.shape[2].value, 1, 1])   # u => [batch_size,
1152, 10, 8, 1]

    # W: [num_caps_input_layer, num_caps_output_layer, len_u_i, len_v_j] as
mentioned in the paper
    W = tf.get_variable('W', shape=(1, u.shape[1].value,
b_ij.shape[2].value,
        u.shape[3].value, CAPS_DIM_CAPS2),dtype=tf.float32,
        initializer=tf.random_normal_initializer(stddev=STDEV))
    W = tf.tile(W, [BATCH_SIZE, 1, 1, 1, 1]) # W => [batch_size, 1152, 10,
8, 16]

    #Computing u_hat (as mentioned in the paper)
    u_hat = tf.matmul(W, u, transpose_a=True)  # [batch_size, 1152, 10, 16,
```

1]

```
    # In forward, u_hat_stopped = u_hat;
    # In backward pass, no gradient pass from  u_hat_stopped to u_hat
    u_hat_stopped = tf.stop_gradient(u_hat, name='gradient_stop')
```

Note that, in the previous code, we are dividing the actual routing function in the code into two parts so that we can focus on the dynamic routing algorithm part. The first part of the function takes vector **u** as input from the lower layer capsule(s). First, it generates the vector $\hat{u}_{j|i}$ using the weight vector **W**. Also, observe that we define a temporary variable called b_{ij}, which is initialized to zero at the start of training. The values of b_{ij} will be updated in the algorithm and will be stored in c_{ij} at the end of the algorithm. The second part of the function implements the actual iterative routing algorithm, as follows:

```
# Routing Algorithm Begins here
for r in range(ROUTING_ITERATIONS):
    with tf.variable_scope('iterations_' + str(r)):
        c_ij = tf.nn.softmax(b_ij, axis=2) # [batch_size, 1152, 10, 1, 1]

        # At last iteration, use `u_hat` in order to back propagate
gradient
        if r == ROUTING_ITERATIONS - 1:
            s_j = tf.multiply(c_ij, u_hat) # [batch_size, 1152, 10, 16, 1]
            # then sum as per paper
            s_j = tf.reduce_sum(s_j, axis=1, keep_dims=True) # [batch_size,
1, 10, 16, 1]

            v_j = squash(s_j) # [batch_size, 1, 10, 16, 1]

        elif r < ROUTING_ITERATIONS - 1:  # No backpropagation in these
iterations
            s_j = tf.multiply(c_ij, u_hat_stopped)
            s_j = tf.reduce_sum(s_j, axis=1, keepdims=True)
            v_j = squash(s_j)
            v_j = tf.tile(v_j, [1, u.shape[1].value, 1, 1, 1]) #
[batch_size, 1152, 10, 16, 1]

            # Multiplying in last two dimensions: [16, 1]^T x [16, 1]
yields [1, 1]
            u_hat_dot_v = tf.matmul(u_hat_stopped, v_j, transpose_a=True) #
[batch_size, 1152, 10, 1, 1]

            b_ij = tf.add(b_ij,u_hat_dot_v)
return tf.squeeze(v_j, axis=1) # [batch_size, 10, 16, 1]
```

First, we define a loop over `ROUTING_ITERATIONS`. This is the parameter that is defined by the user. Hinton mentions in his paper that the typical values of 3 should suffice for this.

Next, we perform a softmax on b_{ij} to compute the initial values of the c_{ij}s. Note that c_{ij}s are not to be included in the back propagation since these can only be obtained through the iterative algorithm. For this reason, all of the routing iterations before the last one are performed on $\hat{u}_{stopped}$ (which helps to stop gradients, as defined earlier).

For each routing iteration, we use the following operations for each higher-level capsule **j**:

$$s_j = \Sigma_i c_{ij} \hat{u}_{j|i} \qquad (1)$$

$$\mathbf{v_j} = \frac{\|s_j\|^2}{1 + \|s_j\|^2} \frac{s_j}{\|s_j\|} \qquad (2)$$

$$\mathbf{b_{ij}} = \mathbf{b_{ij}} + \hat{u}_{j|i} \cdot \mathbf{v_j} \qquad (3)$$

We have explained the first two equations already. Now let's try to understand the third equation.

The third equation is the essence of the iterative routing algorithm. It updates the weights b_{ij}. The formula states that the new weight value is the sum of the old weights: the predicted vector from lower layer capsules and the output of the higher layer capsule. The dot product is essentially trying to capture the notion of similarity between the input vector and the output vector of the capsule. This way, the output from the lower capsule **i** is only sent to the higher-level capsule **j**, which agrees to its input. The dot product achieves the agreement. This algorithm is repeated a number of times equal to the `ROUTING_ITERATIONS` parameter in the code.

This concludes our discussion on the innovative routing algorithm and its applications.

CapsNet for classifying Fashion MNIST images

Now let's take a look at the implementation of CapsNet for classifying Fashion MNIST images. **Zalando**, the e-commerce company, recently released a new replacement for the MNIST dataset, known as **Fashion MNIST** (`https://github.com/zalandoresearch/fashion-mnist`). The Fashion MNIST dataset includes 28 x 28 grayscale images under 10 categories:

Category name	Label (in dataset)
T-shirt/top	0
Trouser	1
Pullover	2
Dress	3
Coat	4
Sandal	5
Shirt	6
Sneaker	7
Bag	8
Ankle boot	9

The following are some sample images from the dataset:

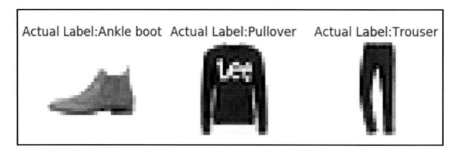

The training set contains 60K examples, and the test set contains 10K examples.

CapsNet implementation

The CapsNet architecture consists of two parts, each consisting of three layers. The first three layers are encoders, while the next three layers are decoders:

Layer Num	Layer Name	Layer Type
1	Convolutional Layer	Encoder
2	PrimaryCaps Layer	Encoder
3	DigitCaps Layer	Encoder
4	Fully Connected Layer 1	Decoder
5	Fully Connected Layer 2	Decoder
6	Fully Connecter Layer 3	Decoder

Let's try to understand these layers in detail.

Understanding the encoder

The following diagram illustrates the structure of the encoder used for modeling. Note that it shows the MNIST digit image as an input, but we are using the Fashion-MNIST data as an input to the model:

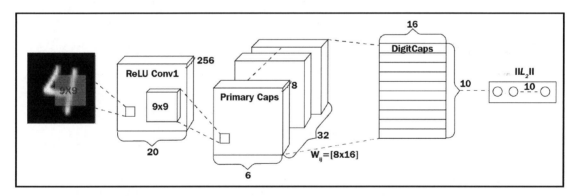

The encoder essentially takes an input of a 28x28 image and produces a 16-dimensional representation of that image. As mentioned previously, the length of the 16D vector denotes the probability that an object is present in the image. The components of the vector represent various instantiation parameters.

The three layers dedicated to the encoder are as follows:

- **Layer 1-convolutional layer**: Layer 1 is a standard convolutional layer. The input to this layer is a 28x28 grayscale image and the output is a 20x20x256 tensor. The other parameters of this layer are as follows:

Parameter name	Value
Filters	256
Kernel Size	9
Activation	ReLU
Strides	1

- **Layer 2-primary caps layer**: Layer 2 is the first layer with capsules. The main purpose of this layer is to use the output of the first convolutional layer to produce higher level features. It has 32 primary capsules. It also takes an input of a 20 x 20 x 256 tensor. Every capsule present in this layer applies the convolutional kernels to the input to produce an output of a 6 x 6 x 8 tensor. With 32 capsules, this output is now a 6 x 6 x 8 x 32 tensor.

    The convolutional parameters that are common for all capsules in the layer are mentioned as follows:

Parameter Name	Value
Filters	256
Kernel Size	9
Activation	ReLU
Strides	2

Note that we also `squash` the output of this layer.

- **Layer 3-DigitCaps layer**: This layer has 10 capsules – one for each class label. Each capsule is a 16D vector. The input to this layer are 6x6x32 8D vectors (**u**, as we defined previously). Each of these vectors have their own weight matrix, $\mathbf{W}_{ij}$, which produces $\hat{u}_{j|i}$. These $\hat{u}_{j|i}$ are then used in the routing by the agreement algorithm that we described previously.

Note that the original paper names this layer as the DigitCaps layer because it uses the MNIST dataset. We are continuing to use the same name for the Fashion MNIST dataset, as it is easier to relate to the original paper.

Understanding the decoder

The structure of the decoder is shown in the following diagram:

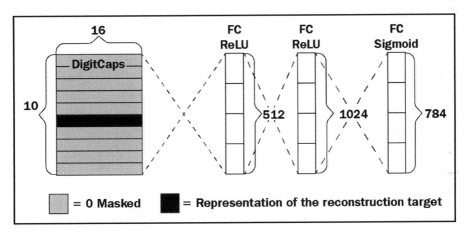

The decoder essentially tries to reconstruct the image from the correct DigitCaps capsule for each image. You can view this as a regularization step, with *loss* being the Euclidean distance between the predicted output and the original label. You could argue that you don't require reconstruction in this application as you are just carrying out classification. However, Hinton specifically shows in his original paper that adding reconstruction loss does improve the accuracy of the model.

The decoder's structure is pretty simple, and consists of only three fully connected layers. The input and the output shapes of all three layers are as follows:

Layer	Input Shape	Output Shape
Fully Connected Layer 4	16 x 10	512
Fully Connected Layer 5	512	1,024
Fully Connected Layer 6	1,024	784

However, before passing the input to the three fully connected layers, during training, we mask all but the activity vector of the correct digit capsule. Since we don't have the correct labels during testing, we pass the activity vector with the highest norm to the fully connected layers.

Defining the loss function

The loss function for capsule networks is composed of two parts:

- **Margin loss**: Margin loss is exactly the same as what's used in **Support Vector Machines (SVM)**. Effectively, we want the digit capsule to have an instantiation vector for class k, but only if the label is class k. For all other classes, we don't require any instantiation parameters. For each digit capsule k, we define separate loss as L_k:

$$L_k = T_k \max(0, m^+ - ||v_k||)^2 + \lambda(1 - T_k)\max(0, ||v_k|| - m^-)^2$$

If an image belongs to class k, then $T_k = 1$ else 0. $m^+ = 0.9$ and $m^- = 0.1$ are the other two parameters. $\lambda = 0.5$ is used for stability when initial learning the model. The total margin loss is the sum of losses of all digit capsules.

To explain this simply, for digit caps k (which is the true label), the loss is zero if we predict a correct label with a probability of > 0.9; otherwise it is non-zero. For all other digit caps, the loss is zero if we predict the probability of all those classes to be less than 0.1; otherwise, it is non-zero.

- **Reconstruction loss**: Reconstruction loss is mainly used as a regularizer for the model so that we can focus on learning the representations to reproduce the image. Intuitively, this can also result in easing the learning of the instantiation parameters of the model. This is generated by taking the Euclidean distance between the pixels of the reconstructed image and the input image. The total loss for the model is given as follows:

Total loss = Margin loss + 0.0005 Reconstruction loss

Note that reconstruction loss is weighted down heavily to ensure that it doesn't dominate the margin loss during training.

Training and testing the model

The following are the steps for training and testing the model:

1. The first step is to read the training and testing datasets. Here are steps we must implement for reading the data:
   - First, we load the training/testing images and label data from the files we downloaded for the **Fashion MNIST** data (`https://github.com/zalandoresearch/fashion-mnist`).
   - Then, we reshape the image data to a shape of 28 x 28 x 1 for our model and normalize it by 255 to keep the input of the model between 0 and 1.
   - We split the training data into train and validation datasets, each with 55,000 and 5000 images respectively.
   - We convert our target array **y** for both training and testing datasets so that we have a one-hot representation of the 10 classes in the dataset that we are going to feed into the model.

Make sure to choose around 10% of data for out validation. In this project, we choose 5000 random images (8% of the total images) for the validation data set.

The code for the preceding steps is as follows:

```
def load_data(load_type='train'):
    '''

    :param load_type: train or test depending on the use case
    :return: x (images), y(labels)
    '''
    data_dir = os.path.join('data','fashion-mnist')
    if load_type == 'train':
        image_file = open(os.path.join(data_dir,'train-images-idx3-
ubyte'))
        image_data = np.fromfile(file=image_file, dtype=np.uint8)
        x = image_data[16:].reshape((60000, 28, 28,
1)).astype(np.float32)

        label_file = open(os.path.join(data_dir, 'train-labels-
idx1-ubyte'))
        label_data = np.fromfile(file=label_file, dtype=np.uint8)
        y = label_data[8:].reshape(60000).astype(np.int32)

        x_train = x[:55000] / 255.
        y_train = y[:55000]
        y_train = (np.arange(N_CLASSES) == y_train[:,
None]).astype(np.float32)

        x_valid = x[55000:, ] / 255.
        y_valid = y[55000:]
        y_valid = (np.arange(N_CLASSES) == y_valid[:,
None]).astype(np.float32)
        return x_train, y_train, x_valid, y_valid
    elif load_type == 'test':
        image_file = open(os.path.join(data_dir, 't10k-images-idx3-
ubyte'))
        image_data = np.fromfile(file=image_file, dtype=np.uint8)
        x_test = image_data[16:].reshape((10000, 28, 28,
1)).astype(np.float)

        label_file = open(os.path.join(data_dir, 't10k-labels-idx1-
ubyte'))
        label_data = np.fromfile(file=label_file, dtype=np.uint8)
        y_test = label_data[8:].reshape(10000).astype(np.int32)
        y_test = (np.arange(N_CLASSES) == y_test[:,
None]).astype(np.float32)
    return x_test / 255., y_test
```

Note that we normalize the image pixels by 255 after loading the dataset for training stability and faster convergence.

2. Implement the encoder by creating the three neural network layers that have been defined in the *Understanding the encoder* section:

```
with tf.variable_scope('Conv1_layer'):
    conv1_layer = tf.layers.conv2d(self.X, name="conv1_layer",
**CONV1_LAYER_PARAMS) # [batch_size, 20, 20, 256]

with tf.variable_scope('PrimaryCaps_layer'):
    conv2_layer = tf.layers.conv2d(conv1_layer, name="conv2_layer",
**CONV2_LAYER_PARAMS) # [batch_size, 6, 6, 256]

    primary_caps = tf.reshape(conv2_layer, (BATCH_SIZE,
NCAPS_CAPS1, CAPS_DIM_CAPS1, 1), name="primary_caps") #
[batch_size, 1152, 8, 1]
    primary_caps_output = squash(primary_caps, name="caps1_output")
    # [batch_size, 1152, 8, 1]

# DigitCaps layer, return [batch_size, 10, 16, 1]
with tf.variable_scope('DigitCaps_layer'):
    digitcaps_input = tf.reshape(primary_caps_output,
shape=(BATCH_SIZE, NCAPS_CAPS1, 1, CAPS_DIM_CAPS1, 1)) #
[batch_size, 1152, 1, 8, 1]
    # [batch_size, 1152, 10, 1, 1]
    self.digitcaps_output = routing(digitcaps_input) # [batch_size,
10, 16, 1]
```

3. Next, implement the decoder layers to reconstruct the images, as described in the *Understanding the decoder* section. Here are the important steps once again for reference:

- First, we calculate the norm of each activity vector in a digit caps output for masking purposes. We also add an epsilon to the norm for stability purposes.

- For training, we mask all of the activity vectors in digit caps output, except the one with the correct label. On the other hand, for testing, we mask all the activity vectors in digit caps output, except the one with the highest norm (or predicted label). We implement this branching mechanism in the decoder with **tf.cond**, which defines a control flow operation in the TensorFlow graph.
- Finally, we flatten the masked output from the digit caps and flatten it as a one-dimensional vector that can be fed to the fully connected layers.

To read up on tf.cond, refer to https://www.tensorflow.org/api_docs/python/tf/cond.

The code for the preceding steps is as follows:

```
# Decoder
with tf.variable_scope('Masking'):
    self.v_norm =
tf.sqrt(tf.reduce_sum(tf.square(self.digitcaps_output), axis=2,
keep_dims=True) + tf.keras.backend.epsilon())

    predicted_class = tf.to_int32(tf.argmax(self.v_norm, axis=1))
#[batch_size, 10,1,1]
    self.y_predicted = tf.reshape(predicted_class,
shape=(BATCH_SIZE,))   #[batch_size]
    y_predicted_one_hot = tf.one_hot(self.y_predicted,
depth=NCAPS_CAPS2)   #[batch_size,10]  One hot operation

    reconstruction_targets = tf.cond(self.mask_with_labels,  #
condition
                                    lambda: self.Y,  # if True (Training)
                                    lambda: y_predicted_one_hot,  # if
False (Test)
                                    name="reconstruction_targets")

    digitcaps_output_masked =
tf.multiply(tf.squeeze(self.digitcaps_output),
tf.expand_dims(reconstruction_targets, -1)) # [batch_size, 10, 16]

    #Flattening as suggested by the paper
    decoder_input = tf.reshape(digitcaps_output_masked,
```

```
                 [BATCH_SIZE, -1]) # [batch_size, 160]


                 with tf.variable_scope('Decoder'):
                     fc1 = tf.layers.dense(decoder_input, layer1_size,
                 activation=tf.nn.relu, name="FC1") # [batch_size, 512]
                     fc2 = tf.layers.dense(fc1, layer2_size, activation=tf.nn.rel ,
                 name="FC2") # [batch_size, 1024]
                     self.decoder_output = tf.layers.dense(fc2, output_size,
                 activation=tf.nn.sigmoid, name="FC3") # [batch_size, 784]
```

4. Implement margin loss using the formula mentioned in the *Defining the loss function* section as follows:

```
                 with tf.variable_scope('Margin_Loss'):
                     # max(0, m_plus-||v_c||)^2
                     positive_error = tf.square(tf.maximum(0., 0.9 - self.v_norm)) #
                 [batch_size, 10, 1, 1]
                     # max(0, ||v_c||-m_minus)^2
                     negative_error = tf.square(tf.maximum(0., self.v_norm - 0.1)) #
                 [batch_size, 10, 1, 1]
                     # reshape: [batch_size, 10, 1, 1] => [batch_size, 10]
                     positive_error = tf.reshape(positive_error, shape=(BATCH_SIZE,
                 -1))
                     negative_error = tf.reshape(negative_error, shape=(BATCH_SIZE,
                 -1))

                     Loss_vec = self.Y * positive_error + 0.5 * (1- self.Y) *
                 negative_error # [batch_size, 10]
                     self.margin_loss = tf.reduce_mean(tf.reduce_sum(Loss_vec,
                 axis=1), name="margin_loss")
```

5. Implement reconstruction loss using the formula mentioned in the *Defining the loss function* section:

```
                 with tf.variable_scope('Reconstruction_Loss'):
                     ground_truth = tf.reshape(self.X, shape=(BATCH_SIZE, -1))
                     self.reconstruction_loss =
                 tf.reduce_mean(tf.square(self.decoder_output - ground_truth))
```

6. Define the optimizer as an Adam optimizer, using the default parameters and an accuracy metric as the usual classification accuracy. These need to be implemented in the CapsNet class itself using the following code:

```
                 def define_accuracy(self):
                     with tf.variable_scope('Accuracy'):
                         correct_predictions =
                 tf.equal(tf.to_int32(tf.argmax(self.Y, axis=1)), self.y_predicted)
```

```
        self.accuracy = tf.reduce_mean(tf.cast(correct_predictions,
tf.float32))

def define_optimizer(self):
    with tf.variable_scope('Optimizer'):
        optimizer = tf.train.AdamOptimizer()
        self.train_optimizer =
optimizer.minimize(self.combined_loss, name="training_optimizer")
```

To learn more about the Adam Optimizer, refer
to `https://www.tensorflow.org/api_docs/python/tf/train/AdamOptim`
`izer`.

7. Implement the support for checkpointing and restoring the model. Select the best model based on validation set accuracy; we checkpoint the model only for the epoch, where we observe a decrease in the validation set accuracy and finally, log the summary output for TensorBoard visualization. We train our model for 10 epochs each having batch size 128. Remember, you can vary these parameters to improve the accuracy of your model:

```
def train(model):
    global fd_train
    x_train, y_train, x_valid, y_valid =
load_data(load_type='train')
    print('Data set Loaded')
    num_batches = int(y_train.shape[0] / BATCH_SIZE)
    if not os.path.exists(CHECKPOINT_PATH_DIR):
        os.makedirs(CHECKPOINT_PATH_DIR)

    with tf.Session() as sess:
        if RESTORE_TRAINING:
            saver = tf.train.Saver()
            ckpt =
tf.train.get_checkpoint_state(CHECKPOINT_PATH_DIR)
            saver.restore(sess, ckpt.model_checkpoint_path)
            print('Model Loaded')
            start_epoch =
int(str(ckpt.model_checkpoint_path).split('-')[-1])
            train_file, val_file, best_loss_val =
load_existing_details()
        else:
            saver = tf.train.Saver(tf.global_variables())
            tf.global_variables_initializer().run()
            print('All variables initialized')
            train_file, val_file = write_progress('train')
            start_epoch = 0
```

```
            best_loss_val = np.infty
        print('Training Starts')
        acc_batch_all = loss_batch_all = np.array([])
        train_writer = tf.summary.FileWriter(LOG_DIR, sess.graph)
        for epoch in range(start_epoch, EPOCHS):
            # Shuffle the input data
            x_train, y_train = shuffle_data(x_train, y_train)
            for step in range(num_batches):
                start = step * BATCH_SIZE
                end = (step + 1) * BATCH_SIZE
                global_step = epoch * num_batches + step
                x_batch, y_batch = x_train[start:end],
y_train[start:end]
                feed_dict_batch = {model.X: x_batch, model.Y:
y_batch, model.mask_with_labels: True}
                if not (step % 100):
                    _, acc_batch, loss_batch, summary_ =
sess.run([model.train_optimizer, model.accuracy,
model.combined_loss, model.summary_],
feed_dict=feed_dict_batch)
                    train_writer.add_summary(summary_, global_ste
                    acc_batch_all = np.append(acc_batch_all,
acc_batch)
                    loss_batch_all = np.append(loss_batch_all,
loss_batch)
                    mean_acc,mean_loss =
np.mean(acc_batch_all),np.mean(loss_batch_all)
                    summary_ =
tf.Summary(value=[tf.Summary.Value(tag='Accuracy',
simple_value=mean_acc)])
                    train_writer.add_summary(summary_, global_step)
                    summary_ =
tf.Summary(value=[tf.Summary.Value(tag='Loss/combined_loss',
simple_value=mean_loss)])
                    train_writer.add_summary(summary_, global_step)

                    train_file.write(str(global_step) + ',' +
str(mean_acc) + ',' + str(mean_loss) + "\n")
                    train_file.flush()
                    print("  Batch #{0}, Epoch: #{1}, Mean Training
loss: {2:.4f}, Mean Training accuracy: {3:.01%}".format(
                        step, (epoch+1), mean_loss, mean_acc))
                    acc_batch_all = loss_batch_all = np.array([])
                else:
                    _, acc_batch, loss_batch =
sess.run([model.train_optimizer, model.accuracy,
model.combined_loss],
feed_dict=feed_dict_batch)
```

```
                                acc_batch_all = np.append(acc_batch_all,
        acc_batch)
                                loss_batch_all = np.append(loss_batch_all,
        loss_batch)

                # Validation metrics after each EPOCH
                acc_val, loss_val = eval_performance(sess, model,
        x_valid, y_valid)
                val_file.write(str(epoch + 1) + ',' + str(acc_val) +
        ',' + str(loss_val) + '\n')
                val_file.flush()
                print("\rEpoch: {}  Mean Train Accuracy: {:.4f}% ,Mean
        Val accuracy: {:.4f}%  Loss: {:.6f}{}".format(
                        epoch + 1, mean_acc * 100, acc_val * 100, loss_val,
                        " (improved)" if loss_val < best_loss_val else ""))

                # Saving the improved model
                if loss_val < best_loss_val:
                        saver.save(sess, CHECKPOINT_PATH_DIR +
        '/model.tfmodel', global_step=epoch + 1)
                        best_loss_val = loss_val
        train_file.close()
        val_file.close()
```

This model achieved almost 99% accuracy with 10 epochs on the validation and test sets, which is quite good.

Reconstructing sample images

We will also reconstruct some sample images to see how the model is performing. We will use the following images as the input:

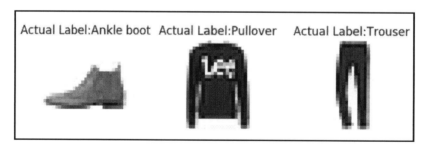

The code for reconstructing the preceding images is as follows:

```
def reconstruct_sample(model, n_samples=5):
    x_test, y_test = load_data(load_type='test')
    sample_images, sample_labels = x_test[:BATCH_SIZE], y_test[:BATCH_SIZE]
    saver = tf.train.Saver()
    ckpt = tf.train.get_checkpoint_state(CHECKPOINT_PATH_DIR)
    with tf.Session() as sess:
        saver.restore(sess, ckpt.model_checkpoint_path)
        feed_dict_samples = {model.X: sample_images, model.Y:
sample_labels}
        decoder_out, y_predicted = sess.run([model.decoder_output,
model.y_predicted],
                                    feed_dict=feed_dict_samples)
    reconstruction(sample_images, sample_labels, decoder_out, y_predicted,
n_samples)
```

The reconstruction function for plotting the images and saving them is given as follows:

```
def reconstruction(x, y, decoder_output, y_pred, n_samples):
    '''
    This function is used to reconstruct sample images for analysis
    :param x: Images
    :param y: Labels
    :param decoder_output: output from decoder
    :param y_pred: predictions from the model
    :param n_samples: num images
    :return: saves the reconstructed images
    '''

    sample_images = x.reshape(-1, IMG_WIDTH, IMG_HEIGHT)
    decoded_image = decoder_output.reshape([-1, IMG_WIDTH,
IMG_WIDTH])

    fig = plt.figure(figsize=(n_samples * 2, 3))
    for i in range(n_samples):
        plt.subplot(1, n_samples, i+ 1)
        plt.imshow(sample_images[i], cmap="binary")
        plt.title("Label:" + IMAGE_LABELS[np.argmax(y[i])])
        plt.axis("off")
    fig.savefig(RESULTS_DIR + '/' + 'input_images.png')
    plt.show()

    fig = plt.figure(figsize=(n_samples * 2, 3))
    for i in range(n_samples):
        plt.subplot(1, n_samples, i + 1)
        plt.imshow(decoded_image[i], cmap="binary")
        plt.title("Prediction:" + IMAGE_LABELS[y_pred[i]])
```

```
        plt.axis("off")
fig.savefig(RESULTS_DIR + '/' + 'decoder_images.png')
plt.show()
```

The reconstructed images now look like this:

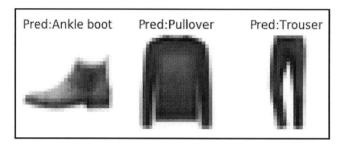

As we can see, the labels are perfect, while the reconstructed images aren't as perfect but very similar. With more hyper parameter tuning, we can generate much better reconstructed images.

Limitations of capsule networks

While capsule networks are great and they address the core issues of convolutional neural networks, they still have a long way to go. Some of the limitations of capsule networks are as follows:

- The network has not been tested on large datasets like ImageNet. This puts a question mark on their ability to perform well on large datasets.
- The algorithm is slow, mainly due to the inner loop of the dynamic routing algorithm. The number of iterations can be fairly large for large datasets.
- Capsule networks definitely have higher complexity in implementation compared to CNNs.

It would be interesting to see how the deep learning community addresses the limitations of capsule networks.

Summary

In this chapter, we looked at the very popular neural network architecture CapsNet, by Geoff Hinton (presumably the father of deep learning).

We started off by understanding the limitations of CNNs in their current form. They use max pooling as a crutch to achieve invariance in activities. Max pooling has a tendency to lose information, and it can't model the relationships between different objects in the image. We then touched upon how the human brain detects objects and are viewpoint invariant. We drew an analogy to computer graphics and understood how we can probably incorporate pose information in neural networks.

Subsequently, we learned about the basic building blocks of capsule networks, that is, capsules. We understood how they differ from the traditional neuron in that they take a vector as the input and produce a vector output. We also learned about a special kind of non-linearity in capsules, namely the `squash` function.

In the next section, we learned about the novel **dynamic routing algorithm,** which helps route the output from lower layer capsules to higher layer capsules. The coefficients c_{ij} are learned through several iterations of the routing algorithm. The crux of the algorithm was the step in which we update the coefficients b_{ij} by using the dot product of the predicted vector $\hat{u}_{j|i}$ and the output vector of the higher-layer capsule v_j.

Furthermore, we implemented CapsNet for the Fashion MNIST dataset. We used a convolutional layer, followed by a PrimaryCaps layer and a DigitCaps layer. We learned about the encoder architecture and how we can get a vector representation of the images. This was followed by an understanding of the decoder architecture to reconstruct the image from the learned representations. The loss function in this architecture was a combination of margin loss (like in SVMs) and weighted-down reconstruction loss. The reconstruction loss was weighted down so that the model could focus more on margin loss during training.

We then trained the model on 10 epochs with a batch size of 128 and achieved over 99% accuracy on the validation and test sets. We reconstructed some sample images to visualize the output and found the reconstruction to be fairly accurate.

In summary, throughout this chapter, we were able to understand and implement capsule networks from scratch using TensorFlow and trained them on the Fashion MNIST dataset.

Now that you have built the basic capsule network, you can try to extend this model by incorporating multiple capsule layers and see how it performs, use on other image datasets and see whether this algorithm is scalable, run it without reconstruction loss, and see whether you can still reconstruct the input image. By doing this, you will be able to develop a good intuition toward this algorithm.

In the next chapter, we will look at the face-detection project using TensorFlow.

11
Making Quality Product Recommendations Using TensorFlow

When you visit Amazon, Netflix, or your other favorite websites, or use any modern app such as Spotify or Pandora, you will have noticed that they recommend different items to you. These recommendations are created using recommendation system algorithms. Before machine learning based recommendations systems, the recommendations were generated with rule-based systems. However, with the advent of machine learning and neural networks, recommendations have become more accurate.

In this chapter, we'll learn about recommendation systems. We'll use the Retailrocket dataset to implement a recommendation system in two different ways, using TensorFlow and Keras.

The following topics will be covered in this chapter:

- Recommendation systems
- Content-based filtering
- Collaborative filtering
- Hybrid systems
- Matrix factorization
- Introducing the Retailrocket dataset
- Exploring the Retailrocket dataset
- Preprocessing the data
- The matrix factorization model for Retailrocket recommendations
- The neural network model for Retailrocket recommendations

Recommendation systems

One of the most common applications of machine learning systems is to recommend things to users that they'll be interested in. Have you noticed how Spotify and Pandora recommend a certain kind of music, or particular songs or radio stations? You may have observed Netflix recommending movies for you, as well, as in the following screenshot:

How about Amazon recommending books based on the book that you are currently browsing, as in the following screenshot:

Such systems are known as recommendation systems.

A recommendation system is one that learns about what items might be of interest to a user, and then recommends those items for buying, renting, listening, watching, and so on. Recommendation systems are broadly classified into two categories: content-based filtering and collaborative filtering.

Content-based filtering

Content-based filtering is based on creating a detailed model of the content from which recommendations are made, such as the text of books, attributes of movies, or information about music. The content model is generally represented as a vector space model. Some of the common models for transforming content into vector space models are TFIDF, the *Bag-of-words* model, Word2Vec, GloVe, and Item2Vec.

Along with the content model, a user profile is also created using information about the user. Content is recommended based on matching the user profile with the content model.

Advantages of content-based filtering algorithms

The following are the advantages of content-based filtering algorithms:

- **Eliminates the cold-start problem for new items:** If we have enough information about the users, and detailed information about the new content, then the cold-start problem found in collaborative filtering algorithms does not affect content-based algorithms. The recommendation can be made based on the user profile and the information about the content.
- **The recommendations are explainable and transparent:** Using content representation models, we'll be able to explain how certain items are selected for recommendations.

Disadvantages of content-based filtering algorithms

The following are the disadvantages of content-based filtering algorithms:

- Content-based filtering algorithms require detailed information about items and content, which is sometimes not available
- Content-based filtering algorithms are prone to overspecialization

Collaborative filtering

Collaborative filtering algorithms do not need detailed information about the user or the items. They build models based on user interactions with items such as song listened, item viewed, link clicked, item purchased or video watched. The information generated from the user-item interactions is classified into two categories: implicit feedback and explicit feedback:

- Explicit feedback information is when the user explicitly assigns a score, such as a rating from 1 to 5 to an item.
- Implicit feedback information is collected with different kinds of interaction between users and items, for example, view, click, purchase interactions in the Retailrocket dataset that we will use in our example.

Further collaborative filtering algorithms can be either user-based or item-based. In user-based algorithms, interactions between users are focused on to identify similar users. Then the user is recommended items that other similar users have bought or viewed. In item-based algorithms, first, the similar items are identified based on item-user interactions, and then items similar to the current item are recommended.

Hybrid systems

Hybrid systems leverage the power of both content-based and collaborative filtering by combing both methods. There are many ways hybrid systems are implemented, such as:

- Creating ensembles of content-based and collaborative filtering algorithms and combining the recommendations of both types of algorithms
- Enhancing collaborative filtering with content details and user information
- Adding user-item interaction models to content-based filtering algorithms

The reader is encouraged to explore more about the three kinds of recommendation systems. We'll explore how to build recommendation systems with matrix factorization and neural networks in the Retailrocket dataset example in the following section.

Matrix factorization

Matrix factorization is a popular algorithm for implementing recommendation systems and falls in the collaborative filtering algorithms category. In this algorithm, the user-item interaction is decomposed into two low-dimensional matrices. For example, let's say all the visitor-item interactions in our dataset are M x N matrix, denoted by A. Matrix factorization decomposes matrix A into two matrices of M x k and k x N dimensions respectively, such that the dot product of these two can approximate matrix A. Some of the more popular algorithms for finding the low-dimensional matrix are based on **Singular Value Decomposition** (**SVD**). In the following example, we'll use the TensorFlow and Keras libraries to implement matrix factorization.

Introducing the Retailrocket dataset

In this chapter, we shall showcase a recommendation system algorithm using the Retailrocket dataset.

 The Retailrocket dataset is available from the Kaggle website, at `https://www.kaggle.com/retailrocket/ecommerce-dataset`.

We download the dataset using the following command:

```
kaggle datasets download -d retailrocket/ecommerce-dataset
```

The downloaded files are moved into the `~/datasets/kaggle-retailrocket` folder. You can keep it in whichever folder you feel comfortable with.

The Retailrocket dataset comes in three files:

- `events.csv`: This file contains the visitor-item interaction data
- `item_properties.csv`: This file contains item properties
- `category_tree.csv`: This file contains the category tree

The data contains the values collected from an e-commerce website but has been anonymized to ensure the privacy of the users. The interaction data represents interactions over a period of 4.5 months.

A visitor can engage in three categories of events: `view`, `addtocart`, or `transaction`. The dataset has a total of 2,756,101 interactions that include 2,664,312 `view` events, 69,332 `addtocart` events, and 22,457 `transaction` events. The interactions are from 1,407,580 unique visitors.

Since the data contains the user-item interactions and not the explicit ranking of items by users, it, therefore, falls under the category of implicit feedback information.

Exploring the Retailrocket dataset

Let's load the dataset and explore it to learn more about the data.

1. Set the path to the folder where we downloaded the data:

```
dsroot = os.path.join(os.path.expanduser('~'),
                      'datasets',
                      'kaggle-retailrocket')
os.listdir(dsroot)
```

2. Load the `events.csv` in a pandas DataFrame:

```
events = pd.read_csv(os.path.join(dsroot,'events.csv'))
print('Event data\n',events.head())
```

The events data has the five columns of `timestamp`, `visitorid`, `event`, `itemid`, and `transactionid`, as shown here:

```
Event data
          timestamp  visitorid event   itemid  transactionid
0    1433221332117     257597  view    355908            NaN
1    1433224214164     992329  view    248676            NaN
2    1433221999827     111016  view    318965            NaN
3    1433221955914     483717  view    253185            NaN
4    1433221337106     951259  view    367447            NaN
```

3. Print the unique items, users, and transactions:

```
print('Unique counts:',events.nunique())
```

We get the following output:

```
Unique counts: timestamp          2750455
visitorid          1407580
event                    3
itemid              235061
transactionid        17672
dtype: int64
```

4. Verify the kinds of events that we mentioned earlier:

```
print('Kind of events:',events.event.unique())
```

We see the three kinds of events that we described before:

```
Kind of events: ['view' 'addtocart' 'transaction']
```

Pre-processing the data

Fields `visitorid` and `itemid` are already numeric, but we still need to convert the events into numeric values.

1. We convert `view` events to 1, `addtocart` events to 2, and `transaction` events to 3 with the following code:

```
events.event.replace(to_replace=dict(view=1,
                                     addtocart=2,
                                     transaction=3),
                     inplace=True)
```

2. Drop the `transcationid` and `timestamp` columns that we don't need:

```
events.drop(['transactionid'],axis=1,inplace=True)
events.drop(['timestamp'],axis=1,inplace=True)
```

3. Shuffle the dataset to get random data for training and test datasets:

```
events = events.reindex(np.random.permutation(events.index))
```

The dataset can also be shuffled with the following command:

```
events = events.sample(frac=1).reset_index(drop=True)
```

4. Split the data in `train`, `valid`, and `test` sets, as follows:

```
split_1 = int(0.8 * len(events))
split_2 = int(0.9 * len(events))
train = events[:split_1]
valid = events[split_1:split_2]
test = events[split_2:]
print(train.head())
print(valid.head())
print(test.head())
```

The `train` and `test` data is printed as follows:

	timestamp	visitorid	event	itemid
1621867	1431388649092	896963	1	264947
1060311	1440610461477	1102098	1	431592
114317	1433628249991	1241997	1	283584
1658382	1431543289648	198153	1	97879
2173151	1436211020113	1278262	1	218178
	timestamp	visitorid	event	itemid
1903213	1432567070061	85425	1	344338
1722815	1431708672912	1085328	1	59691
1388040	1442124865777	1366284	1	248032
2669880	1438030300131	478634	1	388940
1893864	1432416049191	1052918	1	328647
	timestamp	visitorid	event	itemid
1004940	1440383070554	193171	1	11565
642906	1438664048047	704648	1	262522
902126	1439869996568	10212	1	46971
569976	1435624889084	753933	1	29489
1517206	1430856529370	261457	1	154821

The matrix factorization model for Retailrocket recommendations

Now let's create a matrix factorization model in Keras:

1. Store the number of visitors and items in a variable, as follows:

```
n_visitors = events.visitorid.nunique()
n_items = events.itemid.nunique()
```

2. Set the number of latent factors for embedding to 5. You may want to try different values to see the impact on the model training:

```
n_latent_factors = 5
```

3. Import the Input, Embedding, and Flatten layers from the Keras library:

```
from tensorflow.keras.layers import Input, Embedding, Flatten
```

4. Start with the items – create an input layer for them as follows:

```
item_input = Input(shape=[1],name='Ttems')
```

5. Create an Embedding representation layer and then flatten the Embedding layer to get the output in the number of latent dimensions that we set earlier:

```
item_embed = Embedding(n_items + 1,
                       n_latent_factors,
                       name='ItemsEmbedding')(item_input)
item_vec = Flatten(name='ItemsFlatten')(item_embed)
```

6. Similarly, create the vector space representation for the visitors:

```
visitor_input = Input(shape=[1],name='Visitors')
visitor_embed = Embedding(n_visitors + 1,
                     n_latent_factors,
                     name='VisitorsEmbedding')(visitor_input)
visitor_vec = Flatten(name='VisitorsFlatten')(visitor_embed)
```

7. Create a layer for the dot product of both vector space representations:

```
dot_prod = keras.layers.dot([item_vec, visitor_vec],axes=[1,1],
                       name='DotProduct')
```

8. Build the Keras model from the input layers, and the dot product layer as the output layer, and compile it as follows:

```
model = keras.Model([item_input, visitor_input], dot_prod)
model.compile('adam', 'mse')
model.summary()
```

The model is summarized as follows:

```
Layer (type)                    Output Shape          Param #
Connected to
==================================================================
==============
```

Items (InputLayer)	(None, 1)	0
Visitors (InputLayer)	(None, 1)	0
ItemsEmbedding (Embedding) Items[0][0]	(None, 1, 5)	1175310
VisitorsEmbedding (Embedding) Visitors[0][0]	(None, 1, 5)	7037905
ItemsFlatten (Flatten) ItemsEmbedding[0][0]	(None, 5)	0
VisitorsFlatten (Flatten) VisitorsEmbedding[0][0]	(None, 5)	0
DotProduct (Dot) ItemsFlatten[0][0] VisitorsFlatten[0][0]	(None, 1)	0

```
===============================================================
==============
Total params: 8,213,215
Trainable params: 8,213,215
Non-trainable params: 0
```

Since the model is complicated, we can also draw it graphically using the following commands:

```
keras.utils.plot_model(model,
                       to_file='model.png',
                       show_shapes=True,
                       show_layer_names=True)
from IPython import display
display.display(display.Image('model.png'))
```

You can see the layers and output sizes clearly in this plotted visualization:

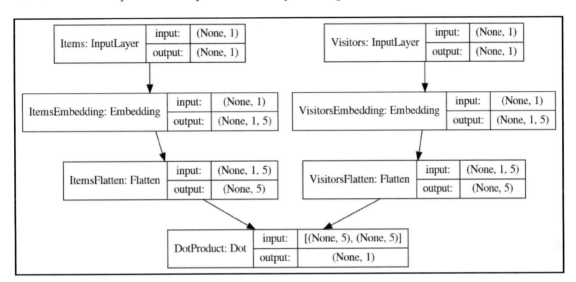

Now let's train and evaluate the model:

```
model.fit([train.visitorid, train.itemid], train.event, epochs=50)
score = model.evaluate([test.visitorid, test.itemid], test.event)
print('mean squared error:', score)
```

The training and evaluation loss will be very high. We can improve this by using advanced methods for matrix factorization.

Now, let's build the neural network model to provide the same recommendations.

The neural network model for Retailrocket recommendations

In this model, we set two different variables for latent factors for users and items but set both of them to 5. The reader is welcome to experiment with different values of latent factors:

```
n_lf_visitor = 5
n_lf_item = 5
```

1. Build the item and visitor embeddings and vector space representations the same way we built earlier:

```
item_input = Input(shape=[1],name='Items')
item_embed = Embedding(n_items + 1,
                        n_lf_visitor,
                        name='ItemsEmbedding')(item_input)
item_vec = Flatten(name='ItemsFlatten')(item_embed)

visitor_input = Input(shape=[1],name='Visitors')
visitor_embed = Embedding(n_visitors + 1,
                          n_lf_item,
name='VisitorsEmbedding')(visitor_input)
visitor_vec = Flatten(name='VisitorsFlatten')(visitor_embed)
```

2. Instead of creating a dot product layer, we concatenate the user and visitor representations, and then apply fully connected layers to get the recommendation output:

```
concat = keras.layers.concatenate([item_vec, visitor_vec],
name='Concat')
fc_1 = Dense(80,name='FC-1')(concat)
fc_2 = Dense(40,name='FC-2')(fc_1)
fc_3 = Dense(20,name='FC-3', activation='relu')(fc_2)

output = Dense(1, activation='relu',name='Output')(fc_3)
```

3. Define and compile the model as follows:

```
optimizer = keras.optimizers.Adam(lr=0.001)
model = keras.Model([item_input, visitor_input], output)
model.compile(optimizer=optimizer,loss= 'mse')
```

Let's see how this model looks visually:

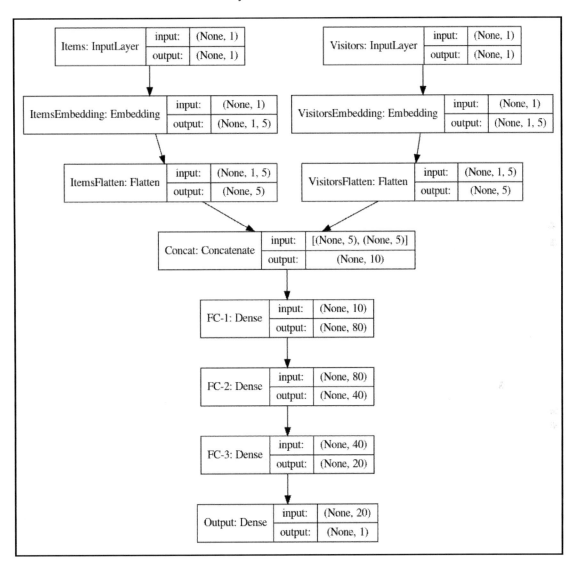

4. Train and evaluate the model:

```
model.fit([train.visitorid, train.itemid], train.event, epochs=50)
score = model.evaluate([test.visitorid, test.itemid], test.event)
print('mean squared error:', score)
```

We get a pretty good accuracy with a very low error rate:

```
275611/275611 [==============================] - 4s 14us/step
mean squared error: 0.05709125054560985
```

That's it. We encourage the reader to learn more about different recommendation system algorithms and try implementing them with Retailrocket or other publicly available datasets.

Summary

In this chapter, we learned about recommendation systems. We learned about different kinds of recommendation systems such as collaborative filtering, content-based filtering, and hybrid systems. We used the Retailrocket dataset to create two models of our recommendation system, one with matrix factorization, and one using a neural network. We saw that the neural network model gave pretty good accuracy.

In the next chapter, we'll learn about object detection at large scale with distributed TensorFlow.

Questions

Enhance your understanding by practicing the following questions:

1. What are the various algorithms for implementing vector space models for text-based content?
2. What are the various advanced algorithms for collaborative filtering?
3. How can we handle overfitting in collaborative filtering models?
4. Experiment with different algorithms apart from the ones implemented in this chapter.
5. Experiment with different values of latent factors for visitors and items.

Further reading

You'll learn more by reading the following materials:

- Tutorials and articles on recommender systems at the following link: `http://recommendation-systems.org`
- *Recommendation Systems Handbook 2nd ed.* by Francesco Ricci, Lior Rokach, and Bracha Shapira, 2015.
- *Recommendation Systems: The Textbook.* by Charu C. Aggarwal, 2016.

12
Object Detection at a Large Scale with TensorFlow

The recent breakthroughs in the field of **Artificial Intelligence** (**AI**) have brought deep learning to the forefront. Today, even more organizations are employing deep learning technologies for analyzing their data, which is often voluminous in nature. Hence, it's imperative that deep learning frameworks such as TensorFlow can be combined with big data platforms and pipelines.

The 2017 Facebook paper regarding training ImageNet in one hour using 256 GPUs spread over 32 servers (`https://research.fb.com/wp-content/uploads/2017/06/imagenet1kin1h5.pdf`) and a recent paper by Hong Kong Baptist University where they train ImageNet in four minutes using 2,048 GPUs (`https://arxiv.org/pdf/1807.11205.pdf`) prove that distributed AI can be a viable solution.

The main idea behind distributed AI is that the task can be divided into different processing clusters. A large number of frameworks have been proposed for distributed AI. We can use either distributed TensorFlow or TensorFlowOnSpark, two popular choices for distributed AI. Both have their own sets of pros and cons, as we'll learn in this chapter.

Applying computationally expensive deep learning applications at a large scale can be an enormous challenge. Using TensorFlowOnSpark, we can distribute these computationally expensive processes in the cluster, enabling us to perform computations at a larger scale.

In this chapter, we'll explore Yahoo's TensorFlowOnSpark framework for distributed deep learning on Spark clusters. Then, we'll apply TensorFlowOnSpark on a large scale dataset of images and train the network to detect objects. In this chapter, we'll cover the following topics:

- The need for distributed AI
- An introduction to the Apache Spark platform for big data

- TensorFlowOnSpark – a Python framework to run TensorFlow on Spark clusters
- Performing object detection using TensorFlowOnSpark and the Sparkdl API

For big data, Spark is the de facto choice, so we'll start with an introduction to Spark. Then, we'll explore the two popular choices: distributed TensorFlow, and TensorFlowOnSpark.

The code for this chapter can be found at `https://github.com/ PacktPublishing/TensorFlow-Machine-Learning-Projects/tree/ master/Chapter12`.

Introducing Apache Spark

If you have worked in big data, there is a high probability that you already know what Apache Spark is, and you can skip this section. But if you don't, don't worry—we'll go through the basics.

Spark is a powerful, fast, and scalable real-time data analytics engine for large scale data processing. It's an open source framework that was developed initially by the UC Berkeley AMPLab around the year 2009. Around 2013, AMPLab contributed Spark to the Apache Software Foundation, with Apache Spark Community releasing Spark 1.0 in 2014.

The community continues to make regular releases and brings new features into the project. At the time of writing this book, we have the Apache Spark 2.4.0 release and active community on GitHub. It's a real-time data analytics engine that allows you to distribute programs across a cluster of machines.

The beauty of Spark lays in the fact that it's **scalable**: it runs on top of a cluster manager, allowing you to use the scripts written in Python (Java or Scala, too) with minimal change. Spark is made up of many components. At the heart, we have the Spark core, which distributes the processing of data and the mapping and reducing of large datasets. There are several libraries that run on top of it. Here are some of the important components of the Spark API:

- **Resilient Distributed Dataset (RDD)**: RDD is the base element of the Spark API. It's a fault-tolerant collection of elements that can be operated on in parallel, which means that the elements in RDD can be accessed and operated upon by the workers in the cluster at the same time.

- **Transformations and actions**: On the Spark RDD, we can perform two types of operations, transformations and actions. Transformations take RDDs as their argument and return another RDD. Actions take an RDD as an argument and return the local results. All transformations in Spark are lazy, which means that the results are not computed right away. Instead, they are computed only when an action requires a result to be returned.

- **DataFrames**: These are very similar to pandas DataFrames. Like pandas, we can read from various file formats in the DataFrame (JSON, Parquet, Hive, and so on) and perform an operation on the entire DataFrame with single command functions. They are distributed across the cluster. Spark uses an engine called Catalyst to optimize their usage.

Spark uses a master/worker architecture. It has a master node/process and many worker nodes/processes. The driver, SparkContext, is the heart of Spark Application. It's the main entry point and the master of the Spark application. It sets up the internal services and establishes a connection with the Spark execution environment. The following diagram shows Spark's architecture:

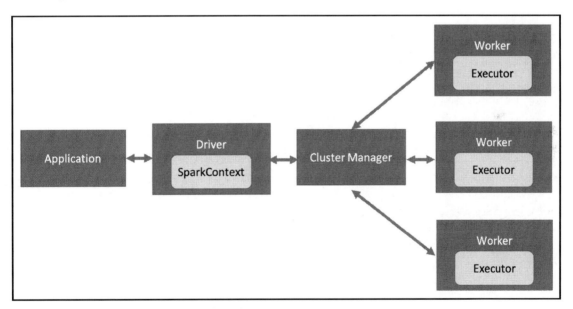

 So far, we have provided an introduction to Apache Spark. It's a big and vast subject, and we would recommend readers to refer to the Apache documentation for more information: `https://spark.apache.org/documentation.html`.

Understanding distributed TensorFlow

TensorFlow also supports distributed computing, allowing us to partition a graph and compute it on different processes. Distributed TensorFlow works like a client-server model, or to be more specific, a master-workers model. In TensorFlow, we first create a cluster of workers, with one being the master-worker. The master coordinates the distribution of tasks to different workers.

The first thing to do when you have to work with many machines (or processors) is to define their name and job type, that is, make a cluster of machines (or processors). Each machine in the cluster is assigned a unique address (for example, worker0.example.com:2222), and they have a specific job, such as type: master (parameter server), or worker. Later, the TensorFlow server assigns a specific task to each worker. To create a cluster, we first need to define cluster specification. This is a dictionary that maps worker processes and jobs. The following code creates a cluster with the job name work and two worker processes:

```
import tensorflow as tf
cluster = tf.train.ClusterSpec({
    "worker":["worker0.example.com:2222",
            "worker1.example.com:2222"]
})
```

Next, we can start the process by using the Server class and specifying the task and task index. The following code will start the worker job on worker1:

```
server = tf.train.Server(cluster, job_name = "worker", task_index = 1)
```

We'll need to define a Server class for each worker in the cluster. This will start all of the workers, making us ready to distribute. To place TensorFlow operations on a particular task, we'll use tf.device to specify which tasks run on a particular worker. Consider the following code, which distributes the task between two workers:

```
import tensorflow as tf

# define Clusters with two workers
cluster = tf.train.ClusterSpec({
    "worker": [
        "localhost:2222",
        "localhost:2223"
        ]})

# define Servers
worker0 = tf.train.Server(cluster, job_name="worker", task_index=0)
worker1 = tf.train.Server(cluster, job_name="worker", task_index=1)
```

```
with tf.device("/job:worker/task:1"):
    a = tf.constant(3.0, dtype=tf.float32)
    b = tf.constant(4.0)
    add_node = tf.add(a,b)

with tf.device("/job:worker/task:0"):
    mul_node = a * b

with tf.Session("grpc://localhost:2222") as sess:
    result = sess.run([add_node, mul_node])
    print(result)
```

The preceding code creates two workers on the same machine. In this case, the work is divided between the two workers via the tf.device function. The variables are created on the respective workers; TensorFlow inserts the appropriate data transfers between the jobs/workers.

This is done by creating a GrpcServer, which is created with the target, grpc://localhost:2222. This server knows how to talk to the tasks in the same job via GrpcChannels. In the following screenshot, you can see the output of the previous code:

```
[13.0, 12.0]
(tensorflow) AKs-Mac-mini:Desktop am$ python distributed.py
2018-11-11 08:56:11.697963: I tensorflow/core/platform/cpu_feature_guard.cc:141] Your CPU supports instructions that this TensorFlow binary was not compiled to use
: SSE4.1 SSE4.2 AVX
2018-11-11 08:56:11.701184: I tensorflow/core/distributed_runtime/rpc/grpc_channel.cc:215] Initialize GrpcChannelCache for job worker -> {0 -> localhost:2222, 1 ->
localhost:2223}
2018-11-11 08:56:11.702310: I tensorflow/core/distributed_runtime/rpc/grpc_server_lib.cc:375] Started server with target: grpc://localhost:2222
2018-11-11 08:56:11.705961: I tensorflow/core/distributed_runtime/rpc/grpc_channel.cc:215] Initialize GrpcChannelCache for job worker -> {0 -> localhost:2222, 1 ->
localhost:2223}
2018-11-11 08:56:11.707046: I tensorflow/core/distributed_runtime/rpc/grpc_server_lib.cc:375] Started server with target: grpc://localhost:2223
2018-11-11 08:56:11.813805: I tensorflow/core/distributed_runtime/master_session.cc:1165] Start master session 3dce8682f0656246 with config:
[7.0, 12.0]
```

The code for this chapter is located in the repository under the Chapter12/distributed.py directory.

This looked easy, right? But what if we want to extend this to our deep learning pipeline?

Deep learning through distributed TensorFlow

At the heart of any deep learning algorithm is the stochastic gradient descent optimizer. This is what makes the model learn and, at the same time, makes learning computationally expensive. Distributing the computation to different nodes on the cluster should reduce the training time. TensorFlow allows us to split the computational graph, describes the model to different nodes in the cluster, and finally merges the result.

This is achieved in TensorFlow with the help of master nodes, worker nodes, and parameter nodes. The actual computation is done by the worker nodes; the computed parameters are kept by the parameter nodes and shared with worker nodes. The master node is responsible for coordinating the workload among different worker nodes. There are two popular approaches that are employed for distributed computing:

- **Synchronous approach**: In this case, the mini-batches are divided among the workers. Each worker has a replica of the model and calculates the gradients separately for the mini-batches allocated to it. Later, the gradients are combined at the master and updates are applied to the parameters at the same time.
- **Asynchronous approach**: Here, the updates to the model parameters are applied asynchronously.

These two approaches are shown in the following diagram:

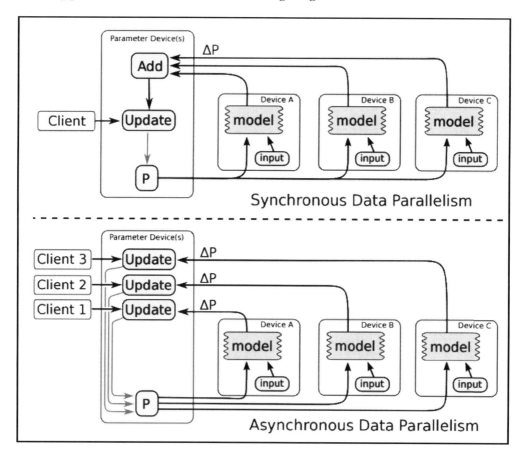

Now, let's look at how we can incorporate distributed TensorFlow in a deep learning pipeline. The following code is based upon the following Medium post, `https://medium.com/@ntenenz/distributed-tensorflow-2bf94f0205c3`:

1. Import the necessary modules. Here, we are importing only the necessary ones to demonstrate the changes needed to convert existing deep learning code to distributed TensorFlow code:

```
import sys
import tensorflow as tf
# Add other module libraries you may need
```

2. Define the cluster. We'll create it with one master at the address and two workers. In our case, the machine we want to make master has an IP address assigned to it, that is, `192.168.1.3`, and we specify port `2222`. You can modify them with the addresses of your machines:

```
cluster = tf.train.ClusterSpec(
        {'ps':['192.168.1.3:2222'],
         'worker': ['192.168.1.4:2222',
                    '192.168.1.5:2222',
                    '192.168.1.6:2222',
                    '192.168.1.7:2222']
})
```

3. The same code executes on each machine, so we need to parse the command-line arguments:

```
job = sys.argv[1]
task_idx = sys.argv[2]
```

4. Create the TensorFlow server for each worker and the master so that the nodes in the cluster can communicate:

```
server = tf.train.Server(cluster, job_name=job, task_index=
int(task_idx))
```

5. Ensure that the variables are allocated on the same worker device. TensorFlow's `tf.train.replica_device_setter()` function helps us to automatically assign devices to `Operation` objects as they are constructed. At the same time, we want the parameter server to wait until the server shuts down. This is achieved by using the `server.join()` method at the parameter server:

```
if job == 'ps':
    # Makes the parameter server wait
    # until the Server shuts down
```

```
        server.join()
else:
    # Executes only on worker machines
    with tf.device(tf.train.replica_device_setter(cluster=cluster,
worker_device='/job:worker/task:'+task_idx)):
        #build your model here like you are working on a single
machine

    with tf.Session(server.target):
        # Train the model
```

 You can access this script from GitHub or from the `Chapter12/tensorflow_distributed_dl.py` directory. Remember that the same script needs to be executed on each machine in the cluster, but with different command-line arguments.

The same script now needs to be executed on the parameter server and the four workers:

Use the following code to execute the script on the parameter server (192.168.1.3:2222):

```
python tensorflow_distributed_dl.py ps 0
```

1. Use the following code to execute the script on worker 0 (192.168.1.4:2222):

   ```
   python tensorflow_distributed_dl.py worker 0
   ```

2. Use the following code to execute the script on worker 1 (192.168.1.5:2222):

   ```
   python tensorflow_distributed_dl.py worker 1
   ```

3. Use the following code to execute the script on worker 2 (192.168.1.6:2222):

   ```
   python tensorflow_distributed_dl.py worker 2
   ```

4. Use the following code to execute the script on worker 3 (192.168.1.6:2222):

   ```
   python tensorflow_distributed_dl.py worker 3
   ```

The major disadvantage of distributed TensorFlow is that we need to specify the IP addresses and ports of all of the nodes in the cluster at startup. This puts a limitation on the scalability of distributed TensorFlow. In the next section, you will learn about TensorFlowOnSpark, an API built by Yahoo. It provides a simplified API to run deep learning models on the distributed Spark platform.

 To find out more about distributed TensorFlow, we suggest that you read the paper *TensorFlow: Large Scale Machine Learning on Heterogeneous Distributed Systems* by Google REsearch teamNIPS, 2012 (`http://download.tensorflow.org/paper/whitepaper2015.pdf`).

Learning about TensorFlowOnSpark

In the year 2016, Yahoo open sourced TensorFlowOnSpark, a Python framework for performing TensorFlow-based distributed deep learning on Spark clusters. Since then, it has undergone a lot of developmental changes and is one of the most active repositories regarding the distributed deep learning framework.

The **TensorFlowOnSpark (TFoS)** framework allows you to run distributed TensorFlow applications from within Spark programs. It runs on the existing Spark and Hadoop clusters. It can use existing Spark libraries such as SparkSQL or MLlib (the Spark machine learning library).

TFoS is automatic, so we do not need to define the nodes as PS nodes, nor do we need to upload the same code to all of the nodes in the cluster. By just performing a few modifications, we can run our existing TensorFlow code. It allows us to scale up the existing TensorFlow apps with minimal changes. It supports all of the existing TensorFlow functionality such as synchronous/asynchronous training, data parallelism, and TensorBoard. Basically, it's a PySpark wrapper for the TensorFlow code. It launches distributed TensorFlow clusters using Spark executors. To support TensorFlow data ingestion, it adds `feed_dict` and `queue_runner`, allowing direct HDFS access from TensorFlow.

Understanding the architecture of TensorFlowOnSpark

The following diagram depicts the architecture of TFoS. We can see that TFoS does not involve Spark drivers in tensor communication, giving the same scalability as standalone TensorFlow clusters:

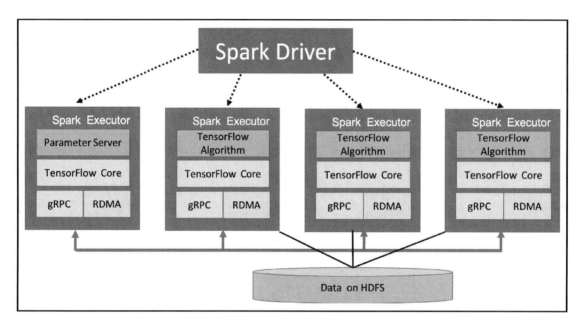

TFoS provides two input modes to take in data for training and inference:

- **Spark RDD**: Spark RDD data is fed to each Spark executor. The executor, in turn, feeds the data to the TensorFlow graph using `feed_dict`. However, in this mode, TensorFlow worker failures stay hidden from Spark.
- **TensorFlow QueueRunners**: Here, the TensorFlow worker runs in the foreground. TFoS takes advantage of the TensorFlow file readers and QueueRunners to read data directly from HDFS files. TensorFlow worker failures are retired as Spark Tasks, and it restores them from the checkpoint.

Deep delving inside the TFoS API

The use of TFoS can be divided into three basic steps:

1. Launch the TensorFlow cluster. We can launch the cluster using `TFCluster.run`:

   ```
   cluster = TFCluster.run(sc, map_fn, args, num_executors, num_ps,
   tensorboard, input_mode)
   ```

2. Feed the data into the TensorFlow app. The data is given for both training and inference. To train, we use the `train` method:

   ```
   cluster.train(dataRDD, num_epochs)
   ```

   We perform the inference with the help of `cluster.inference(dataRDD)`.

3. Finally, shut down the TensorFlow cluster with `cluster.shutdown()`.

We can modify any TensorFlow program to work with TFoS. In the following section, we'll look at how we can train a model to recognize handwritten digits using TFoS.

Handwritten digits using TFoS

In this section, we'll look at how to convert our TensorFlow code to run on TFoS. To do this, first, we need to build an EC2 cluster on Amazon AWS. One of the easy ways to do this is to use Flintrock, a CLI tool for launching Apache Spark clusters from your local machine.

The following are the prerequisites that you'll need to complete this section:

- Hadoop
- PySpark
- Flintrock
- Python
- TensorFlow
- TensorFlowOnSpark

Now, let's see how we can do this. We're using the MNIST dataset (`http://yann.lecun.com/exdb/mnist/`). The following code is taken from the TensorFlowOnSpark GitHub. The repository contains the links to documentation and more examples (`https://github.com/yahoo/TensorFlowOnSpark`):

1. Define the model architecture and training in the `main(argv, ctx)` function, where the `argv` parameter contains the arguments supplied at the command line, and `ctx` contains the node metadata such as `job` and `task_idx`. The `cnn_model_fn` model function is the CNN model that's defined as a function:

```
def main(args, ctx):
    # Load training and eval data
    mnist =
tf.contrib.learn.datasets.mnist.read_data_sets(args.data_dir)
        train_data = mnist.train.images # Returns np.array
        train_labels = np.asarray(mnist.train.labels, dtype=np.int32)
        eval_data = mnist.test.images # Returns np.array
        eval_labels = np.asarray(mnist.test.labels, dtype=np.int32)

        # Create the Estimator
        mnist_classifier =
tf.estimator.Estimator(model_fn=cnn_model_fn, model_dir=args.model)

        # Set up logging for predictions
        # Log the values in the "Softmax" tensor with label
"probabilities"

        tensors_to_log = {"probabilities": "softmax_tensor"}
        logging_hook = tf.train.LoggingTensorHook(
tensors=tensors_to_log, every_n_iter=50)

        # Train the model
        train_input_fn = tf.estimator.inputs.numpy_input_fn(
            x={"x": train_data}, y=train_labels,
            batch_size=args.batch_size, num_epochs=None,
```

```
        shuffle=True)

    eval_input_fn = tf.estimator.inputs.numpy_input_fn(
        x={"x": eval_data},
        y=eval_labels,
        num_epochs=1,
        shuffle=False)

    #Using tf.estimator.train_and_evaluate
    train_spec = tf.estimator.TrainSpec(
        input_fn=train_input_fn,
        max_steps=args.steps,
        hooks=[logging_hook])
    eval_spec = tf.estimator.EvalSpec(
        input_fn=eval_input_fn)
    tf.estimator.train_and_evaluate(
        mnist_classifier, train_spec, eval_spec)
```

2. In the `if __name__=="__main__"` block, add the following imports:

```
from pyspark.context import SparkContext
from pyspark.conf import SparkConf
from tensorflowonspark import TFCluster
import argparse
```

3. Launch the Spark Driver and initiate the TensorFlowOnSpark cluster:

```
sc = SparkContext(conf=SparkConf()
        .setAppName("mnist_spark"))
executors = sc._conf.get("spark.executor.instances")
num_executors = int(executors) if executors is not None else 1
```

4. Parse the arguments:

```
parser = argparse.ArgumentParser()
parser.add_argument("--batch_size",
        help="number of records per batch",
        type=int, default=100)
parser.add_argument("--cluster_size",
        help="number of nodes in the cluster",
        type=int, default=num_executors)
parser.add_argument("--data_dir",
        help="path to MNIST data",
        default="MNIST-data")
parser.add_argument("--model",
        help="path to save model/checkpoint",
        default="mnist_model")
```

```
parser.add_argument("--num_ps",
            help="number of PS nodes in cluster",
            type=int, default=1)
parser.add_argument("--steps",
            help="maximum number of steps",
            type=int, default=1000)
parser.add_argument("--tensorboard",
            help="launch tensorboard process",
            action="store_true")


args = parser.parse_args()
```

5. Use `TFCluster.run` to manage the cluster:

```
cluster = TFCluster.run(sc, main, args,
        args.cluster_size, args.num_ps,
        tensorboard=args.tensorboard,
        input_mode=TFCluster.InputMode.TENSORFLOW,
        log_dir=args.model, master_node='master')
```

6. Once the training is over, shut down the cluster:

```
cluster.shutdown()
```

The complete code is available in the GitHub repository in the `Chapter12/mnist_TFoS.py` directory.

To execute the code on the EC2 cluster, you'll need to submit it to Spark cluster using `spark-submit`:

```
${SPARK_HOME}/bin/spark-submit \
--master ${MASTER} \
--conf spark.cores.max=${TOTAL_CORES} \
--conf spark.task.cpus=${CORES_PER_WORKER} \
--conf spark.task.maxFailures=1 \
--conf spark.executorEnv.JAVA_HOME="$JAVA_HOME" \
${TFoS_HOME}/examples/mnist/estimator/mnist_TFoS.py \
--cluster_size ${SPARK_WORKER_INSTANCES} \
--model ${TFoS_HOME}/mnist_model
```

The model learned in 6.6 minutes on the EC2 cluster with two workers:

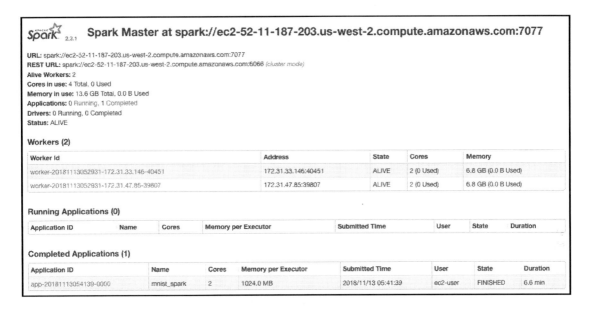

We can use TensorBoard to visualize the model architecture. Once we run the code successfully, the event file is created and it can be viewed on the TensorBoard.

When we visualize loss, we can see that the loss decreases as the network learns:

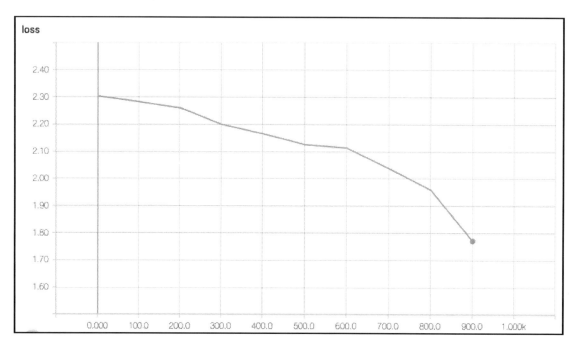

The model provides 75% accuracy on the test data set on only 1,000 steps, with a very basic CNN model. We can further optimize the result by using a better model architecture and tuning hyperparameters.

Object detection using TensorFlowOnSpark and Sparkdl

Apache Spark has a higher level API Sparkdl for scalable deep learning in Python. In this section, we'll use the Sparkdl API. In this section, you will learn how to build a model over the pre-trained Inception v3 model to detect cars and buses. This technique of using a pre-trained model is called **transfer learning**.

Transfer learning

Learning in humans is a continuous process—whatever we learn today is built upon the learning we have had in the past. For example, if you know how to drive a bicycle, you can extend the same knowledge to drive a motorcycle, or drive a car. The driving rule remains the same—the only thing that changes is the control panel and actuators. However, in deep learning, we often start afresh. Is it possible to use the knowledge the model has gained in solving a problem in one domain, to solve the problem in another related domain?

Yes, it's indeed possible, and it's called transfer learning. Though a lot of research is still going on in the field, a great deal of success has been achieved in applying transfer learning in the area of computer vision. This is due to the fact that for computer vision tasks **Convolutional Neural Networks** (**CNNs**) are preferred since they are good in extracting features from the image (features such as lines, circles, and squares, at lower layers, and higher abstract features such as ears and nose at the higher layers). Hence, the features extracted by convolutional layers while learning one type of image dataset can be reused in other similar domain images. This can help in reducing the training time.

In this section, we'll use Inception v3 (`https://arxiv.org/pdf/1512.00567v1.pdf`), a state-of-the-art CNN trained on the ImageNet dataset. ImageNet (`http://image-net.org/`) contains over 14 million labelled high-resolution hand-annotated images that have been classified into 22,000 categories. Inception v3 was trained on a subset of it consisting of about 1.3 million images with 1,000 categories.

In the transfer learning approach, you keep the feature extractor CNN layers but replace the classifier layers with a new classifier. This new classifier is then trained on the new images. Two approaches are generally followed: either we only train the new classifier or we fine-tune the entire network. In the first case, we extract the features from our new dataset, called **bottleneck features**, by feeding the new dataset into CNN layers. The extracted bottleneck features are then used to train the final classifier. In the second case, we train the entire network, the original CNN, along with the new classifier on the training dataset.

Understanding the Sparkdl interface

To access Spark functionality in the deep learning pipeline, we need to use a Spark driver program. From Spark 2.0.0, we have a single point entry using `SparkSession`. The simplest way to do this is by using `builder`:

```
SparkSession.builder().getOrCreate()
```

This can allow us to get an existing session or create a new session. At the time of instantiation, we can use the `.config()`, `.master()`, and `.appName()` methods to set configuration options, set the Spark master, and set the application name.

To read and manipulate images, Sparkdl provides the `ImageSchema` class. Out of its many methods, we'll be using the `readImages` method to read the directory of images. It returns a Spark DataFrame with a single column – `image`, of images.

We can add or remove column/rows from the Spark DataFrames using transformations. The example code in this section uses the `withColumn` transformation to add a column named `label` and assign label classes to our dataset. Just like with a pandas Dataframe, we can view the rows of the Spark DataFrame with the help of the `show()` method. The Spark DataFrames can also be split or combined together.

The Sparkdl API has methods to enable fast transfer learning. It provides the `DeepImageFeaturizer` class, which automatically peels the classifier layer from the pre-trained model and uses the features (bottleneck features) from the pre-trained CNN layers as an input to the new classifier.

One advantage of working with Sparkdl is that we can access all of the Spark APIs—even its machine learning API MLlib from the same `SparkSession` instance. Using MLlib, we can easily combine multiple algorithms into a single a pipeline. The Spark machine learning API MLlib also provides support for various classification and regression methods.

Building an object detection model

We'll now make some code by using TFoS and Sparkdl. The dataset consists of images of buses and cars that have been curated from a Google image search. The aim is to train a model so that it can differentiate between cars and buses. The following is a list of prerequisites that you will need for this code to work:

- PySpark
- Python
- TensorFlow
- TensorFlowOnSpark
- Pillow
- Keras
- TensorFrames

- Wrapt
- pandas
- FindSpark
- py4j

First, let's explore our dataset. Inception v3 was trained on ImageNet data with 1,000 categories. These included images of various vehicles as well. We have 49 images for buses and 41 images of cars. Here, you can see the sample images from the dataset:

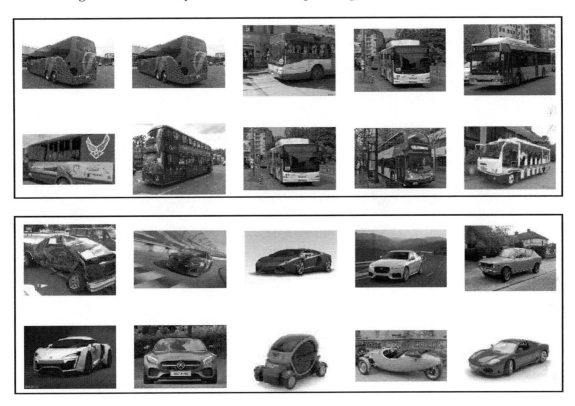

Now, let's build the code:

1. This time, we'll not be using `spark-submit`. Instead, we'll run the code like any standard Python code. Therefore, we'll define the location of spark driver and the Spark deep learning package in the code itself and create a Spark session using PySpark's `SparkSession` builder. One thing to keep in mind here is the memory allocated to the heap: Spark executor and Spark driver. The values should be based on your machine's specifications:

```
import findspark
findspark.init('/home/ubuntu/spark-2.4.0-bin-hadoop2.7')

import os
SUBMIT_ARGS = "--packages databricks:spark-deep-learning:1.3.0-
spark2.4-s_2.11 pyspark-shell"
os.environ["PYSPARK_SUBMIT_ARGS"] = SUBMIT_ARGS

from pyspark.sql import SparkSession
spark = SparkSession.builder \
    .appName("ImageClassification") \
    .config("spark.executor.memory", "70g") \
    .config("spark.driver.memory", "50g") \
    .config("spark.memory.offHeap.enabled",True) \
    .config("spark.memory.offHeap.size","16g") \
    .getOrCreate()
```

2. The images are loaded in the Spark DataFrame using PySpark's `ImageSchema` class. The bus and cars images are loaded in different Spark DataFrames:

```
import pyspark.sql.functions as f
import sparkdl as dl
from pyspark.ml.image import ImageSchema

dfbuses = ImageSchema.readImages('buses/').withColumn('label',
f.lit(0))
dfcars = ImageSchema.readImages('cars/').withColumn('label',
f.lit(1))
```

3. You can see the top five rows of the Spark DataFrame here:

```
dfbuses.show(5)
dfcars.show(5)
```

The output of the preceding code is as follows:

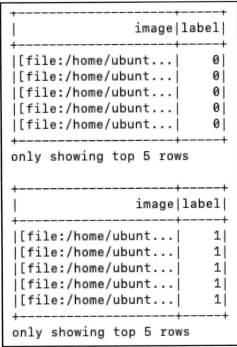

4. We split the dataset into the training-test datasets, with a ratio of 60% training and 40% test. Remember that these values are random and you can vary them accordingly:

```
trainDFbuses, testDFbuses = dfbuses.randomSplit([0.60,0.40], seed =
123)
trainDFcars, testDFcars = dfcars.randomSplit([0.60,0.40], seed =
122)
```

5. The training dataset for buses and cars is combined. The same is done for the test dataset:

```
trainDF = trainDFbuses.unionAll(trainDFcars)
testDF = testDFbuses.unionAll(testDFcars)
```

6. We use the Sparkdl API to get the pre-trained Inception v3 model and on top of the CNN layers of Inception, we add a logistic regressor. Now, we'll train the model on our dataset:

```
from pyspark.ml.classification import LogisticRegression
from pyspark.ml import Pipeline
vectorizer = dl.DeepImageFeaturizer(inputCol="image",
        outputCol="features",
        modelName="InceptionV3")

logreg = LogisticRegression(maxIter=30, labelCol="label")
pipeline = Pipeline(stages=[vectorizer, logreg])
pipeline_model = pipeline.fit(trainDF)
```

7. Let's see how the trained model fairs on the test dataset. Let's use a perfect confusion matrix:

```
predictDF = pipeline_model.transform(testDF)
predictDF.select('prediction', 'label').show(n =
testDF.toPandas().shape[0], truncate=False)
predictDF.crosstab('prediction', 'label').show()
```

The output of the preceding code is as follows:

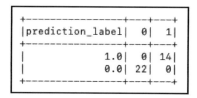

8. For the test dataset, the model gives 100% accuracy:

```
from pyspark.ml.evaluation import MulticlassClassificationEvaluator
scoring = predictDF.select("prediction", "label")
accuracy_score =
MulticlassClassificationEvaluator(metricName="accuracy")
rate = accuracy_score.evaluate(scoring)*100
print("accuracy: {}%" .format(round(rate,2)))
```

Our model is giving such a good performance because the Inception v3 model that we have used as the base model for transfer learning has already been trained on a lot of vehicle images. A word of caution, however—100% accuracy doesn't mean it's the best model, just that it does well on the present test images.

Developed by DataBricks, Sparkdl is part of the Deep Learning Pipelines. They provide high-level APIs for scalable deep learning in Python with Apache Spark. You can learn more about its features and how to use it here: https://github.com/databricks/spark-deep-learning.

Summary

Deep learning models provide better performance when the training dataset is large (big data). Training models for big data is computationally expensive. This problem can be handled using the divide and conquer approach: we divide the extensive computation part to many machines in a cluster, in other words, distributed AI.

One way of achieving this is by using Google's distributed TensorFlow, the API that helps in distributing the model training among different worker machines in the cluster. You need to specify the address of each worker machine and the parameter server. This makes the task of scaling the model difficult and cumbersome.

This problem can be solved by using the TensorFlowOnSpark API. By making minimal changes to the preexisting TensorFlow code, we can make it run on the cluster. The Spark framework handles the distribution among executor machines and the master, shielding the user from the details and giving better scalability.

In this chapter, the TensorFlowOnSpark API was used to train a model to recognize handwritten digits. This solved the problem of scalability, but we still had to process data so that it's available in the right format for training. Unless you are well-versed with the Spark infrastructure, especially Hadoop, this can be a difficult task.

To ease the difficulty, we can make use of another API, Sparkdl, which provides the complete deep learning pipeline on Spark for training using Spark DataFrames. Finally, this chapter used the Sparkdl API for object detection. A model was built over the pre-trained Inception v3 model to classify images of buses and cars.

In the next chapter, you will learn how to generate book scripts using RNN. Who knows—it may win the Booker Prize!

13
Generating Book Scripts Using LSTMs

Natural language generation (**NLG**), which is a sub-field of artificial intelligence, is a natural language processing task of generating human-readable text from various data inputs. It is an active area of research that has achieved great popularity in recent times.

The ability to generate natural language through machines can have wide variety of applications, including text autocomplete feature in phones, generating the summary of a document, and even generating new scripts for comedies. Google's Smart Reply also uses a technology that runs on similar lines to give reply suggestions when you're writing an email.

In this chapter, we will look at an NLG task of generating a book script from another Packt book that goes by the name of *Mastering PostgreSQL 10*. We took almost 100 pages of this book and removed any figures, tables, and SQL code. The data is fairly large and has enough words for a neural network to learn the nuances of the dataset.

We will learn how to generate book scripts using reinforcement neural networks by going through the following topics:

- Introduction to recurrent neural networks and LSTMs
- Description of the book script dataset
- Modeling using LSTMs and generating a new book script

Understanding recurrent neural networks

Recurrent neural networks (**RNNs**) have become extremely popular for any task that involves sequential data. The core idea behind RNNs is to exploit the sequential information present in the data. Under usual circumstances, every neural network assumes that all of the inputs are independent of each other. However, if we are trying to predict the next word in a sequence or the next point in a time series, it is imperative to use information based on the words used prior or on the historical points in the time series.

One way to perceive the concept of RNNs is that they have a memory that stores information about historical data in a sequence. In theory, RNNs can remember history for arbitrarily long sequences, however, in practice, they do a bad job in tasks where the historical information needs to be retained for more than a few steps back.

The typical structure of a RNN is as follows:

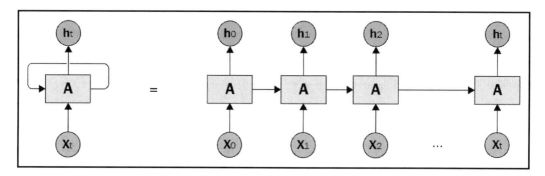

In the preceding diagram, Xt is the sequence value at different time steps. RNNs are called **recurrent** as they apply the exact same operation on every element of the sequence, with the output being dependent on the preceding steps. The connection between cells can be clearly observed. These connections help to transfer information from the previous step to the next.

As mentioned previously, RNNs are not great at capturing long-term dependencies. There are different variants of RNNs. A few of them are as follows:

- **Long Short-Term Memory (LSTMs)**
- **Gated recurrent units (GRU)**
- Peephole LSTMs

LSTMs are better at capturing long-term dependencies in comparison to vanilla RNNs. LSTMs have become very popular regarding tasks such as word/sentence prediction, image caption generation, and even forecasting time series data that requires long-term dependencies. The following are some of the advantages of using LSTMs:

- Great at modeling tasks involving long-term dependencies
- Weight sharing between different time steps greatly reduces the number of parameters in the model
- Suffers less from the vanishing and exploding gradient problem faced by traditional RNNs

The following are some of the disadvantages of using LSTMs:

- LSTMs are data-hungry. They usually require a lot of training data to produce any meaningful results.
- Slower to train than traditional neural networks.
- There are computationally more efficient RNN variants such as GRU that achieve a similar performance as LSTMs.

A discussion of other types of RNNs is outside the scope of this chapter. If you are interested, you can refer to the sequential modeling chapter in the *Deep Learning Book* (https://www.deeplearningbook.org/contents/rnn.html).

Pre-processing the data

As mentioned previously, the dataset used in this project is from a popular Packt book that goes by the name of *Mastering PostgreSQL 10*, and was written by Hans-Jürgen Schönig (`https://www.cybertec-postgresql.com`). We considered text from the first 100 pages of the book, excluding any figures, tables, and SQL code. The cleaned dataset is stored, alongside the code, in a text file. The dataset contains almost 44,000 words, which is just enough to train the model. The following are a few lines from the script:

"PostgreSQL Overview

PostgreSQL is one of the world's most advanced open source database systems, and it has many features that are widely used by developers and system administrators alike. Starting with PostgreSQL 10, many new features have been added to PostgreSQL, which contribute greatly to the success of this exceptional open source product. In this book, many of these cool features will be covered and discussed in great detail.

In this chapter, you will be introduced to PostgreSQL and the cool new features available in PostgreSQL 10.0 and beyond. All relevant new functionalities will be covered in detail. Given the sheer number of changes made to the code and given the size of the PostgreSQL project, this list of features is of course by far not complete, so I tried to focus on the most important aspects that are relevant to most people.

The features outlined in this chapter will be split into the following categories Database administration

SQL and developer related Backup, recovery, and replication Performance related topics

What is new in PostgreSQL 10.0.

PostgreSQL 10.0 was released in late 2017 and is the first version that follows the new numbering scheme introduced by the PostgreSQL community. From now on, the way major releases are done will change and therefore, the next major version after PostgreSQL

10.0 will not be 10.1 but PostgreSQL 11. Versions 10.1 and 10.2 are merely service releases and will only contain bug fixes."

For pre-processing the data so that we prepare it for a LSTM model, go through the following steps:

1. **Tokenize punctuation**: While pre-processing, we consider the splitting criteria as words using spaces. However, in this scenario, the neural network will have a hard time distinguishing words such as Hello and Hello!. Due to this limitation, it is required that you tokenize the punctuations in the dataset. For example, ! will be mapped to _Sym_Exclamation_. In the code, we implement a function named `define_tokens`. This is used to create a dictionary. Here, each piece of punctuation is considered a key, and its respective token is a value. In this example, we will create tokens for the following symbols:

   - Period (.)
   - Comma (,)
   - Quotation mark (")
   - Semicolon (;)
   - Exclamation mark (!)
   - Question mark (?)
   - Left parenthesis (( )
   - Right parenthesis ( ))
   - Dash (--)
   - Return (\n)

   Avoid using a token that will probably be a word in the dataset. For example, ? is replaced by _Sym_Question_, which is not a word in the dataset.

2. **Lower and split**: We must convert all of the uppercase letters in the text to lowercase so that the neural network will learn that the two words "Hello" and "hello" are actually the same. As the basic unit of input to neural networks will be words, the very next step would be to split the sentences in the text into words.

3. **Map creation**: Neural networks do not accept text as an input, and so we need to map these words to indexes/IDs. To do this, we must create two dictionaries, as follows:

   - `Vocab_to_int`: Mapping of each word in the text to its unique ID
   - `Int_to_vocab`: Inverse dictionary which maps IDs to their corresponding words

Defining the model

Before training the model using the pre-processed data, let's understand the model definition for this problem. In the code, we define a model class in the `model.py` file. The class contains four major components, and are as follows:

- **Input**: We define the TensorFlow placeholders in the model for both input (X) and target (Y).
- **Network definition**: There are four components of the network for this model. They are as follows:
  - **Initializing the LSTM cell**: To do this, we begin by stacking two layers of LSTMs together. We then set the size of the LSTM to be a `RNN_SIZE` parameter, which is as defined in the code. RNN is then initialized with a zero state.
  - **Word embeddings**: We encode the words in the text using word embeddings rather than one-hot encoding. This is done, mainly, to reduce the dimension of the training set, which can help neural networks learn faster. We generate embeddings from a uniform distribution for each word in the vocabulary and use TensorFlow's `embedding_lookup` function to get embedding sequences for the input data.
  - **Building LSTMs**: To obtain the final state of LSTMs, we use TensorFlow's `tf.nn.dynamic_rnn` function with the initial cell and the embeddings of the input data.
  - **Probability generation**: After obtaining the final state and output from LSTM, we pass it through a fully connected layer to generate logits for predictions. We convert those logits into probability estimates by using the `softmax` function. The code is as follows:
- **Sequence loss**: We must define the loss, which in this case is the Sequence loss. This is nothing but a weighted cross entropy for a sequence of logits. We equally weight the observations across batch and time.

- **Optimizer**: We will use the Adam optimizer, along with its default parameters. We will also clip the gradients to keep it within the range of -1 to 1. Gradient clipping is a common phenomenon in recurrent neural networks. When gradients are backpropagated in time, they can vanish if they are constantly multiplied by numbers less than 1, or can explode due to being multiplied by numbers greater than 1. Gradient clipping will help to resolve both of these problems by restricting the gradient to be between -1 and 1.

Training the model

Before understanding the implementation of the training loop, let's take a closer look at how we can generate batches of data.

It is common knowledge that batches are used in neural networks to speed up the training of the model and to consume less memory. Batches are samples of the original dataset that are used for a forward and backward pass to the network. The forward pass refers to the process of multiplying inputs with weights of different layers in the network and obtaining the final output. The backward pass, on the other hand, refers to the process of updating the weights in the neural network based on the loss obtained from the outputs of the forward pass.

In this model, since we are predicting the next set of words given a set of previous words to generate the TV script, the targets are basically the next few (depending on sequence length) words in the original training dataset. Let's consider an example where the training dataset contains the following line:

The quick brown fox jumps over the lazy dog

If the sequence length (the number of words to process together) used is 4, then the following are true:

- X is the sequence of every four words, for example, [*The quick brown fox, quick brown fox jumps* .....] .
- Y is the sequence of every four words, skipping the first word, for example, [*quick brown fox jumps, brown fox jumps over* ...].

Defining and training a text-generating model

1. Begin by loading the saved text data for pre-processing with the help of the `load_data` function:

```
def load_data():
"""
Loading Data
"""
input_file = os.path.join(TEXT_SAVE_DIR)
with open(input_file, "r") as f:
data = f.read()

return data
```

2. Implement `define_tokens`, as defined in the *Pre-processing the data* section of this chapter. This will help us create a dictionary of the key words and their corresponding tokens:

```
def define_tokens():
"""
Generate a dict to turn punctuation into a token. Note that Sym
before each text denotes Symbol
:return: Tokenize dictionary where the key is the punctuation and
the value is the token
"""
dict = {'.':'_Sym_Period_',
',':'_Sym_Comma_',
'"':'_Sym_Quote_',
';':'_Sym_Semicolon_',
'!':'_Sym_Exclamation_',
'?':'_Sym_Question_',
'(':'_Sym_Left_Parentheses_',
')':'_Sym_Right_Parentheses_',
'--':'_Sym_Dash_',
'\n':'_Sym_Return_',
}
return dict
```

The dictionary that we've created will be used to replace the punctuation marks in the dataset with their respective tokens and delimiters (space in this case) around them. For example, `Hello!` will be replaced with `Hello _Sym_Exclamation_`.

Note that there is a space between `Hello` and the token. This will help the LSTM model treat each punctuation marks as its own word.

3. Map the words to indexes/IDs with the help of the `Vocab_to_int` and `int_to_vocab` dictionaries. We are doing this since neural networks do not accept text as input:

```
def create_map(input_text):
    """
    Map words in vocab to int and vice versa for easy lookup
    :param input_text: TV Script data split into words
    :return: A tuple of dicts (vocab_to_int, int_to_vocab)
    """
    vocab = set(input_text)
    vocab_to_int = {c: i for i, c in enumerate(vocab)}
    int_to_vocab = dict(enumerate(vocab))
    return vocab_to_int, int_to_vocab
```

4. Combine all of the preceding steps to create a function that will pre-process the data that's available for us:

```
def preprocess_and_save_data():
    """
    Preprocessing the TV Scripts Dataset
    """
    generate_text_data_from_csv()
    text = load_data()
    text= text[14:] # Ignoring the STARTraw_text part of the dataset
    token_dict = define_tokens()
    for key, token in token_dict.items():
        text = text.replace(key, ' {} '.format(token))

    text = text.lower()
    text = text.split()

    vocab_to_int, int_to_vocab = create_map(text)
    int_text = [vocab_to_int[word] for word in text]
    pickle.dump((int_text, vocab_to_int, int_to_vocab, token_dict),
    open('processed_text.p', 'wb'))
```

We will then generate integer text for the mapping dictionaries and dump the pre-processed data and relevant dictionaries in a `pickle` file.

5. To define our model, we will create a model class in the `model.py` file. We will begin by defining the input:

```
with tf.variable_scope('Input'):
    self.X = tf.placeholder(tf.int32, [None, None], name='input')
    self.Y = tf.placeholder(tf.int32, [None, None], name='target')
    self.input_shape = tf.shape(self.X)
```

We must define variable type to be integers since the words in the dataset have been transformed to integers.

6. Define the network of our model by defining the LSTM cell, word embeddings, building LSTMs, and probability generation. To define the LSTM cell, stack two LSTM layers and set the size of the LSTM to be a `RNN_SIZE` parameter. Assign RNN the value 0:

```
lstm = tf.contrib.rnn.BasicLSTMCell(RNN_SIZE)
cell = tf.contrib.rnn.MultiRNNCell([lstm] * 2) # Defining two LSTM
layers for this case
self.initial_state = cell.zero_state(self.input_shape[0],
tf.float32)
self.initial_state = tf.identity(self.initial_state,
name="initial_state")
```

To reduce the dimension of the training set and increase the speed of the neural network, generate and look up embeddings using the following code:

```
embedding = tf.Variable(tf.random_uniform((self.vocab_size,
RNN_SIZE), -1, 1))
embed = tf.nn.embedding_lookup(embedding, self.X)
```

Run the `tf.nn.dynamic_rnn` function to find the final state of the LSTMs:

```
outputs, self.final_state = tf.nn.dynamic_rnn(cell, embed,
initial_state=None, dtype=tf.float32)
self.final_state = tf.identity(self.final_state,
name='final_state')
```

Convert the logits obtained from the final state of the LSTMs to a probability estimate by using the `softmax` function:

```
self.final_state = tf.identity(self.final_state,
name='final_state')
self.predictions = tf.contrib.layers.fully_connected(outputs,
self.vocab_size, activation_fn=None)
# Probabilities for generating words
probs = tf.nn.softmax(self.predictions, name='probs')
```

7. Define a weighted cross entropy or sequence loss for a sequence of logits, which further helps fine-tune our network:

```
def define_loss(self):
# Defining the sequence loss
with tf.variable_scope('Sequence_Loss'):
self.loss = seq2seq.sequence_loss(self.predictions, self.Y,
tf.ones([self.input_shape[0], self.input_shape[1]]))
```

8. Implement the Adam optimizer with the default parameters, and clip the gradients to keep it within the range of –1 to 1 to avoid diminishing the gradient when it is backpropagated in time:

```
def define_optimizer(self):
with tf.variable_scope("Optimizer"):
optimizer = tf.train.AdamOptimizer(LEARNING_RATE)
# Gradient Clipping
gradients = optimizer.compute_gradients(self.loss)
capped_gradients = [(tf.clip_by_value(grad, -1., 1.), var) for
grad, var in gradients]
self.train_op = optimizer.apply_gradients(capped_gradients)
```

9. Define the sequence length using the `generate_batch_data` function. This helps generate batches that are necessary for the neural network training:
   - The input for this function will be the text data that is encoded as integers, batch size, and sequence length.
   - The output will be a numpy array with the shape [# batches, 2, batch size, sequence length]. Each batch contains two parts, defined as follows:
     - X with shape [batch size, sequence length]
     - Y with shape [batch size, sequence length]:

```
def generate_batch_data(int_text):
"""
Generate batch data of x (inputs) and y (targets)
:param int_text: Text with the words replaced by their ids
:return: Batches as a Numpy array
"""
num_batches = len(int_text) // (BATCH_SIZE * SEQ_LENGTH)

x = np.array(int_text[:num_batches * (BATCH_SIZE * SEQ_LENGTH)])
y = np.array(int_text[1:num_batches * (BATCH_SIZE * SEQ_LENGTH) +
1])

x_batches = np.split(x.reshape(BATCH_SIZE, -1), num_batches, 1)
```

```
y_batches = np.split(y.reshape(BATCH_SIZE, -1), num_batches, 1)
batches = np.array(list(zip(x_batches, y_batches)))
return batches
```

10. Train the model using the following parameters:

  - Num Epochs = 500
  - Learning Rate = 0.001
  - Batch Size = 128
  - RNN Size = 128
  - Sequence Length= 32:

```
def train(model,int_text):
# Creating the checkpoint directory
 if not os.path.exists(CHECKPOINT_PATH_DIR):
 os.makedirs(CHECKPOINT_PATH_DIR)

batches = generate_batch_data(int_text)
with tf.Session() as sess:
 if RESTORE_TRAINING:
 saver = tf.train.Saver()
 ckpt = tf.train.get_checkpoint_state(CHECKPOINT_PATH_DIR)
 saver.restore(sess, ckpt.model_checkpoint_path)
 print('Model Loaded')
 start_epoch = int(str(ckpt.model_checkpoint_path).split('-')[-1])
 else:
 start_epoch = 0
 tf.global_variables_initializer().run()
 print('All variables initialized')

for epoch in range(start_epoch, NUM_EPOCHS):
 saver = tf.train.Saver()
 state = sess.run(model.initial_state, {model.X: batches[0][0]})

for batch, (x, y) in enumerate(batches):
 feed = {
 model.X: x,
 model.Y: y,
 model.initial_state: state}
 train_loss, state, _ = sess.run([model.loss, model.final_state,
model.train_op], feed)

if (epoch * len(batches) + batch) % 200 == 0:
 print('Epoch {:>3} Batch {:>4}/{} train_loss = {:.3f}'.format(
 epoch,
 batch,
```

```
len(batches),
train_loss))
# Save Checkpoint for restoring if required
saver.save(sess, CHECKPOINT_PATH_DIR + '/model.tfmodel',
global_step=epoch + 1)

# Save Model
saver.save(sess, SAVE_DIR)
print('Model Trained and Saved')
save_params((SEQ_LENGTH, SAVE_DIR))
```

Since the dataset wasn't very large, the code was executed on the CPU itself. We will save the output graph, since it will come in useful for generating book scripts.

Generating book scripts

Now that the model has been trained, we can have some fun with it. In this section, we will see how we can use the model to generate book scripts. Use the following parameters:

- Script Length = 200 words
- Starting word = `postgresql`

Follow these steps to generate the model:

1. Load the graph of the trained model.
2. Extract four tensors, as follows:
   - Input/input:0
   - Network/initial_state:0
   - Network/final_state:0
   - Network/probs:0

Extract the four tensors using the following code:

```
def extract_tensors(tf_graph):
    """
    Get input, initial state, final state, and probabilities tensor
    from the graph
    :param loaded_graph: TensorFlow graph loaded from file
    :return: Tuple
    (tensor_input,tensor_initial_state,tensor_final_state,
    tensor_probs)
    """
```

```
tensor_input = tf_graph.get_tensor_by_name("Input/input:0")
tensor_initial_state =
tf_graph.get_tensor_by_name("Network/initial_state:0")
tensor_final_state =
tf_graph.get_tensor_by_name("Network/final_state:0")
tensor_probs = tf_graph.get_tensor_by_name("Network/probs:0")
return tensor_input, tensor_initial_state, tensor_final_state,
tensor_probs
```

3. Define the starting word and obtain an initial state from the graph, which will be used later:

```
# Sentences generation setup
sentences = [first_word]
previous_state = sess.run(initial_state, {input_text:
np.array([[1]])})
```

4. Given a starting word and an initial state, proceed to iterate over a for loop to generate the next word for the script. In each iteration of the for loop, generate the probabilities from the model using the previously generated sequence as input and select the word with a maximum probability using the select_next_word function:

```
def select_next_word(probs, int_to_vocab):
    """
    Select the next work for the generated text
    :param probs: list of probabilities of all the words in vocab
    which can be selected as next word
    :param int_to_vocab: Dictionary of word ids as the keys and words
    as the values
    :return: predicted next word
    """
    index = np.argmax(probs)
    word = int_to_vocab[index]
    return word
```

5. Create a loop to generate the next word in the sequence:

```
for i in range(script_length):

    # Dynamic Input
    dynamic_input = [[vocab_to_int[word] for word in sentences[-
seq_length:]]]
    dynamic_seq_length = len(dynamic_input[0])

    # Get Prediction
    probabilities, previous_state = sess.run([probs, final_state],
```

```
{input_text: dynamic_input, initial_state: previous_state})
 probabilities= np.squeeze(probabilities)

pred_word = select_next_word(probabilities[dynamic_seq_length - 1],
int_to_vocab)
 sentences.append(pred_word)
```

6. Join all of the words in the sentences using a space delimiter and replace the punctuation tokens with the actual symbols. The obtained script is then saved in a text file for future reference:

```
# Scraping out tokens from the words
book_script = ' '.join(sentences)
for key, token in token_dict.items():
    book_script = book_script.replace(' ' + token.lower(), key)
book_script = book_script.replace('\n ', '\n')
book_script = book_script.replace('( ', '(')
```

7. Here is a sample of the text that was generated from the execution:

```
    postgresql comparatively).
one transaction is important, you can be used



create index is seen a transaction will be provided this index.
an index scan is a lot of a index
the index is time.
to be an index.
you can see is to make expensive,
the following variable is an index

the table will index have to a transaction isolation level
the transaction isolation level will use a transaction will use the
table of the following index creation.
the index is marked.
the following number is one of the following one lock is not a good
source of a transaction will use the following strategies
in this is not, it will be a table
in postgresql.
the postgresql cost errors is not possible to use a transaction.
postgresql 10. 0. 0. you can see that the data is not free into
more than a transaction ids, the same time. the first scan is an
example
the same number.
one index is not that the same time is needed in the following
strategies

in the same will copy block numbers.
```

```
the same data is a table if you can not be a certain way, you can
see, you will be able to create statistics.
postgresql will
```

Interestingly, the model learns to use a full stop after a sentence, leaves a blank line between paragraphs, and follows basic grammar. The model has learned all of this by itself, without us having to provide any guidance/rules. Despite the fact that the script is far from perfect, it's amazing how a machine is able to generate real-sounding sentences of a book. We can further fine-tune the hyperparameters of the model to generate more meaningful text.

Summary

In this chapter, we learned about how LSTMs can be used to generate book scripts.

We began by looking at the basics of RNNs and its popular variant, commonly known as LSTMs. We learned that RNNs are hugely successful in predicting datasets that involve sequences such as time series, next word prediction in natural language processing tasks, and so on. We also looked at the advantages and disadvantages of using LSTMs.

This chapter then helped us understand how to pre-process text data and prepare it so that we can feed it into LSTMs. We also looked at the model's structure for training. Next, we looked at how to train the neural networks by creating batches of data.

Finally, we understood how to generate book script using the TensorFlow model we trained. Although the script that was generated doesn't make complete sense, it was amazing to observe the neural network generate a book's sentences. We then saved the generated book script in a text file for future reference.

In the next chapter, we shall play Pac-Man using deep reinforcement learning.

Questions

The following are the questions:

1. Can you try to use from a different book to see how well the model is able to generate new text?
2. What happens to the generated text if you double the batch size and decrease the learning rate?
3. Can you train the model without gradient clipping and see if the result improves?

14
Playing Pacman Using Deep Reinforcement Learning

Reinforcement learning refers to a paradigm where an agent learns from environment feedback by virtue of receiving observations and rewards in return for actions it takes. The following diagram captures the feedback-based learning loop of reinforcement learning:

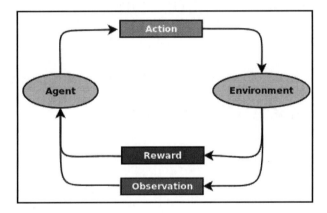

Although mostly applied to learn how to play games, reinforcement learning has also been successfully applied in digital advertising, stock trading, self-driving cars, and industrial robots.

In this chapter, we will use reinforcement learning to create a PacMan game and learn about reinforcement learning in the process. We will cover the following topics:

- Reinforcement learning
- Reinforcement learning versus supervised and unsupervised learning
- Components of reinforcement learning
- OpenAI Gym

- A PacMan game in OpenAI Gym
- DQN for deep reinforcement learning:
    - Q Learning
    - Deep Q Network
- Applying DQN to a PacMan game

Let's get started!

Reinforcement learning

Reinforcement learning is a type of machine learning in which an agent learns from the environment. The agent takes actions and, as a result of the actions, the environment returns observations and rewards. From the observation and rewards, the agent learns the policy and takes further actions, thus continuing the sequence of actions, observations, and rewards. In the long run, the agent has to learn the policy such that, when it takes actions based on the policy, it does so in such a way as to maximize the long-term rewards.

Reinforcement learning versus supervised and unsupervised learning

Machine learning solutions can be of three major types: supervised learning, unsupervised learning, and reinforcement learning. So how is reinforcement learning different from the other two types?

1. **Supervised learning**: In supervised learning, the agent learns the model from a training dataset consisting of features and labels. The two most common types of supervised learning problems are regression and classification. Regression refers to predicting the future values based on the model, and classification refers to predicting the categories of the input values.

2. **Unsupervised learning**: In unsupervised learning, the agent learns the model from a training dataset consisting of only features. The two most common types of unsupervised learning problems are dimensionality reduction and clustering. Dimensionality reduction refers to reducing the number of features or dimensions in a dataset without altering its natural distribution. Clustering refers to dividing the input data into multiple groups, thus producing clusters or segments.

3. **Reinforcement learning**: In reinforcement learning, the agent starts with an initial model and then continuously learns the model based on feedback from the environment. An RL agent updates the model by applying supervised or unsupervised learning techniques on a sequence of actions, observations, and rewards. The agent only learns from a reward signal, not from a loss function as in other machine learning approaches. The agent receives the feedback after it has already taken the action, while, in other ML approaches, the feedback is provided at the time of training in terms of loss or error. The data is not i.i.d. (independent and identically distributed) because it depends on previous actions taken, while in other ML approaches data is i.i.d.

Components of Reinforcement Learning

In any RL formalization, we talk in terms of a **state space** and an **action space**. Action space is a set of finite numbers of actions that can be taken by the agent, represented by A. State space is a finite set of states that the environment can be in, represented by S.

The goal of the agent is to learn a policy, denoted by π. A **policy** can be **deterministic** or **stochastic**. A policy basically represents the model, using which the agent to select the best action to take. Thus, the policy maps the rewards and observations received from the environment to actions.

When an agent follows a policy, it results in a sequence of state, action, reward, state, and so on. This sequence is known as a **trajectory** or an **episode**.

An important component of reinforcement learning formalizations is the **return**. The return is the estimate of the total long-term reward. Generally, the return can be represented by the following formula:

$$G = \sum_{t=0}^{T} \gamma^t r_t$$

Here γ is a discount factor with values between (0,1), and r_t is the reward at time step t. The discount factor represents how much importance should be given to the reward at later time steps. If γ is 0 then only the rewards from the next action are considered, and if it is 1 then the future rewards have the same weight as the rewards from the next action.

However, since it is difficult to compute the value of the return, hence it is estimated with **state-value** or **action-value** functions. We shall talk about action-value functions further in the q-learning section in this chapter.

For simulating our agent which will play the PacMan game, we shall be using the OpenAI Gym. Let's learn about OpenAI Gym now.

 You can follow along with the code in the Jupyter Notebook `ch-14_Reinforcement_Learning` in the code bundle of this book.

OpenAI Gym

OpenAI Gym is a Python-based toolkit for the development of reinforcement learning algorithms. It provides more than 700 open source contributed environments at the time of writing this book. Custom environments for OpenAI can also be created. OpenAI Gym provides a unified interface for working with reinforcement learning environments and takes care of running the simulation, while the user of OpenAI can focus on designing and implementing the reinforcement learning algorithms.

 The original research paper on OpenAI Gym is available at the following link: `http://arxiv.org/abs/1606.01540`.

Let's take a look at the following steps to learn how to install and explore OpenAI Gym:

1. Install OpenAI Gym using the following command:

   ```
   pip3 install gym
   ```

    If the preceding command does not work, then refer to the following link for further help with installation: `https://github.com/openai/gym#installation`.

2. Print the number of available environments in the OpenAI Gym with the following code:

   ```
   all_env = list(gym.envs.registry.all())
   print('Total Environments in Gym version {} : {}'
       .format(gym.__version__,len(all_env)))
   ```

The preceding code generates the following output:

```
Total Environments in Gym version 0.10.5 : 797
```

3. Print the list of all environments, as shown in the following code:

```
for e in list(all_env):
    print(e)
```

The partial list from the output is as follows:

```
EnvSpec(Copy-v0) EnvSpec(RepeatCopy-v0) EnvSpec(ReversedAddition-
v0) EnvSpec(ReversedAddition3-v0) EnvSpec(DuplicatedInput-v0)
EnvSpec(Reverse-v0) EnvSpec(CartPole-v0) EnvSpec(CartPole-v1)
EnvSpec(MountainCar-v0) EnvSpec(MountainCarContinuous-v0)
EnvSpec(Pendulum-v0)
```

Each environment, represented by the `env` object, has a standardized interface:

- An `env` object can be created with the `env.make(<game-id-string>)` function by passing the `id` string.
- Each `env` object contains the following main functions:
  - The `step()` function takes an action object as an argument and returns four objects:
    - `observation`: An object implemented by the environment, representing the observation of the environment.
    - `reward`: A signed float value indicating the gain (or loss) from the previous action.
    - `done`: A Boolean value representing whether or not the scenario is finished.
    - `info`: A Python dictionary object representing the diagnostic information.
  - The `render()` function creates a visual representation of the environment.
  - The `reset()` function resets the environment to the original state.
- Each `env` object comes with well-defined actions and observations, represented by `action_space` and `observation_space`.

Creating a Pacman game in OpenAI Gym

In this chapter, we will use the PacMan game as an example, known as **MsPacman-v0**. Let's explore this game a bit further:

1. Create the `env` object with the standard `make` function, as shown in the following command:

   ```
   env=gym.make('MsPacman-v0')
   ```

2. Let's print the action space of the game with the following code:

   ```
   print(env.action_space)
   ```

   The preceding code generates the following output:

   ```
   Discrete(9)
   ```

   `Discrete 9` refers to the nine actions, such as up, down, left, and right.

3. We can now see the observation space, as shown in the following example:

   ```
   print(env.observation_space)
   ```

   The preceding code generates the following output:

   ```
   Box(210, 160, 3)
   ```

   Thus, the observation space has three color channels and is of size 210 x 160. The observation space gets rendered as in the following screenshot:

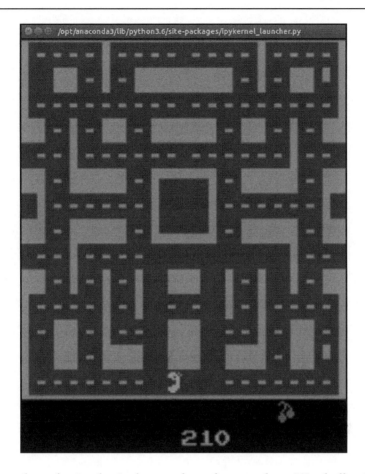

4. The number of episodes is the number of game plays. We shall set it to one, for now, indicating that we just want to play the game once. Since every episode is stochastic, in actual production runs you will run over several episodes and calculate the average values of the rewards. Let's run the game for one episode while randomly selecting one of the actions during the gameplay with the following code:

```
import time

frame_time = 1.0 / 15 # seconds
n_episodes = 1

for i_episode in range(n_episodes):
    t=0
    score=0
    then = 0
```

```
        done = False
        env.reset()
        while not done:
            now = time.time()
            if frame_time < now - then:
                action = env.action_space.sample()
                observation, reward, done, info = env.step(action)
                score += reward
                env.render()
                then = now
                t=t+1
        print('Episode {} finished at t {} with score
{}'.format(i_episode,
t,score))
```

We then get the following output:

```
Episode 0 finished at t 551 with score 100.0
```

5. Now, let's run, the game 500 times and see what maximum, minimum, and average scores we get. This is demonstrated in the following example:

```
import time
import numpy as np

frame_time = 1.0 / 15 # seconds
n_episodes = 500

scores = []
for i_episode in range(n_episodes):
    t=0
    score=0
    then = 0
    done = False
    env.reset()
    while not done:
        now = time.time()
        if frame_time < now - then:
            action = env.action_space.sample()
            observation, reward, done, info = env.step(action)
            score += reward
            env.render()
            then = now
            t=t+1
    scores.append(score)
    #print("Episode {} finished at t {} with score
{}".format(i_episode,t,score))
print('Average score {}, max {}, min {}'.format(np.mean(scores),
```

```
                                        np.max(scores),
                                        np.min(scores)
                                        ))
```

The preceding code generates the following output:

Average 219.46, max 1070.0, min 70.0

Randomly picking an action and applying it is probably not the best strategy. There are many algorithms for finding solutions to make the agent learn from playing the game and apply the best actions. In this chapter, we shall apply Deep Q Network for learning from the game. The reader is encouraged to explore other algorithms.

DQN for deep reinforcement learning

The **Deep Q Networks** (**DQN**) are based on Q-learning. In this section, we will explain both of them before we implement the DQN in Keras to play the PacMan game.

- **Q-learning**: In Q-learning, the agent learns the action-value function, also known as the Q-function. The Q function denoted with $q(s,a)$ is used to estimate the long-term value of taking an action a when the agent is in state s. The Q function maps the state-action pairs to the estimates of long-term values, as shown in the following equation:

$$Q : S \times A \to \mathbb{R}$$

Thus, under a policy, the q-value function can be written as follows:

$$q_\pi(s, a) = E_\pi[G_t | s_t, a_t]$$

The q function can be recursively written as follows:

$$q_\pi(s, a) = E_\pi[R_{t+1} + \gamma q_\pi(s_{t+1}, a_{t+1}) | s_t, a_t]$$

The expectation can be expanded as follows:

$$q_\pi(s, a) = R(s, a) + \gamma \sum_{s' \in S} p(s' | s, a) \sum_{a' \in A} \pi(a' | s') q_\pi(s', a')$$

An optimal q function is the one that returns the maximum value, and an optimal policy is the one that applies the optimal q function. The optimal q function can be written as follows:

$$q_* (s, a) = R(s, a) + \gamma \sum_{s' \in S} p (s' | s, a) \, max_{a'} \, [q_* (s', a')]$$

This equation represents the **Bellman Optimality Equation**. Since directly solving this equation is difficult, Q-learning is one of the methods used to approximate the value of this function.

Thus, in Q-learning, a model is built that can predict this value, given the state and action. Generally, this model is in the form of a table that contains all the possible combinations of state s and action a, and the expected value from that combination. However, for situations with a large number of state-action combinations, this table becomes cumbersome to maintain. The DQN helps to overcome this shortcoming of table-based Q-learning.

- The DQN: In DQN, instead of tables, a neural network model is built that learns from the state-action-reward-next state tuples and predicts the approximate q-value based on the state and action provided. Since the sequence of states-action-rewards is correlated in time, deep learning faces the challenge, since, in deep learning, the input samples need to be i.i.d. Thus, in DQN algorithms, **experience replay** is used to alleviate that. In the experience replay, the previous actions and their results are sampled randomly to train the network.

The basic Deep Q-learning algorithm is as follows:

1. Start the play in its initial state
2. Select to explore or exploit
3. If you selected exploit, then predict the action with the neural network and take the predicted action
4. If you selected explore, then randomly select an action
5. Record the previous state, action, rewards, and next state in the experience buffer
6. Update the `q_values` using `bellman` function
7. Train the neural network with `states`, `actions`, and `q_values`
8. Repeat from *step 2*

To improve the performance, and implement experience replay, one of the things you can do is to randomly select the training data in *step 7*.

Applying DQN to a game

So far, we have randomly picked an action and applied it to the game. Now, let's apply DQN for selecting actions for playing the PacMan game.

1. We define the q_nn policy function as follows:

```
def policy_q_nn(obs, env):
    # Exploration strategy - Select a random action
    if np.random.random() < explore_rate:
        action = env.action_space.sample()
    # Exploitation strategy - Select the action with the highest q
    else:
        action = np.argmax(q_nn.predict(np.array([obs])))
    return action
```

2. Next, we modify the episode function to incorporate calculation of q_values and train the neural network on the sampled experience buffer. This is shown in the following code:

```
def episode(env, policy, r_max=0, t_max=0):

    # create the empty list to contain game memory
    #memory = deque(maxlen=1000)
    # observe initial state
    obs = env.reset()
    state_prev = obs
    #state_prev = np.ravel(obs) # replaced with keras reshape[-1]
    # initialize the variables
    episode_reward = 0
    done = False
    t = 0
    while not done:
        action = policy(state_prev, env)
        obs, reward, done, info = env.step(action)
        state_next = obs
        #state_next = np.ravel(obs) # replaced with keras
reshape[-1]
        # add the state_prev, action, reward, state_new, done to
memory
        memory.append([state_prev,action,reward,state_next,done])
        # Generate and update the q_values with
        # maximum future rewards using bellman function:
        states = np.array([x[0] for x in memory])
        states_next = np.array([np.zeros(n_shape) if x[4] else x[3]
for x in memory])
        q_values = q_nn.predict(states)
```

```
        q_values_next = q_nn.predict(states_next)
        for i in range(len(memory)):
            state_prev,action,reward,state_next,done = memory[i]
            if done:
                q_values[i,action] = reward
            else:
                best_q = np.amax(q_values_next[i])
                bellman_q = reward + discount_rate * best_q
                q_values[i,action] = bellman_q
        # train the q_nn with states and q_values, same as updating
the q_table
        q_nn.fit(states,q_values,epochs=1,batch_size=50,verbose=0)
        state_prev = state_next
        episode_reward += reward
        if r_max > 0 and episode_reward > r_max:
            break
        t+=1
        if t_max > 0 and t == t_max:
            break
    return episode_reward
```

3. Define an `experiment` function that will run for a specific number of episodes; each episode runs until the game is lost, namely when `done` is `True`. We use `rewards_max` to indicate when to break out of the loop as we do not wish to run the experiment forever, as shown in the following code:

```
# experiment collect observations and rewards for each episode
def experiment(env, policy, n_episodes,r_max=0, t_max=0):
    rewards=np.empty(shape=[n_episodes])
    for i in range(n_episodes):
        val = episode(env, policy, r_max, t_max)
        #print('episode:{}, reward {}'.format(i,val))
        rewards[i]=val
    print('Policy:{}, Min reward:{}, Max reward:{}, Average
reward:{}'
        .format(policy.__name__,
            np.min(rewards),
            np.max(rewards),
            np.mean(rewards)))
```

4. Create a simple MLP network with the following code:

```
from collections import deque
from tensorflow.keras.models import Sequential
from tensorflow.keras.layers import Dense, Flatten

# build the Q-Network
model = Sequential()
```

```
model.add(Flatten(input_shape = n_shape))
model.add(Dense(512, activation='relu',name='hidden1'))
model.add(Dense(9, activation='softmax', name='output'))
model.compile(loss='categorical_crossentropy',optimizer='adam')
model.summary()
q_nn = model
```

The preceding code generates the following output:

Layer (type)	Output Shape	Param #
flatten_3 (Flatten)	(None, 100800)	0
hidden1 (Dense)	(None, 8)	806408
output (Dense)	(None, 9)	81

```
Total params: 806,489
Trainable params: 806,489
Non-trainable params: 0
```

5. Create an empty list to contain the game memory and define other hyperparameters and run the experiment for one episode, as shown in the following example:

```
# Hyperparameters

discount_rate = 0.9
explore_rate = 0.2
n_episodes = 1

# create the empty list to contain game memory
memory = deque(maxlen=1000)

experiment(env, policy_q_nn, n_episodes)
```

The result we get is as follows:

Policy:policy_q_nn, Min reward:490.0, Max reward:490.0, Average reward:490.0

That is definitely an improvement in our case, but, in your case, it might be different. In this case, our game has only learned from a limited memory and only from game replay in one episode.

6. Now, run it for 100 episodes, as shown in the following example:

```
# Hyperparameters

discount_rate = 0.9
explore_rate = 0.2
n_episodes = 100

# create the empty list to contain game memory
memory = deque(maxlen=1000)

experiment(env, policy_q_nn, n_episodes)
```

We get the following results:

```
Policy:policy_q_nn, Min reward:70.0, Max reward:580.0, Average
reward:270.5
```

Thus we see that, on average, the results did not improve, although we reached a high max reward. Tuning the network architecture, features, and hyperparameters might produce better results. We would encourage you to modify the code. As an example, instead of MLP, you can use the simple one-layer convolutional network, as follows:

```
from collections import deque
from tensorflow.keras.models import Sequential
from tensorflow.keras.layers import Dense, Flatten
from tensorflow.keras.layers import Conv2D, MaxPooling2D

# build the CNN Q-Network
model = Sequential()
model.add(Conv2D(16, kernel_size=(5, 5),
                 strides=(1, 1),
                 activation='relu',
                 input_shape=n_shape))
model.add(MaxPooling2D(pool_size=(2, 2), strides=(2, 2)))
model.add(Flatten())
model.add(Dense(512, activation='relu',name='hidden1'))
model.add(Dense(9, activation='softmax', name='output'))
model.compile(loss='categorical_crossentropy',optimizer='adam')
model.summary()
q_nn = model
```

The preceding code displays the network summary as follows:

Layer (type)	Output Shape	Param #
conv2d_4 (Conv2D)	(None, 206, 156, 16)	1216
max_pooling2d_4 (MaxPooling2	(None, 103, 78, 16)	0
flatten_8 (Flatten)	(None, 128544)	0
hidden1 (Dense)	(None, 512)	65815040
output (Dense)	(None, 9)	4617

```
Total params: 65,820,873
Trainable params: 65,820,873
Non-trainable params: 0
```

Summary

In this chapter, we learned what reinforcement learning is. Reinforcement learning is an advanced technique that you will find is often used to solve complex problems. We learned about OpenAI Gym, a framework that provides an environment for simulating many popular games in order to implement and practice reinforcement learning algorithms. We touched on deep reinforcement learning concepts, and we encourage you to explore books (mentioned in the further reading) specifically written about reinforcement learning to learn deeply about the theories and concepts.

We learned how to play the PacMan game in OpenAI Gym. We implemented DQN and used it to learn to play the PacMan game. We only used an MLP network to keep things simple, but, for complex examples, you may end up using complex CNN, RNN, or Sequence-to-Sequence models.

In the next chapter, we shall learn about future opportunities in the fields of machine learning and TensorFlow.

Further Reading

- Deep Reinforcement Learning Hands-On by Maxim Lapan, Packt Publications
- Reinforcement Learning: An Introduction by Richard S. Sutton and Andrew G. Barto
- Statistical Reinforcement Learning: Modern Machine Learning Approaches by Masashi Sugiyama
- Algorithms for reinforcement learning by Csaba Szepesvari

15
What is Next?

Congratulations on making it this far. So far, have learned to implement a variety of cutting-edge AI algorithms in TensorFlow and built cool projects on the side. Specifically, we have built projects on reinforcement learning, Bayesian neural networks, capsule networks, and **Generative Adversarial Networks (GANs)**, among others. We have also learned about several modules of TensorFlow, including TensorFlow.js, TensorFlow Lite, and TensorFlow Probability, among others. This surely deserves a pat on the back and a well-earned rest.

Before we go out to play, there are a few more things that we should consider reading about before we are prime-time ready to deploy these cutting edge techniques in production. As we will realize in this chapter, there is more to deploying a machine learning model in production than just implementing the latest research paper in AI. To understand what I mean by this, let's read through the following topics:

- TensorFlow utilities to deploy models in production
- General rules for building AI applications
- Limitations of deep learning
- Applications of AI across different industries
- Ethical Considerations in AI

Implementing TensorFlow in production

When it comes to software engineering, we see several best practices, like version control through GitHub, reusable libraries, continuous integration, and others, which have made developers more productive. Machine learning is a new field where there is a definite need for some tooling to make model deployment simple and improve a data scientist's productivity. In that respect, TensorFlow has released a host of tools recently.

Understanding TensorFlow Hub

Software repositories have a real benefit in the field of software engineering as they enhance the reusability of code. This not only helps to improve developer productivity, but also helps in sharing expertise among different developers. Also, because developers now want to share their code, they develop their code in a manner that is more clean and modular so that it can benefit the entire community.

Google introduced TensorFlow Hub to achieve the similar purpose of reusability in machine learning. It is designed so that you can create, share, and reuse the components of machine learning models. Reusability in machine learning is even more important than software engineering because we are not only using the algorithm/architecture and the expertise—we are also using an enormous amount of compute power that went into training the model and all of the data as well.

 TF hub comprises of several machine learning models which are trained using state-of-the-art algorithms and huge amounts of data by experts at Google. Each of this trained model is termed as **Module** in TF hub. A module and can be shared on the **TensorFlow Hub**, where they can then be imported by anyone into their code. The following diagram depicts the flow of what how a trained TensorFlow model can be used by other applications/models:

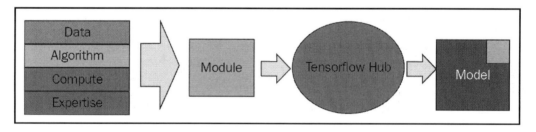

Modules in **TensorFlow Hub** contain both the model's architecture or the TensorFlow graph and the weights of the trained **Model**. **Modules** have the following properties:

- **Composable:** Composable means that we can use modules as building blocks and add stuff on top of them.
- **Reusable:** Reusable means that modules have a common signature so that we can swap one with another. This is mainly useful when we are iterating over models to get the best accuracy on our dataset.
- **Retrainable:** Modules come with pre-trained weights, but they are flexible enough to be retrained on the new dataset. This means that we can back propagate through the model to generate new set of weights.

Let's understand this with the help of an example. Say we have a dataset of different Toyota cars such as the Camry, the Corolla, and other models. If we don't have a lot of images of each category, it won't be prudent to train the entire model from scratch.

Instead, what we can do is take a general purpose model that has been trained on a giant set of images from TensorFlow Hub and take the reusable part of the model, such as its architecture and pre-trained weights. On top of the pre-trained model, we can add a classifier that classifies the images that are present in our dataset appropriately. This procedure is sometimes also referred to as transfer learning. This is illustrated in the following diagram:

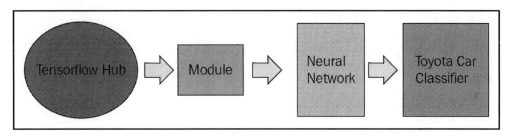

 If you want to learn more about Transfer Learning, please refer to the Stanford's course notes (http://cs231n.github.io/transfer-learning/)

You can visit TensorFlow Hub (https://www.tensorflow.org/hub/) to get state-of-the-art, research-oriented image models that you can directly import into your custom models. Let's say we are using NasNet (https://tfhub.dev/google/imagenet/nasnet_large/feature_vector/1), which is an image module that's trained through architecture search. Here we are going to use the URL for the NasNet module in our code to import the module, as follows:

```
module =
hub.Module("https://tfhub.dev/google/imagenet/nasnet_large/feature_vect
        or/1")
features = module(toyota_images)
logits = tf.layers.dense(features, NUM_CLASSES)
probabilities = tf.nn.softmax(logits)
```

We added a dense layer with softmax non-linearity on top of the module. We train the weights of the dense layer through backpropagation to classify the Toyota car images.

Note that we don't need to download the module, nor do we need to instantiate it.

TensorFlow takes care of all of those low-level details, which makes the module reusable in a true sense. Another great thing about using this module is that you get thousands of hours of compute required to train NasNet for free.

Let's say we do have a large dataset. In that case, we can train the reusable part of the module as follows:

```
module =
hub.Module("https://tfhub.dev/google/imagenet/nasnet_large/feature_vector/1"
,trainable = True, tags {"train"})features = module(toyota_images)
logits = tf.layers.dense(features, NUM_CLASSES)
probabilities = tf.nn.softmax(logits)
```

TensorFlow Hub has pre-trained models for image classification, word embeddings, sentence embeddings, and other applications. Let's consider our movie sentiment detection project from Chapter 3, *Sentiment Analysis in your browser using Tensorflow.js* in this book. We could have used a pre-trained embedding for each piece of work in the dataset from TensorFlow Hub. This availability of pre-trained modules across domains will potentially help many developers build new applications without having to worry about the math behind the models.

You can find more details about this on the official web page of TensorFlow Hub (https://www.tensorflow.org/hub/).

TensorFlow Serving

TensorFlow Serving is a highly flexible serving system for deploying machine learning models in production. Before we go into the details, first let's try to understand what serving is by taking a look at its architecture:

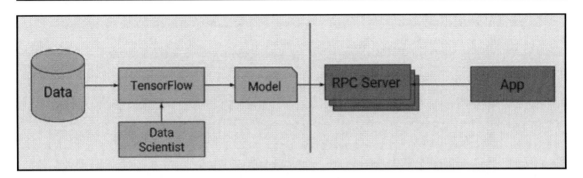

We have some **Data** and we use that to train a machine learning **Model**. Once the **Model** is trained, it needs to be deployed onto a web or mobile **App** to serve the end users. One way to do that is through a **remote procedure call** (**RPC**) server (`https://www.ibm.com/support/knowledgecenter/en/ssw_aix_72/com.ibm.aix.progcomc/ch8_rpc.htm`). TensorFlow Serving can be used both as an **RPC Server** and as a set of libraries, both inside an app or embedded device.

TensorFlow Serving has three pillars:

- **C++ libraries:** Low-level C++ libraries primarily contain the functions and methods required for TensorFlow serving. These are the libraries that Google uses to generate the binaries used by applications. They are also open sourced.
- **Binaries:** If we want standard settings for our serving architecture, we can use pre-defined binaries, that incorporate all the best practices from Google. Google also provides Docker containers (`https://www.docker.com/`) to scale the binaries on Kubernetes (`https://kubernetes.io/`).
- **Hosted services:** TensorFlow Serving also has hosted services across Google Cloud ML, which makes it pretty easy to use and deploy.

Here are some of the advantages of TensorFlow Serving:

- **Online and low latency:** Users don't want to wait to see predictions on their application. With TF serving, predictions are not only fast—they are consistently fast.
- **Multiple models in a single process:** TF serving lets you load multiple models in the same process. Let's say we have a model that is serving great predictions to the customers. However, if we want to run an experiment, then we might want to load another model, along with the production model.

- **Auto-loading and training of versions of the same model:** TF serving has support for auto-loading a newly trained model without downtime and switching from an old version of the same model in production.
- **Scalable:** TF Serving is auto-scalable with Cloud ML, Docker, and Kubernetes.

For more details on how to deploy your models using TF Serving, refer to the official documentation here (`https://www.tensorflow.org/serving/`).

TensorFlow Extended

TensorFlow Extended (TFX) is a general-purpose machine learning platform that was built at Google. Some components of it are open sourced, and there was a recent paper (`https://www.kdd.org/kdd2017/papers/view/tfx-a-tensorflow-based-production-scale-machine-learning-platform`) in a KDD conference illustrating the capabilities and vision of TFX.

In this book, we primarily understood the semantics of building a TensorFlow model. However, when we look at the actual machine learning applications in production, there are many more components. The following diagram illustrates these components:

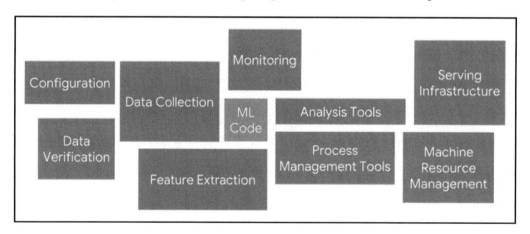

As we can see, ML code is a very small component of the overall system. Other blocks take the maximum amount of time to build and occupy the maximum lines of code. TFX provides the libraries and tools to construct the other components of machine learning pipeline.

Let's look at an example of the machine learning process to understand the different open source components of TensorFlow Extended:

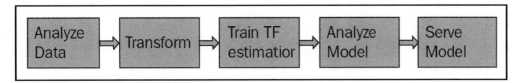

- **Analyze Data**: Exploratory data analysis is a requirement for building any machine learning model. TFX has a tool named Facets (`https://github.com/PAIR-code/facets`), which lets us visualize the distribution of each variable and identify missing data or outliers, or inform others about what data transformations might be required on the data.
- **Transform**: TensorFlow transforms (`https://www.tensorflow.org/tfx/transform/get_started`) provide out-of-the-box functions to perform a full transform on the base data to make it suitable for training a model. It is also very much attached to the TF graph itself, which ensures that you are applying the same transforms in training, as well as serving.
- **Train TF estimator**: After transforming the data, we can use the TF Estimator (`https://www.tensorflow.org/api_docs/python/tf/estimator/Estimator`), which provides a high-level API to quickly define, train, and export a model. TF Estimators also let you export models in different formats for inference and serving.
- **Analyze Model**: Once the model is built, we can directly push it to production, but that would be a very bad idea. Instead, we should analyze the model predictions and make sure that the model is predicting things that we want it to predict. TF Model Analysis (`https://www.tensorflow.org/tfx/model_analysis/get_started`) lets us evaluate the model over a large dataset and provides a UI to slice the predictions by different values of attributes.
- **Serve Model**: After analyzing our model and getting comfortable with its model predictions, we want to serve the model to production. One way this can be achieved is by using TensorFlow Serving, which was described in the previous section.

TensorFlow Extended is heavily used inside Google for building products. It definitely has more features than the ones that are open sourced. For people working at startups or companies that don't have their own internal ML platform, TFX is highly recommended for building end-to-end ML applications.

Recommendations for building AI applications

Now that we understand some of the tools from TensorFlow that can help us in developing and deploying models at scale, let's try to understand the general rules of thumb when building AI applications.

- **Engineering over machine learning**: Almost all the solutions to problems start with engineering. It is very important to get the data pipeline right before building any machine learning model.

- **Keep it simple**: Generally, data scientists have a natural tendency to build the most complex model for the problem. However, it is great to start with a simple, interpretable model—say, a logistic regression model for classification. It helps in discovering and debugging data or engineering pipeline issues better. Only when you are not satisfied with the results of the basic model should you use advanced techniques like deep learning.

- **Distributed processing**: In the era of big data, you will almost always run into issues where you can't fit the data into RAM. Learning about distributed frameworks like Spark can help a lot in processing and building scalable machine learning applications.

- **Automated model retraining**: Once the model is deployed, its performance can degrade over time. It is important to keep checking the model's accuracy so that automated training of the model can be kicked off with new data. This will help in maintaining prediction accuracy for the product.

- **Training and testing pipelines**: With separate pipelines for training and testing, there is always a possibility of divergence between training and testing features. Try to have as much overlap as possible between training and testing pipelines. This can help make debugging model predictions easier.

- **Launch new models with A/B testing**: A/B testing is a method of comparing two versions of model/webpage and others. It is a statistical experiment conducted where two different versions are shown to the users at random. You can read more about them in lecture notes from Purdue (https://www.cs.purdue.edu/homes/ribeirob/courses/Fall2016/lectures/hyp_tests.pdf)

If you build a better model than the one already existing in production, you will see some uplift in accuracy for testing datasets. However, there is a real chance that you might not see the same uplift in production compared to the existing model because of a variety of issues like correlations versus causation, change in user behavior, and so on. It is very important to perform A/B tests with a new model in production before rolling them out to all users.

- **One model over ensemble**: Ensemble models (a combination of many single models) might give better accuracy over a single model. However, if the gain is not significant, always prefer using a single model. This is because ensemble models are difficult to maintain, debug, and scale in production systems.

Limitations of deep learning

In this project, almost all of the projects involved some sort of deep learning. Deep learning has been pivotal in powering most of the advances in the last few years. However, there are obvious limitations to deep learning that we should understand before applying them to real-world situations. Here are some of them:

- **Data-hungry**: Usually, we don't have big datasets for every problem we want to solve using machine learning. On the contrary, deep learning algorithms only work when we have huge datasets for the problem.
- **Compute intensive**: Deep learning training usually requires GPU support and a huge amount of RAM. However, this makes it impossible to train deep neural networks on edge devices like mobiles and tablets.
- **No prediction uncertainty**: Deep learning algorithms are, by default, poor at representing uncertainty. Deep neural networks can confidently misclassify a cat image as that of a dog.

  There is no notion of confidence intervals or uncertainty in predictions. For applications like self-driving cars, it is very important to take uncertainty into account before making any decision. In this book, we touched on concepts like Bayesian neural networks, which are an attempt to incorporate uncertainty in deep neural networks.

- **Uninterpretable black boxes**: Deep learning models are hard to interpret and trust. For example, the loan department at a bank decides whether to give a loan to an individual based on their past purchases or credit history using a deep neural network.

If the model denies the loan, the bank has to give an explanation to the individual regarding why their loan was denied. However, with deep neural networks, it is almost impossible to provide an explicit reason about why the loan was denied. Uninterpretability is a major reason why these models are not ubiquitous across different industries.

AI applications in industries

AI is the new paradigm that every company is trying to move to. As per the Mckinsey report (`https://www.mckinsey.com/featured-insights/artificial-intelligence/notes-from-the-ai-frontier-modeling-the-impact-of-ai-on-the-world-economy`), by 2030, 70% of companies are expected to adopt at least one AI technology. Let's look at different applications of AI by industries:

- **Retail**:
    - Supply chain optimization
    - Customization of shopping experiences by micro targeting
    - Pricing of products and holiday discount calculations
    - Custom product placement in retail stores to increase sales

- **Social Networks (Facebook, LinkedIn, Twitter)**:
    - Friend/follower recommendations
    - Home feed customization to increase engagement based on past history
    - Fake news/fraud detection

- **Healthcare**:
    - New drug discovery
    - Automated medical imaging
    - Recommending workouts/food through data stored in Apple Watch or other devices

- **Finance**:
    - Stock market prediction
    - Credit card fraud detection
    - Loan qualification
    - Chatbots for customer support

- **Manufacturing**:
  - Predictive maintenance
  - Demand forecasting
  - Inventory management
- **Logistics**:
  - ETA optimization
  - Surge pricing
  - Shared rides/pool
  - Pricing
  - Self-driving cars

Ethical considerations in AI

We are seeing an extraordinary rise in Artificial Intelligence and its applications. However, the growing sophistication of AI applications has raised a number of concerns around bias, fairness, safety, transparency, and accountability. This is mainly because AI models don't have a conscience and can't distinguish good from bad all by themselves. They are as good as the data they are trained on. So, if the data is biased in some sense, so will the predictions be. There are other concerns around rising unemployment due to automation, the use of AI for terrorism, and racist predictions from AI models, among others.

The good news is that many universities are spending time and resources to come up with solutions on how to make AI more fair and free from bias. At the same time, regulators are trying to frame new rules so that AI applications are safe and secure for humans.

As an AI practitioner, it is imperative that we understand these issues before using AI in our own products. I urge you to make yourself aware of the ethical issues in your products and correct them accordingly.

Summary

In this chapter, we looked at various extensions of TensorFlow for improving the productivity of data scientists and enabling the easier deployment of cutting-edge models in production at a large scale.

We looked at TensorFlow Hub, which is similar to the GitHub repository of trained deep learning models from various areas like Computer Vision, Natural Language Processing, and so on. Thereafter, we understood how TensorFlow Serving provide tools and libraries to deploy deep learning models at scale. Lastly, we learned about the open source components of **TensorFlow Extended** (**TFX**), which is a machine learning platform from Google. TFX helps in the entire model building pipeline, from data analysis to model deployment.

Next, we learned about several best practices when building scalable AI products. Building a robust engineering pipeline and trying out simple models before deep learning and always launching new models with A/B tests are few of them.

Thereafter, we dispensed the hype around deep learning by understanding the limitations of deep neural networks. Specifically, we learned that they require huge amounts of data and compute power for building good, accurate models. Also, the fact that they are not interpretable makes them unusable in many AI applications. We also looked at various applications of AI across different industries and learned about the importance of ethics in AI.

Lastly, if you have made it this far and completed the projects, I thank you and congratulate you for your awesome achievement. You have acquired the necessary skills to build practical AI applications using state-of-the-art techniques in reinforcement learning, computer vision, and natural language processing, among others. I would request that you now use your knowledge for good and make this world a better place.

I would like to end this book with my favorite quote:

> *The future is not some place we are going, but one we are creating.*

- John H. Schaar

Other Books You May Enjoy

If you enjoyed this book, you may be interested in these other books by Packt:

TensorFlow Machine Learning Cookbook - Second Edition
Nick McClure

ISBN: 9781789131680

- Become familiar with the basic features of the TensorFlow library
- Get to know Linear Regression techniques with TensorFlow
- Learn SVMs with hands-on recipes
- Implement neural networks to improve predictive modeling
- Apply NLP and sentiment analysis to your data
- Master CNN and RNN through practical recipes
- Implement the gradient boosted random forest to predict housing prices
- Take TensorFlow into production

Hands-on Artificial Intelligence with TensorFlow
Amir Ziai

ISBN: 9781788998079

- Explore the core concepts of AI and its different approaches
- Use the TensorFlow framework for smart applications
- Implement various machine and deep learning algorithms with TensorFlow
- Design self-learning RL systems and implement generative models
- Perform GPU computing efficiently using best practices
- Build enterprise-grade apps for computer vision, NLP, and healthcare

Leave a review - let other readers know what you think

Please share your thoughts on this book with others by leaving a review on the site that you bought it from. If you purchased the book from Amazon, please leave us an honest review on this book's Amazon page. This is vital so that other potential readers can see and use your unbiased opinion to make purchasing decisions, we can understand what our customers think about our products, and our authors can see your feedback on the title that they have worked with Packt to create. It will only take a few minutes of your time, but is valuable to other potential customers, our authors, and Packt. Thank you!

Index

model class
  designing 256
model
  testing 199, 204
  training 93, 199, 204, 257
Module
  about 286
  composable 286
  retrainable 286
  reusable 286
Monte Carlo methods 144
MsPacman-v0 274
multiclass 29
multiple graphs 26

N

Natural language generation (NLG) 251
Natural Language Processing (NLP) 61
network definition
  about 256
  LSTM cell, initializing 256
  LSTMs, building 256
  probability generation 256
  word embedding 256
Neural Information Processing Systems (NIPS)
  reference link 44
neural network architecture
  about 92
  deep neural network module 92
  feature extraction module 92
neural network model
  for Retailrocket recommendations 221, 222,
    223, 224

O

object detection
  model, building 244, 245, 246, 247, 248
  Sparkdl, used 242
  TensorFlowOnSpark (TFoS), used 242
  transfer learning 243
OpenAI Gym
  about 272, 273
  Pacman game, creating 274, 275
  reference link 272
optimize for inference 80

P

Pacman game
  creating, in OpenAI Gym 274, 275
posterior 100
prior 100

R

rank 8
recommendation systems 212, 213
reconstruction error 127
Rectified linear (ReLU) 148
rectified linear units (ReLU) 172
recurrent 252
recurrent neural networks (RNNs)
  about 252, 253
  Gated recurrent units (GRU) 253
  Long Short-Term Memory (LSTMs) 253
  Peephole LSTMs 253
reinforcement learning
  about 27, 270, 271
  components 271
  versus supervised learning 270
  versus unsupervised learning 270
remote procedure call (RPC) 289
Retailrocket dataset
  about 215, 216
  exploring 216, 217
  reference link 215
Retailrocket recommendations
  used, for matrix factorization model 218, 219,
    221
  used, for neural network model 221, 222, 223,
    224

S

sample images
  reconstructing 206, 208
scalable 228
sentiment analysis
  about 57
  model, building 62, 64
  model, data preprocessing 63, 64
  model, pre-processing data 62
shape 8